AF575262

# *Who Killed the Holy Ghost?*

OTHER BOOKS BY RUFUS GOODWIN

*Dreamlife: How Dreams Happen*

*Give Us This Day: The Story of Prayer*

# *Who Killed the Holy Ghost?*

## A Journalist Reports on the Holy Spirit

Rufus Goodwin

Lindisfarne Books
*2005*

2005

Lindisfarne Books
610 Main Street
Great Barrington, MA 01230
www.lindisfarne.org



Interior design by William Jensen

Library of Congress Cataloging-in-Publication Data

Goodwin, Rufus.

Who killed the Holy Ghost? : a journalist reports on the Holy Spirit / Rufus Goodwin. — 1st ed.

p. cm.

Includes bibliographical references and index.

ISBN 1-58420-033-2

1. Holy Spirit. I. Title.

BT121.3.G66 2005

231'.3 — dc22

2005001527

10 9 8 7 6 5 4 3 2 1

# Contents

"The world grows younger."
—*anonymous*

"I heard the light."
—*folk saying*

"No man is nearly as great as his story—nor his woman."
—*popular saying*

"The Holy Ghost is the sum total of the toil of unknown saints."
—*anonymous*

"As legend has it, a holy man once came across a boy digging in the sand. He asked the boy what he was doing. 'Digging a hole so that the whole sea can pour out and go down the hole,' the boy answered. The holy man said, 'But that's impossible.' 'No more impossible,' said the boy, 'than you telling what the Holy Spirit is.'"
—*anonymous*

"Walk with the Spirit!"
—*St. Paul*

# Introduction

The tale of the Holy Ghost is just that: a ghost story. That means, among other things, scary. I tell the story journalistically, which means a report, a dossier, a documentary. The Holy Ghost's story is also a mystery, a thriller. It even has a victim, a *corpus delicti,* like all great detective stories. That victim, the corpse, is the body of the Holy Ghost itself. And, like a mystery story, it has an unexpected ending because none has ever found the body, of course, because the Holy Ghost is a spirit. Otherwise, this notice might be an obituary for the Holy Ghost, and obituaries are sad. But they are also informative. They tell us what went on before our times—before the funeral.

In this story, the Holy Ghost haunts itself, and it haunts history. The mystery here is how a spirit, the Holy Ghost, lived. But who knows what a spirit is? For centuries now, since Galileo, since Newton, science has taught that we are bodies that fall, like apples to earth. Or else like clocks, wound up and running down. Or atoms and molecules. Or genomes. According to the Church, we are rotten apples, too, riddled by Original Sin. But Chinese Tao, Buddhist Zen, Hindu Brahma, the Egyptians, and the Greeks all had good heroes and Gods before us, and they were spirits, too, before the apple fell. Long before even Columbus got to America, the Great Spirit lived here, so say the American Indians. Does that mean that the Holy Ghost lived in the new world before the Jesuits and the Puritans showed up?

This is not a "God is Dead" book; it is a cognitive treatment dealing strictly with the record of, and working of, Spirit—the Holy Ghost. If anything, it is more than even an advanced obituary; it is in the mood of a requiem. Moreover, it is specific to the Holy Ghost, not a tract on God, religion, or Church history. The need for this book rose out of the experience that many people, in casual conversation, held strong views about mind/body problems, or about spirituality, but were at a loss to say what spirit, indeed, is. Everyone knew of the

Holy Ghost, but that was about all—even among some churchgoers and believers. Meanwhile, a Google search on the Internet turned up 4,220 hits for the Holy Ghost, including a fourteen-karat Holy Ghost lapel pin and a ten-karat gold Holy Ghost ring.

Many believers had only vague notions of the history or nature of the Holy Ghost—much less its relation to that category, spirit, which plays such a role in disputes about mind and body and between religion and science. Furthermore, the view here is that what is called the "Holy Ghost" is not just a precinct of the churches, theology, and religion, but covers a zone of life that all persons in some way deal with: conscience, consciousness, thinking, emotion, and encounters with the self and the other. Spirituality is not just the life of churches or institutional religions—it is lived and explored and met by many in all walks of life in one guise or another. The Holy Ghost is an expression of one guise of spirit, one guise of God. What is that guise; how did it come into history; how did it touch other forms of spirituality, even secularism?

Animation, vigor, and ardor—liveliness—were signs of the spirit, the breath. Yet the word *Spirit* has often come to be associated in people's minds with the vapors, melancholy, brooding, detachment, otherworldliness, and renunciation. An oft-repeated saying, too, goes, "The spirit is willing, but the flesh is weak." The flesh is blamed for failure and falling into temptation. But more often in these cases the opposite is true; the flesh is strong enough—fit and full of appetite and muscle and impulse—but the spirit is weak; the spirit loses strength, control, and focus. Flesh takes over—the spirit weakens. People lose their goals, their discipline, their resistance, their peace and calm.

Fitness centers train and strengthen the flesh. A healthy mind in a healthy body, the Romans were fond of saying: "*mens sano in corpore sano.*" The Greeks thought that a beautiful body was a sign of superior character. It was later left to the priesthood to train the soul and the mind. Monasteries, in earlier times, were the fitness centers of the Medieval Ages.

The very concept of Spirit is related to two streams of evolution: divinity and humanity. One source of Spirit is the divine source—the

Supreme Being, cosmic essence. But another aspect of spirit belongs to the individual person, the character, the ego, the personal soul. It belongs, in a word, to men and women. A lot of religion is about how to mediate between these two. The Holy Ghost is one of these links. The Holy Ghost is, as well as a supreme Divine Spirit in the universe, a mediator. But human beings do not go to God when dealing with the Holy Ghost; the Holy Spirit comes to him or her.

It is very important to distinguish between the theological and philosophers' names for the Holy Spirit and the reality, or presence, of the Holy Spirit. This distinction, or the lack of it, has plagued the fate of religions, history, and the faithful. Arab and Jew, who both experience God as a presence, see eye-to-eye; Arab and Jew, who are caught in the war because of the name of Allah and the name of God, fight instead.

There are two histories of the Holy Ghost: one is the history of the name, its theology, its place in religion, the definitions, creeds, and formulas. The other story is of the role, the presence, and action of the Holy Spirit—its being and essence, and its intervention in history, visible or invisible. Both histories are important, but the documentary record, or written history, is far stronger in testifying to the names, creeds, formulas, and disputes than it is to the presence, which, often, takes place in ordinary people and in ordinary lives. The file and dossier of names and disputes is longer; it is written. The actual presence, so often invisible, is unwritten and cannot be pictured easily. It is often ineffable according to witnesses and sometimes indescribable. As in physics, if you can locate it and pinpoint it, you no longer can measure it. The differences about these two natures of the Holy Ghost—let us say the nominal, or written one, and the existential and sometimes invisible one—have dogged the life of the spirit through the ages. People have clashed, struggled, fought over this. Thrones and kingdoms, as well as personal salvation, have hung in the balance.

This book, then, means to base itself on both skepticism and respect for the Holy Ghost. It is not a work of demystification or deconstruction. My attitude is that of one invited to a funeral—I at least take my hat off and show reverence. And, if the Holy Ghost is not dead yet, then this is merely what journalists call an "advance" obituary. If anything, however, my purpose is not to deflate mystery but to bring the mystery closer, both to the faith and to reasonableness. It is not to analyze and dispute and to argue, but to record, to probe, to take a close up. To inform, familiarize, report, and clarify.

Some critics feel that the Spirit has been overly "churchified," or that it sits in pews, attends church suppers, shakes hands with the pastor, and gossips with old ladies too much. The Holy Spirit, in this view, is devout and pious and looks like an old gothic married pair. Others think the Holy Ghost only hangs out with nuns and monks, and has nothing to do with real life. Other critics say the priests, long ago, abandoned the Holy Spirit in favor of offices, rents, income, big buildings, jewels and finery, high living, secularism and the state — even profaneness, clericalism, powers, and the sexual abuse of young boys. However this may be, the Church has also been the champion through history of the Holy Ghost.

This book tries, in the spirit of the Spirit, to take a loftier view. One does not need to be a churchman or even a Christian to read this. It is meant to be a thoughtful, but popular, history of the Holy Ghost and Spirit as experienced, too, by real and often unknown people. The story of the Holy Ghost is too broad and too important to get bogged down either in secular rejection or in the petty bickering of some church disputes. Some conflicts of doctrine and theology are noteworthy, of course, because they are about the nature of the Spirit itself, of humankind, and of life on earth. Often the story of the Spirit is fascinating and riveting. The story of Spirit touches our deepest concerns not just about things religious, but also about who we are, where we are going, how we get there, and what we mean to ourselves when we get there.

# WHO KILLED THE HOLY GHOST?

## Chapter 1

# The Spirit that Blows Where It Will

Some say that an obituary for the Holy Ghost is premature, that he, she, or it never died—that the Holy Spirit is merely in exile. A spirit never dies, others say; only the body dies. And stars. Others say the world will die one day, and that then the world's dead body will be a Holy Ghost wandering the Heavens. Others say the Holy Ghost is the mind. But scientists and physiologists say there is no mind—only the brain. Ergo, they also say, there is a cosmos—space, gas, galaxies—but no Holy Ghost. He, she, or it is long gone, just like the ether that the physicists banned from the universe. Others say the Holy Ghost is just a name—the same name as the Holy Spirit. In ancient times, names themselves were holy—the name of God, like Yahweh of the Jews, was too holy to be spoken. Names and images in those days were magical. They invoked the thing they stood for. In fact, the name and the thing were not yet separated. Mere symbols had not arrived yet; words and pictures became symbols only after the name and thing were separated, after the words lost the meaning, after nominalism was born. So in the beginning was the Word. Then, sometime after the beginning, priests and prophets came up with the term *Holy Ghost,* or *Holy Spirit.* But Jesus, the prophets, and Paul had used just the word *Spirit.*

In English, *Holy Spirit*—from the Hebrew, Greek, Aramaic, and Latin—was translated as "Holy Ghost." The word *ghost* did not yet mean apparition, phantom, or specter, as it did later on. In the old Anglo Saxon, and Middle English, it came from the word *gast,* which meant breath or spirit. This was the same, then, as the Latin word *spirare*—to breathe, which is the root of the word *spirit.* The translators of the King James version of the Bible—which was authorized in 1604 by the Hampton Conference dealing with the Puritans—used the term *Holy Ghost* for the Holy Spirit. Only gradually did the word come to signify the departed soul of a dead person, or a phantom, a specter, an apparition. Shakespeare used it this way in *Venus and Adonis* in 1592. Originally, like breath itself, the word meant something that animated things. Thus the very word *Spirit*—apart from the mystery of the Holy Spirit—from Roman times and before meant something that animates, something much closer to vivacity and vigor than our meaning of haunted castles and attics. Spirit meant vivacity, animation, ardor, enthusiasm courage, and vigor for the Romans.

Perhaps nowadays the haunted attic, however, is a more apt image for the Holy Ghost. Because the attic, so to speak, is fairly empty and pretty much haunted. Science, philosophy, metaphysics, theology, and even the Churches are sometimes empty as far as the spirit is concerned. Ever since Newton's model of the universe as a clock, commentators have talked about the "ghost in the machine," but it had become mostly a phantom.

Ordinary people often have a lot of common respect for the Holy Ghost, or Holy Spirit, although they sometimes have little idea of what it is or means. Other people, the secular, atheists, agnostics, and materialists—a lot of educated people, unless they go often to Church—just think the Holy Ghost is a joke and that the Holy Spirit is essentially a lot of nonsense. Even Churchgoers who respect the Father and Son, unless they are a special sort of evangelical, Quaker, or Pentecostal, usually don't know much about the Holy Ghost. Catholics—though the faithful and the Church are supposed to be the temple of the Holy Spirit—often have little grasp of the Holy Spirit, even though it is part of their Trinity: Father, Son, and Holy Spirit. One of the reasons for this is that the Father God, or Creator, had a clear function: creation. Everyone, too, has a father. And fathers have sons, and everybody knows what a son is. Besides, Jesus Christ, the second person of the Trinity was a person. Everybody knows his story. But when it comes to the Holy Ghost, or the Holy Spirit, nobody seems to know exactly what, who, and where it is going on. Even the traditional theology of the Holy

Spirit is much less developed and less voluminous than the theology of the Father God, of the sacraments, of creation, or of the Son. Besides, people's eyes glaze over nowadays when one speaks about the Spirit being a person. Science teaches that people are not spirits, so how could the Holy Ghost be a person?

Because the Holy Ghost was incorporated into the Trinity in Christendom, and because the Church monopolized the Trinity, people associate the Holy Spirit with some kind of technical specialty of religion. Particularly nonreligious people think this way. For them, the Holy Ghost is some kind of mumbo jumbo that the Christian priests cooked up long ago, and that is, as we said, dead—though no one knows when the Holy Ghost died or where his or her body is. This is the difference between the Holy Ghost and the Greek Gods and Jesus; everyone knows how, when, and where Jesus died, and what happened to his body. No one seems to know the story of what happened to the Holy Ghost.

The Arabs, the Jews, the Hindus, and the Taoists—not to mention the African animists and America Indians—also deal in spirits, but very differently. None of them have a Trinity, and usually their spirits are not persons. The Greeks dealt in Gods, but no one on Olympus resembles the Holy Ghost. In fact, while a lot of people think the Holy Ghost is dead, no one seems to know when the Holy Ghost was born. Was it in the first chapter of Genesis in the Bible, when God created Heaven and Earth? Verse two says the earth was waste and void. Darkness covered the abyss. Then "the spirit of God was stirring above the waters."

Is the Spirit of God the same as the Holy Ghost, or did the Holy Ghost create God? If the Holy Ghost proceeds from Father and Son, how could he have existed before Jesus? According to the theologians, God created the universe out of nothing; the Hebrew word means "a making out of nothing." But wasn't the Divine Spirit always there? Divine Spirit is still another name for Holy Ghost and Holy Spirit. And doesn't it say the Divine Spirit will always be there? So did the Spirit come before the creation? And, if so, was the Spirit nothing—nothing before and nothing after? Or did God create the

Holy Spirit? Apparently not; the Holy Spirit proceeds out of God, just as the Son does. In fact, how could the spirit be a creation? Creation is the natural world, the material world. And what about the Big Bang? Was the Holy Ghost the Big Bang?

The American Indians speak of the Great Spirit; so did they posses the Holy Spirit before the Christians and the Jesuits arrived, and, if so, why did they convert them? Or, as St. John said, "In the beginning was the Word," or the Logos. Was the Logos the Great Spirit? Again, apparently not. John says the Word was God. So is the Logos and the word the same as the Holy Ghost? Or, as the linguists say—and the semiotics people, and the man in the street—the Logos is just a name, and names are not the same as things, and language is pretty meaningless anyway.

It is pretty much accepted by the faithful that the Divine Spirit inspired the Bible. This is generally thought to be the same as the Holy Ghost. The Church, the Vatican, and Martin Luther, as well as Calvin, have long taught that the scriptures are the word of the Holy Ghost, or God, writ through human beings. In the nineteenth century, the High Criticism and Biblical scholars tore all that talk apart and pretty much proved that people of a particular time and place wrote relative accounts of Biblical events, and some claimed that, therefore, the Bible is not the revelation of God, but just another sort of fake history.

But just the fact that people wrote the Bible doesn't mean that the Holy Ghost didn't inspire them. In fact, how are poets generally inspired with the divine madness? Aren't they maybe, just as possessed by spirits—maybe even by the Holy Ghost? Plato said that all poets were mad and expelled them from the Republic. Plato did not want a state run by madmen, or inspired poets. He did not want a theocracy either. He wanted a Republic run by good men.

The Jewish prophets were familiar with the Holy Ghost long before the Christians discovered her or him or it; and long before she, him, or it belonged to any Trinity. The prophet Joel in particular speaks of the Holy Spirit and predicts that the Holy Spirit will one day pour out its gifts into the world when the Messiah comes. This, the Christians claim, was Pentecost.

But Moses never seems to deal with the Holy Spirit; he always deals with God the Father, the father of Abraham. Even when Moses gets the tablets on the mountain with the Ten Commandments, he is not dealing with the Holy Ghost, as one might expect, or with the spirit, but with God, a person, whom he meets face to face, but never sees. The burning bush is not a spirit but God himself in flames; there is nothing ghostly about it, nothing phantom or specter-like. It is vibrantly real, just as creation is.

For Buddhists, God is not a person at all. Their religion, in the parlance, is not theistic. But enlightenment, the goal of the Buddhist path, is a matter nevertheless of spiritual enlightenment. What does spiritual mean? Not bodily? Or does it also mean the breath. Maybe this is why Buddhists and yoga have so many breathing exercises. In yoga, the Buddhist passes into a state of individual illumination—sometimes into a kind of nirvana, a nothingness. Is this the same uncreated nothingness that we met in Genesis before the beginning of heaven and earth? And if so, why would the Buddhist want to go there? The Holy Spirit is supposed to look ahead, to guide the future. The Christian, after all, is not supposed to return to the Garden of Eden, but to proceed onward to the Last Judgment and Doomsday, when all the gifts of the Holy Ghost are bestowed on the righteous. Do Buddhists, in enlightenment, already participate in the Holy Spirit? Or are they getting some other kind of message?

Since all these religions have different gods, and different sons—or no son at all—is there any chance that by not discussing the Father and the Son, or any Gods at all, people can agree on something in the way of Holy Spirit—something that is common to Jesus, the Koran, the Buddhists, and all the others? If so, how do we define *spirit* and *spiritual?* The New Agers and Aquarians, with their fourth dimension of consciousness, may have something to say about all this. The new cosmic consciousness of the New Age may be the presentiment of the coming of the Holy Spirit—or is it just the death of the Holy Ghost?

The last thing I want to do—that is, the thing I don't want to do—is kill the mystery surrounding the Holy Ghost. Science, in the name of the brain and reason and in the name of scornfulness, has already created enough sense of demystification in all branches of life. But a gene does not need to demystify life. It can raise life's factor of wonder and mystery. But I do want to clarify and explain the story of the Holy Ghost. An explanation does not remove the wonder. An explanation need not kill the mystery. Mystery novels unravel the crime without undoing the suspense. And even then, at the denouement, or Last Judgment, a good thriller does not take away from the read. An explanation that solves the mystery does not necessarily belie the truth that, in the story, it was good Fido, the dog, who bit the man. An explanation, or clarification, does not undo the mystery. *Mystery* is a word that has to do with myth and mysticism. The word *mystery,* like *myth,* comes from the Greek word *musteion:* to close the eyes or mouth—in other words, to shut up. For the Greek Orthodox and Byzantine Fathers of the East, to whom the Holy Spirit was always more important than to the West, this also meant the way of silence: reaching God through silence, through negation, through darkness. This is known as the *via negativa,* the apophatic path affirming the greatest truths of life.

So it is not demystification I seek—not another deconstruction of wonder and mystery. But I do want to set down a record of the name the Holy Ghost, and the history, in some small part, of the Holy Spirit, and also consider what the difference is, or the connection, between the name and the reality of the thing, or the spirit, itself—or herself, or himself. History at best can only skim a record of the thing and say even less of the spirit, often leaving even salient acts unnoted or unrecorded, and the truth submerged. But the history of what happened to Caesar, or how DNA was discovered, need not kill the mystery of Caesar's life or the mystery of matter. In fact, a good explanation should increase the mystery. Chemistry does not deconstruct the crystal or its place in the awe and poetry of humankind. Wonder and awe, like a sense of mystery itself, are functions of the human mind and attitude. The chemist does not destroy a crystal with a formula; people destroy the mystery by saying, "Oh, it's just a crystal, just a damn crystal." Love does not exist for those who destroy it because it is just damn chemistry—nothing but atoms at work. Love for them is mere cathection—the loss of self, a person becoming a damn fool. Because it is chemistry, it doesn't exist as a spirit. It's a joke. Never mind that it still happens. That falling in love is still magic. They still scoff. They still scorn.

The same is true of mystery and the spirit—and with myth. If the Holy Ghost turned out to be Santa Claus for real, the deconstructionists and scientific cynics, the perpetual scoffers and denigrators, the people with degrees who think a course in social psychology has illuminated them, will make fun of the mystery. It's an industry and it's a way of being smart to devalue mystery and life itself. It happens at work; it happens at school; it happens at universities; it happens in bars and in the locker room. A sense of mystery, in our world, is ridiculed as superstition, ignorance, and stupidity. Get real, they say. But mystery, like life itself—and like the Spirit—is a part of wonder, of suspense, of awe, of thrill, of faith, of a way of knowing things, of finding out things, and of the pursuit of happiness. It has to do with the attitude of the beholder, not just the object itself. A stone is not a mystery, some say; it's just a stone—unless it is the grain of sand that the poet William Blake found heaven in, or unless it's the Kaaba, the black stone in Mecca. The Kaaba is a simple black stone, a cube. But the Iranian philosopher Ali Shariati called the Kaaba "the world's sun, whose face attracts you into its orbit." Near the Kaaba, "you have been transformed into a particle that is gradually melting and disappearing. This is absolute love at its peak." This, too, is Spirit. A rose may be just a rose. A stone is just a stone—unless, of course, it is the rock of Peter, or the Foundation Stone. Or a ruby. Or a diamond.

But why should such things be so ridiculous to even an Isaac Newton, who wrote a disdainful, scathing, and scornful pamphlet against the mystery of the Trinity and the Holy Ghost—or to Nobel prize winners like James Watson and Francis Crick, discovers of DNA, or brain theorist John Searle, who all claim that there is no soul, no mind, and that this idea of mind or soul is just a cheap shot. Why is the sublime itself so often just a bad joke in American locker rooms and labs?

For centuries, simple people who worshipped the Holy Ghost without knowing much about it were put off by the priests who, even with the very word *ghost,* surrounded the Holy Spirit with a kind of spooky taboo. Because the Holy Spirit is not bodily and is invisible, people kept their distance. The Holy Ghost has never been big table talk. Modern people on the whole think of the Holy Ghost as some kind of spook that hangs around the shadowy nooks of Churches. Except for simple people who worship from their hearts, mostly they don't know the difference between the Holy Ghost and an idol. Yet there are technical literature and specifications on the Holy Ghost, just the way there is on the brain in physiology and on the mind in the cognitive sciences. In fact, for many thousands of years the mind was the realm of the Holy Ghost before we even heard from the cognitive sciences.

Aside from Newton (and the Devil), the Holy Ghost, although it was for a short time at the center of world politics, has few nominal enemies. Not many people target the Holy Ghost personally, as Karl Marx did God, or as the agnostics, atheists, and some scientists generally go after religion. The Holy Ghost is like shooting at a target that isn't there. Newton placed a clock in the universe instead of any God or any Holy Ghost. The wonderful history of painting, except for the pictures of the Dove, never depicted the Holy Spirit the way they did Jesus, Mary, the prophets, the saints, and God himself. There was nothing to show, nothing to paint. God can be shown anthropomorphically—that is, in the image of a man, because God is supposed to have created humankind in his own image. But the Holy Ghost has no image. You can't paint invisibility.

The Spanish painter Salvador Dali made a joke on Newton by painting the world as a desert inhabited by dead clocks. His clocks were not wound up anymore. They were limp and lifeless. Dali's joke was on the people who destroyed mystery. His surrealism—more than realism—depicted a mystery of the world without life, without the Holy Ghost. Giorgio De Chirico did the same; the world was a desert haunted by a few Greek ruins and empty temples. They were pictures of emptiness: the Holy Ghost seen as a kind of death. Small spiritual morphs, forms, or souls in empty, shrouded hoods come as close to depicting the Holy Ghost as anything, although the abstractionists

Klee and Kandinsky portrayed something fantastical—maybe spirits, maybe Holy Ghosts. As Emily Dickinson wrote:

> Death is a dialogue between
> The Spirit and the dust.

The closest that the Greeks had to a Holy Spirit was the Goddess Athene. She sprang full blown out of the mind of Zeus, the creator. This is known as a procession; it is a way of reproducing without coming out of the loins. Her province was thought. She is portrayed as a woman with a helmet. Giotto, too, painted her almost, in the birth of Venus, which is also a picture of a birth by procession. Only Venus was the Goddess of Beauty—Aphrodite in Greek—a sister of Athene.

In Greek, the poets were inspired—the word *inspiration* again coming from the same word as Sprit: *spirare,* to breathe—by the Muses. They were in turns the daughters of Zeus and Mnemosyne. Mnesmosyne was herself memory. But one could later have said, with some justice, that the Muses were really the Daughters of the Holy Ghost. Since paganism was out, of course, Christianity never said this. The Muses did. So did the orphic spirits—the oracles—and the Sybils. These were all female spirits, and the Hebrew tradition and the Patristic Fathers of Christianity were interested mainly in the male line. But at Herculaneum in Italy, the archeologists who uncover the tombs of things found pictures of the nine Muses: Calliope, the queen of muses; Clio, muse of heroic epic and history; Euterpe, muse of Dionsiac music, the flute, and lyric poetry; Thalia, the muse of gaiety country life, and comedy; Melpomene, the muse of song, harmony, and tragedy; Terpsichore, the muse of dance; Erato, the muse of lyre and erotic poetry; Polhymnia, the muse of choral singing and hymns; and Thanius, the muse of celestial events and astronomy. These were spirits.

In modern parlance, they are cognitive disciplines, no longer spirits of the mind. The gradual evolution of the Spirit of the prophets in Hebrew tradition into the Holy Ghost of the early Christians was a loss of gods, goddesses, spirits, and idols. In some ways, the shift from these spirits to one Holy Spirit was a consolidation, or an abstraction, of the supernatural into the one Divine Spirit. Superstition, in one sense, receded, yes, but then became invisible in a new mystery. But mystery, too, once had an archaic sense; it once meant "handicraft." This sense of the original word still comes down to us in the French word *métier:* trade, craft, or profession. This side of mystery had to do with the mysterious skills of antiquity and came through the Middle English as *mistere,* from Medieval Latin, *misterium,* which was related to *ministerium,* the word for ministry.

The ancient Greek mysteries were places where the eyes and lips were shut, only then to open, or initiate, people into the greater truths of the world. This sometimes involved near-death experiences in which the novice was introduced to the spirit. Resurrection, one of the great mysteries of the Holy Spirit, has to do with the initiate returning from the dead, now referred to as the return of the body. The three so-called greater mysteries of the Church, incidentally, are now the Trinity (which includes the Holy Ghost), Original Sin, and the Incarnation.

The Incarnation—God becoming man—is really a mystery about our nature. It was long a dispute in the Church, because early Fathers of the Church tried to figure—just as the genome now tries to sort genes—what was the substance, the essence, and the spirit of the human being, and of God, or the universe. A museum, incidentally, now arguably a house of the Holy Ghosts of humankind, was originally a house for spirits—the Muses. Kingdom Come, instead, was death, the grave, the next world, and the realm of the Holy Ghost. Or does the Holy Spirit really dwell in life—not death—in this world, not the next. This is another riddle of speculation that theology has never wholly developed, and that we can examine in a further chapter when we trace who the Holy Spirit is supposed to be—and what she, he, or it is supposed to do.

The tradition of touching the anointed one, the Pope, or the King, may also have to do with the supposed spark of the Holy Spirit passing by hands from one to one. The Pope in the late

Middle Ages, incidentally, had the word *Mysterium* inscribed on his tiara, or headdress, and the letters of the word were supposed to amount cabalistically to 666, the number of the Beast in the Book of Revelation. That book, in turn, like Scripture itself, could be interpreted only through the Holy Spirit. The sense of holy touch passed, too, from Jesus to Peter and to the Popes and Kings — called the "King's Evil." The scrofula could be cured by the King's touch, and this gift of the Holy Spirit was established later as divine hereditary right. King Charles of England was said to have touched 92,107 persons, and this right of touch remained in the prayer book until 1712. Whether the right of touch is an incorporation of the Holy Ghost is open to conjecture, but it is a mystery even today, when millions of people still try to touch the Pope. The tradition of touching or shaking hands with the President of the United States stems from the same origins: the tradition that the Holy Spirit passes from the King's touch, although no American would probably know that they are dealing with the Holy Ghost. The practice lives on; the idea is dead.

Is the Holy Spirit then an Idea? Or is it a living person? The Holy Ghost is not a member of the Holy Family, as are the Infant, Joseph, Mary, Elizabeth, Anne, and John the Baptist. There was in France, until the Revolution of 1830 after Napoleon's time, an order of the Holy Ghost (*Ordre du Saint Esprit*), instituted by Henry III in 1878 to replace the Order of St. Michael. It was limited to a hundred knights.

If the Holy Ghost is just an idea (with a small "i"), then it belongs to the world of Platonic ideas; or does it incarnate? Is truth, which the Holy Ghost represents, an idea that never incarnates, or is truth something that lives in the mind and in the world? In history, Peter, Paul, Mark, Luke, and John dealt with this problem. Journalists deal with it still today.

The German philosopher Hegel, an abstract idealist, spent his life writing about the spirit; his main book is called, *The Phenomenology of the Sprit.* He is remembered mainly by the logic of dialectic method: thesis antithesis, synthesis. Was his work about the Holy Ghost in disguise? The Holy Ghost got abstracted by the philosophers. Did

Karl Marx—who adapted the dialectic method to history—really stumble on the workings in history of the Holy Ghost, the thesis of history, the counter-thesis, the synthesis? He reduced the spirit of history to dialectic materialism. Was this the same as Darwin's theory of evolution—the struggle for survival reducing the history of the Holy Ghost to the cloth of nature raw in tooth and claw? Indeed, do animals have spirit—or the Spirit—or is the lack of spirit in them what actually separates human from beast. Is the Eternal Feminine of Goethe the Holy Spirit in disguise, distinguishing man from woman? As Hamlet said, "There are more things in Heaven and Earth, Horatio, than are dreampt of in your philosophy." He had started on his tragedy and his illumination—"to be or not to be"—when he saw his father's ghost.

Or, as some have asserted, is the Holy Spirit not the language itself—the word breathed into the human being—the gift of language. As the poet Shelley said:

> Language is a perpetual Orphic song,
> Which rules with harmony a throng
> Of thoughts and forms,
> which else were senseless and shapeless.

The Egyptians did not have the Holy Ghost, but they had the God Toth, who gave us alchemy, the science of the spirit. The Greeks had the oracles, which came not from breath but from the mystery of speaking, of praying. Speech takes place on the breath—the outgoing breath. Inspiration takes place on the incoming breath. Inhalation, Exhalation. The apostrophe in Greek, for the sound "H," a breath, was called "a spirit." The oracle of the Greeks—in most temples interpreted by a woman sitting on a tripod—was the answer of a god or inspired priest to an inquiry respecting the future. These oracles came to be held as not only profoundly wise, but also infallible, even dogmatic. A dogma, in the original meaning of a teaching, was not something dogmatic in our sense, but an esoteric teaching that was a mystery, something beyond normal understanding. The oracles often were housed in dark, in mist, next to vents of steam from the earth. At Delphi, the priestess was called the Pythoness. The python was a monster serpent hatched from the mud of the great deluge. It was slain by Apollo, God of light, near Delphi. But maybe the python was just another incarnation of the serpent of the Garden of Eden who tempted Adam and Eve with the fruit of knowledge—knowledge, the reality, the Holy Spirit.

Apollo himself was not a spirit, however, he was a God who typified the sun in its light and life-giving as well as its destroying power. Light would later play a tremendous role in the efforts of those trying to approach, apprehend, and "process" the Holy Spirit in theology.

But first were the oracles. As Shakespeare, in the Merchant of Venice said,

> I am Sir Oracle,
> And when I open my lips let no dog bark.

After the oracles died, the Holy Ghost was born and then, from Egypt, Jerusalem, Greece, and Rome, moved on in a new form, went into exile, or lived on in history.

This record is written as the advance obituary—the postmortem of the Holy Ghost. Or, if the Holy Spirit is not dead and nobody seems to know except the cocky materialists and science, always so sure of everything, then this is a mere advance, as the journalists are accustomed to write—a premature obituary ready for the day should the Holy Ghost and death actually collide; and that day, according to the tradition, would be Doomsday.

## Chapter 2

# The Spirit and the Dust

The Holy Ghost's tale reaches far back into the first mists of time; the book of Genesis in the Bible tells of when darkness was upon the face of the deep, and then, "The Spirit of God moved upon the face of the waters." So the Spirit was even before the light, which was only created on the first day.

The Holy Ghost came to have many names: the Spirit, the Spirit of God, the Wind; the Breath, the Paraclete (the Greek word for "advocate"), the Comforter, the Gift, Divine Spirit, the Spirit of Truth, and, most simply of all, Love. The word *ghost* is ancient and is used for the Spirit as soon as English is used to translate the Bible from the Vulgate. *Ghost* came from cognates in German into Old English before 800. Dutch, Old Saxon, and Old Frisian used *gast, jest, gest, gheist,* and *geist,* meaning, variously, soul, spirit, angel, and sometimes demon. Old Icelandic used *geiska,* as in *geiskafulls,* meaning "of fright." The Gothic *usgaisjan* means to frighten and relates to Sanskrit words for wrath and terror. The English spelling "ghost," with the "h," emerged around 1425, at the time of Caxton. Shakespeare uses it in 1592 for an apparition or specter. The word *ghost* was used in the St. James Version of the Bible (translated c.1904) for the Latin *Spiritus Sanctus.*

In Hebrew, the word was *Ruah,* meaning breath or wind. The Greek word was *pneuma,* also meaning breath. In Roman, however, the word *spiritus*—from which we eventually get *spirit* and *spiritual* through the French *esprit*—came from *spirare,* to breathe. In Latin, far from being a phantasm or spiritually wimpish, *spiritus* suggested rather a sense of courage and vigor—as in Elizabethan English when one spoke of a man of spirit or wit. *Spirare,* in Latin, is related to old words like *pysketi* ("to bang" in Lithuanian) and the Old Slavic *piskah* ("to play a pipe"). The word was related to vigor in life, not to death and the otherworldly. The extended sense of a supernatural incorporeal being came later in Middle English, under the influence of popular folklore and theology, which spooked the Holy Ghost, party because of Medieval and ascetic theology. It was not even the original meaning of spirit when, for the early Jewish and Christian communities, the word from Jesus also meant a rushing wind and energy and imbued the early believers with courage.

The Hebrew prophets, Joel, Isaiah, and Jeremiah speak of spirit and of the Spirit. Joel quotes God as saying, "And it shall come to pass afterward that I will pour out my spirit upon all flesh; and your sons and your daughters shall prophesy, your old men shall dream dreams, your young men shall see visions. And also upon the servants and upon the handmaids in those days will I pour my spirit" (Joel 2: 28,29). According to the Gospels of the New Testament, this happened at Pentecost, or Whitsuntide, ten days after the Ascension. It came upon the disciples fifty days after Easter in the Upper Room in Jerusalem with "a might rushing of wind" and with "tongues of fire."

But the Patristic Fathers of the Church don't get to an intense discussion of the doctrinal development of Holy Spirit until the fourth century, and then the Church largely buries the matter for hundreds of years—even a thousand—and it is still hushed over. Theology of the Holy Spirit is widely admitted to be greatly underdeveloped in comparison to the theology of God the Father, Christology, God the Son, and the Sacraments. During the thirteenth century, St. Thomas Aquinas skims over the Holy Ghost in the *Summa Theologica* in a few pages during the Scholastic Medieval Ages, and the Holy Ghost again fades even further until the Evangelicals, and later the Pentecostals, revive the flagging spirit in various forms. And the Holy Ghost even makes a recent reappearance under the impetus of science, after the New Physics and after the enunciation in 1927 of Werner Heisenberg's indeterminacy principle.

But what is the Spirit? Is spirit with a small s the same as in Holy Spirit with a capital "S"? Like the chicken and the egg, which came first: matter or spirit? Is the Holy Ghost the same as the American Indians' Great Spirit? Is the *ch'ai* of the Eastern tradition—the Chinese word for spirit—the same as the word *spirit* in the West? Is the primal energy, *ch'ai*, the same as the Holy Ghost? Or is it the Brahma of the Hindus? The Greeks had Gods—but did they have a Holy Spirit? No. Does the spirit start before time, or after! In Christianity, is the Holy Spirit the same as God the Father and God the Son? Or is the Spirit the same as mind, as in mind and body. Or is it a person? Is the Holy Ghost a person or an immaterial essence? Is the spirit of the philosopher George W. F. Hegel (1770–1831) the same spirit as that of the Holy Ghost? Indeed, are spirit and soul, or psyche, the same thing? And does philosophy recognize the Holy Ghost or only spirit in the form of mind, or essence, as in philosophical idealism?

Nor was it only Jesus, St. Paul, and St. John who thought about the Holy Ghost or Holy Spirit in history; the American founding fathers had views on the spirit, too. So did Newton, Galileo, Einstein, Samuel Johnson, Washington, Jefferson, and the astronaut John Glenn. The poets Wordsworth and Gerald Manley Hopkins wrote about the Holy Spirit, as did Dante and Shakespeare. The Holy Ghost, before and after Christianity, has a long history, and indeed one question that arises is, "Does the Holy Ghost manifest itself in history?" Even gender is a question. Is the Holy Spirit masculine, neuter, or feminine? And political questions also come up: Is the Holy Ghost a royalist, totalitarian, Republican, or Democrat? Is the Holy Ghost in favor of communism, or for democracy?

The Holy Ghost is no dead, dry idea, nor idol, but an adventure—an adventure of the mind, of history, and of salvation. But more, he, she, or it is a personal adventure. The Holy Ghost does not transcend; it indwells in human beings. From the New Age spirituality to the personal biography of everyday people, the Holy Ghost is a cognitive challenge. The theological entity—the person of the Holy Ghost—is only one aspect. The Holy Ghost has to do with our very thinking about life—whether we are animal, human, or spirit. And, traditionally, the Holy Ghost has to do with the future. It has to do with our views of our selves and our becoming—our personal biography, our personal lives, and how we think about what we are: genes, chemistry, matter, or perhaps also soul and spirit. The Holy Ghost sometimes has to do with thinking itself—it is a cognitive realm. It is in the realm of knowing—not to mention revelation and religion. It has to do with the very animation of human beings—how we receive the Creation, what we think of the Cosmos, and how we interact with God—if there is one.

Christian theology and views of the Holy Spirit are only part of the story—a fascinating one of personalities, politics society, religion, and evolution. But the Jews believed in the Holy Spirit. The Greeks deal with the philosophy of heroes and warriors and their fate in the land of the dead—the land of Spirits. The Egyptians embalmed their dead to send them on a voyage to the afterworld—the land of the Holy Spirit for them. The prophets sought to bring the messages from the Holy Spirit, to warn their people.

Culture is an interlay on many levels of what humankind envisions as the spirit of the times. Personal identity is a struggle with definitions of the self—myself, yourself—as bodies, soul, and spirit, or not. More and more, culture is without mystery; science, the media, the critics, and universities increasingly deconstruct the mystery. God was rationalized by the Scholastics, then by the Enlightenment, then by science. Divinity slowly died not only in the hands of Friedrich Nietzsche, but *Time* magazine also once advertised that God was dead. Culture has deconstructed the marvels of the past, and some say the Holy Spirit, the Holy Ghost, has long gone into exile. But the Holy Ghost is just that—a mystery. The Patristic Fathers of the Church intentionally set out to mystify themselves in dealing with the Holy Ghost, and so did the Greeks and the Russians. They didn't want a patent answer. They wanted to tease the intellect, to challenge other levels of psychology—the emotions, inspiration, and intuition. Clashes over the Holy Ghost involve clashes between East and West, between Rome and Byzantium. The Buddhists, the Hindus, and the Arabs also struggled with their experience of the Holy Spirit and with their version of how the human spirit, the individual, meets the spirit of the universe, the Holy Ghost.

Jesus delivers information about the Holy Ghost to the Apostles in the most personal and direct way at the Last Supper, but hides information about the Holy Ghost, too. The *kerygma,* or teachings of the Church, deals with the mysteries of the Holy Ghost in *exoteric* teaching, while the dogmas—those reviled pronouncements of the Church—deal with the nature of the Holy Ghost in an *esoteric* fashion. This is little understood.

The Jewish *Shekinah,* the female dwelling of the spirit, becomes the wandering spirit of redemption exiled from the destroyed Temple, appearing, like a tent, in Babylon, in Syria, and in Auschwitz. And Sophia, the lost wisdom—they are sisters of the Holy Spirit.

Freud, Jung, Kant, Washington, Jefferson, Loyola, St. Francis, Theresa d'Avila, Martin Luther, Calvin, the Pilgrims, Henry the IV, czars, the Baptists, the Quakers, and evangelicals all deal with the Holy Ghost. St. John, Peter, Mark, Luther, and the Apostles all deal with the Holy Spirit. The individual in the street, even without knowing it, deals with the Holy Ghost when the wind blows around the corner.

One hears a lot about Christ, about Jesus, about God, about Buddha, about Muhammad, but lurking in all these religious traditions and in New Age spirituality is an encounter with that reality of experience, the indwelling, called the Holy Ghost. We have partly seen how the Holy Ghost got that name, but we need to know the relationship of the Holy Ghost to spirituality, to religion, and to the very term *Spirit.* There are prayers to the Holy Ghost, but does the Holy Ghost intercede? Is the Holy Ghost a bridge between the living and the dead? How is the Holy Ghost the same as God—and in what ways distinct? What was Jesus' relationship to the Holy Ghost? What is the Holy Ghost's relationship to the unconscious? What, in fact, do psychologists think of the Holy Ghost? We saw how for thought the Greeks proceeded from Athena, but we need to check on how the Holy Ghost proceeded from the Father—and the Son—and indeed, what the difference is between *psyche* and *pneuma.*

Let's take a look at the ghosts in general and what the relationship of the Holy Ghost is to ordinary ghosts. To the *Jinnin* of Islam. Let us look at how the Holy Ghost wrote Scripture and why and how we need the Holy Ghost for hermeneutics, or the interpretation of Scripture. Let us examine what it means to be inspired, which also comes from the word *spirare*, the root of spirit. How does a poet tap into the Muses, his own psyche, or the Holy Ghost when writing poems? Does the Holy Ghost have to do with the Last Judgment and the evolution of humanity on earth between then and now? What are the Catholic definitions of the Holy Ghost and what did the Protestants reject? Did they change the concept of the Holy Ghost? Is the Holy Ghost just a theological construct or a living person, a living spirit? Did the Holy Spirit die on the Cross when Jesus was crucified, or was she, he, or it spared? If so, how? Why is Holy Spirit for the Jews sometimes feminine—and let us look at the relationship between the Holy Ghost and Sophia, the ancient tradition of wisdom, that appears in John's Revelation, the Apocalypse. Are they the same? Is the Holy Ghost, in fact, the feminine side of the Godhead?

The Arabs reject their feminine Godesses as pagan and ban them from the Koran—maybe because they are somehow related to the Christian and Jewish Holy Spirit. The Prophets contacted the Holy Spirit, but how? What does the Holy Ghost have to do with intellect, wit, cognition, and thinking? Or is it just a construct of Faith? These are some of the concerns that the history and story of the Holy Ghost pose—both in factual history out there, and in this book. This is not speculation but a reading of the record, historical, religious, and theological. The Holy Spirit meant different things to St. Augustine, to Teilhard de Chardin, to the Rosicrucians, to Descartes, to Charles Peguy, to Madame Blavatsky, and to Rudolf Steiner.

The prophet Joel of the Old Testament prophesied that the Holy Spirit would "pour out" when the time came. The Church claimed that the Twenty-First Ecumenical Council, from 1962 to 1966, was the second coming of Pentecost. On the fiftieth day after Passover in the year that Christ died, the Apostles thought that was exactly what happened at Pentecost, or Whitsuntide. The twelve disciples of Jesus from the Upper Room spoke to a multitude "in tongues"—speaking in one language and being understood in another. True? False? Why did John and Paul view the Holy Ghost as the Spirit of Truth—a concept almost without meaning in our times? A concept also meaningless to Pilate, who judged Jesus, or refused to, and asked him, "What is truth?"

Maybe the tale of the Holy Spirit has something to say to countless non-Christians and agnostics and atheists—maybe it is part of human hardwiring, our very thinking. Or is it just an epiphenomenon of theology? Does it, she, or him have anything to say to our daily lives? Our training of ourselves? Our values? To some churchgoers—to fundamentalists, to evangelicals, and to some faithful—such questions may seem startling, or downright sacrilegious. The Holy Ghost is, after all, one of the most sacrosanct ideas of all times, of all religion. For believers, the very idea of questioning the Holy Spirit's nature may seem like a taboo venture into free inquiry. But on closer examination, even the faithful may have clear feelings about God, about Jesus Christ, but retain unclear understandings or even woozy views of the Holy Spirit—even confusion and fear. The religious may take their understanding for granted or, in the case of many Christians, have given up on the Holy Spirit as a confusing term of the Trinity. Many Jews have historically found the Christian procession of the Trinity an abomination, not only because of its acceptance of Jesus Christ's divinity, but also because it seems to make nonsense of the great Judaic idea of monotheism and one God. But the Holy Spirit is a great ecumenical challenge, too. Where Arabs and Jews differ from Christians over the person of Jesus, they differ far less over the presence of the Spirit and the one God. Nor is all humanity Christian. The Great Spirit of the North American Indians may, as we noted, be the same as the Holy Ghost.

Much of culture today is secular. Methodologically and philosophically, science as a whole is almost entirely materialistic in orientation. The genome is at the forefront of human frontiers in the third millennium. But the question continues, even in biotech, as to whether we are no more than atoms and cells. Since Newton's time, when the clock became the symbol for the universe at odds with the Holy Spirit and the old Earth-centered system, the industrial revolution brought us to the brink of a robotic universe; now biotech brings us new ethical questions of whether humanity is all just a matter of engineering genes and of how to engineer evolution.

In this brave new world, is there also a brooding spirit with great wings? Is there a soul? Is our being one that participates in the Great Spirit of the Indians, the world as a living being, or in the traditional presence of the Holy Ghost, of the Holy Spirit? We laughed at the ancients' spirits in trees and the animism of Africans, but now our children laugh at us—the space age is interested in whether there are live aliens, not angels. Maybe the angels, the archangels, and the Holy Spirit itself are like forgotten aliens. Personal witness, even personal existential fate, may be more tied up with this encounter or denial of the Holy Ghost than with anything in the common routine of the everyday or adventures with Hollywood space odysseys. Psychology, the mass media, the global village, the internet and modernity itself may have shortchanged itself by relegating the Holy Ghost—a paradigm in its way for spirituality—to the dustbin of history.

But attacks against and resistance to the presence of a Holy Spirit have not come from the scientific sector or materialism alone. Within the Church through history long and bitter disputes took place over the nature of the Holy Spirit, and more recently the Unitarians, Universalists and Congregationlists all rejected the triune nature of God and removed the references to the Holy Spirit from the Godhead. In Geneva, in neutral and ostensibly tolerant Switzerland, Servetus was burned at the stake in 1533 for expressing that view. The covenant in use for Unitarians today is simply: "In the love of truth, and in the spirit of Jesus, we unite for the worship of God and for the service of man." The Unitarians claim that the early Church was Unitarian in creed—before definitions and deification of the Holy Ghost. But St. Paul claimed, in the early days, that the Spirit was indeed the Spirit of Truth.

America's Ralph Waldo Emerson, while moving on to claim the transcendental spirit in New England, first rejected the idea that the Holy Spirit had written the books of the Bible, accepting instead the new methods of higher Biblical criticism, which relativized the origins of the texts and stressed the authorship of men of a particular time and place. Emerson also rejected the Last Supper and the Eucharistic communion and refused to administer the sacrament, which was for him a "dead form." And this raises an interesting question that should concern some Christians, churchgoers, and Catholics: Is the transubstantiation—the mystery of the transformation of the bread into body and wine into blood—an action of God, of Christ, or of the minister—or of the Holy Spirit?

Along with the modern secularization and materialization of culture and society and the loss of religion, broad movements of spiritual renewal have swept America, from fundamentalism to New Age spirituality and longings to connect with Eastern disciplines such as yoga and meditation. Do these participate in any history of the Holy Spirit? As the peoples and races and nations increasingly mix in this pluralistic culture, will American spirituality jettison the old gods and Jesus Christ and even the "In God We Trust" on the coin of the realm? Will they mingle in some form of revival or participation of the Holy Spirit—perhaps in the brooding Great Spirit of the Indians, the original spirit of the continent? These are not sectarian or denominational questions, nor are they, strictly speaking, theological questions. They are not so much confessional questions or creedal questions as they are spiritual and cultural questions.

In Jewish tradition the High Priest was allowed to enter the Holy of Holies at the Temple only once a year. The sacred was that which was shut off from common use, separate and sanctified, by the agency of men or priests. The holy was not just the sacred, but derived from the word *wholeness*—and was always more divine and more spiritual than the merely sacred. It is, in spiritual experience, not just human beings who approach the traditionally taboo areas or who are kept out of them. In the tradition of the Holy Ghost, it is the Holy Spirit that enters the human being. Darwinian evolution did not evolve just the physical body; the very concept of the inward human and the experience of the divine—or the experience of experience, of conscience and consciousness themselves—was an evolution that goes hand in hand not just with monkeys but also with the passing of the propitiatory blood sacrifices to the ancient gods.

The very idea of a Holy Spirit goes hand in hand with culture's development and evolution, just as does the idea of a human being as more than a tribal and blood member of the family and is also an individual. In the evolution of culture, awareness in religion of the Holy Spirit—not just idols—was something new and accorded with the philosophical and even juridical development of individual rights—the right to life, liberty, and the pursuit of happiness. This makes the story of the Holy Ghost—either as a religious construct for nonbelievers or as a spiritual force or living being and person—more than an academic question. If artificial intelligence and the robot and the internet computer become the models of the mind, the development of culture and life will be at least different, and differently inspired, than when the model was a clock—or an animal monkey, a pagan god, or the Holy Spirit.

This aspect of the Godhead—not just in common parlance, but even in traditional theology—has always received less attention and been treated with less familiarity than God the Father and God the Son. In Chinese Taoist culture and in Buddhist and Hindu cultures, the questions of the spirit were closer to the main core, because the quest itself was more privatized. Enlightenment there is a path of accessing something spiritual, an object of study and practice, but not so much a politically correct creedal definition and communitarian and moral rule, stricture, or norm. Nor was there the awe and internecine strife to such a degree over the possession of the Holy Spirit for political and societal reasons.

Traditionally the dove has been the symbol of the Holy Spirit recognized in the West. Originally, the temple space, or *templum,* was set off and reserved for the augury of birds—the reading of omens, in Rome at least. In St. Peter's Cathedral in Rome, in the apse to the rear of the Basilica, the wall is covered with a grand gilt replica of a throne—the throne that comes down to us from ancient kingdoms and the hierarchies themselves. A dove descends over this empty throne, which is a symbol of the teaching authority of the Church and the dissemination of truth. This dove represents the Holy Spirit. It is not just an emblem of our own personal striving, self-reliance, feelings, or opinions; it is also an esoteric symbol that envisions what comes to humankind—from space.

From the cosmos, from life, the breath, and the spirit. From heaven. Religion tried to defend, nurture and teach what the dove brought. But the Spirit listeth where it will. The Spirit comes into and out of the focus of history—like a proton that cannot be measured and seen at the same time. Or, in more natural times and poetic cultures, like the morning doves that fly in and out of the garden.

# Chapter 3

# The Unwanted Guest

Originally, Spirit meant life, not the otherworld and death. It was only relatively later, nearly the fourteenth century, that a ghost became a specter or apparition, someone who had died—a dead soul. In a way, religion by this time had abstracted the spirit, or soul, from life. Today, if you ask anyone, they will usually say a spirit, as opposed to a body, is something "immaterial." That is, a spirit is not composed of matter, while a body is. A body is made of atoms and molecules; a body is made of matter. A soul or a spirit, however, is not made of matter. Bodies are physical; souls and spirits are not physical. A lot of trouble has been caused by this otherworldliness—a lot of suffering, war, and pestilence. Many Arabs, for instance, who see things very differently from the average American, believe that spirits or souls enjoy material life. Paradise (an Arab word) is a garden for them, in which you eat and drink well and get to enjoy the virgins—in the flesh. For Arabs—like heavenly playboys—paradise is physical, and its virgins have bodies. A good Arab—one who does something for Allah (like fly into the Trade Towers)—receives life eternal and a good time in paradise, with fruits and virgins and palaces. The good Arab is a martyr and receives eternal life, like the Christian martyrs eaten by lions in the Coliseum in Rome, the Eternal City. The Christian, however, gets eternal life *in the spirit*—at least until Doomsday. The Arab martyr, on the other hand, gets eternal life right now, in the flesh. After hitting the Towers he doesn't have to wait till Doomsday. He gets his reward from Allah immediately.

The Greeks also thought very differently. "Go to Hell" did not mean damnation to the Greeks; it meant losing your body. Hell was called Hades. There was no sunshine, no eating and drinking, and no virgins. You became "a shade" when you went there—and everybody did, good or bad, because there was no heaven for the Greeks, only Olympus where the gods lived. Being a shade was no fun. Odysseus, Achilles, and all the other Greek heroes who were afraid of nothing in this world were terrified of Hades. They didn't want to be shades. They wanted to be full-blooded heroes, full of spirit and enjoying, well, the same thing that the Arabs want to enjoy in heaven—food, drink, and virgins. The Greeks had no heavenly afterlife—only Mt. Olympus, where the gods lived. The gods weren't dead either; they weren't spirits in our sense. The Greek gods wanted the same thing as the Greek heroes and the Arabs—to eat, drink, and make merry. That's what the Greek gods enjoyed: banquets, partying, and a very heavy love life. Greek gods and goddesses spent a lot of time doing the unprintable word—loving around. Virgins did not last long on Mt. Olympus. Nor were they in endless supply, as they are in the Arab paradise. As Vestal Virgins in Rome, however, they did preserve an altered consciousness from that of the everyday forum, and guarded the eternal flame.

The French have always been somewhat different, too. They also like partying and banquets and gourmet food, but many Frenchmen have something against virgins; that is why—like the French poet Charles Baudelaire, who wrote the *Flowers of Evil* (*Fleurs des Mal*)—they go to hell seducing the virgins on the way. As the old joke goes, there are not many virgins in France, but there are a lot of virgins in hell. A good Frenchman does not go to heaven to enjoy himself, but to hell.

Science, meanwhile, is supposed to be the art of weights and measures. If you can't weigh or measure it, it is not a body—and for science, only bodies are real. Science does not really believe in ghosts. You can't weigh a ghost (although the Egyptians weighed souls against a feather), and you can't measure a ghost. A ghost is a dead soul. Souls are not supposed to be real. Not even the mind is real anymore for science. The scientist Francis Crick, his colleague James Watson, and California's Daniel Dennet have all proved to their liking that "the mind" is not real and that the soul is not real. They are just part of the body—chemistry, like everything else.

Naïvely enough, they call this "the astonishing hypothesis"—the idea that there is no such thing as spirit.

But the ancient Egyptians were even more astonishing. Before there were even Arabs—or at least Muslims—the Egyptians used to weigh souls, not bodies. There is a famous picture in the Egyptian Book of the Dead showing the God Psychopompus weighing a soul on an actual scale. This was real science, in the ancient sense, like burial of the dead. When Egyptians died, they didn't become just spirits; one became "a body," or a mummy. The body went on a journey in a boat, and guess what? The boat, like Pyramids, was crammed with food and everything else a body would need. The life was all wrapped up and preserved for eternity, and the material things were all there—combs, gold, jewelry, food, and drink. A dead body for the Egyptians was not "immaterial" in our sense, nor was it a ghost. It was a mummy: a lived life. A mummy had no virgins with it, but often enough the Egyptians killed a man's wife so she could be a mummy, too, and ride along with her husband to Eternity.

The ancient Jews were also different. They got out of Egypt at the time of the Exodus not only because they were slaves, but also because they did not believe as the Egyptians did. The Jews in the ancient Hebraic and Judaic cultures, long before Jesus, did not really believe there was any difference between the body and the soul. The soul was life, and it was part of the body. The Jews always like to think monotheistically of one God, instead of many Gods like the Greeks and the Egyptians. And they liked to think of the body and soul as one, too.

Before then, there was nothing but the uncreated. God belonged, before Moses, to the uncreated. In Genesis, God breathed on the nothing, which was chaos, and then there was light. And there was light and the darkness. The first thing God did—and this was the Spirit before the Holy Ghost came to be—was to breath on the waters. This was *ruah,* the original meaning of spirit: breath. It was life. It was no ghost, not in our sense. It was the Spirit of God. God had done the same thing to man, to Adam. God breathed onto the dust. He didn't dress up in a white sheet and turn into a spook to terrify Adam and Eve in the Garden of Eden. God was a Spirit, a breath.

No one was allowed even to say the name of God; it was too holy. The name, however, was not the Lord, then, but Yahweh: the Spirit of God. He was incomprehensible, immeasurable, and unknowable. Of course, there was no science yet, not in our sense. So people did not deny God, but they also could not know God, not in the cognitive sense; God was a presence, a breath of life. That was unknowable, because it was still a mystery. The irony is that today we have science, and we are supposed to know things, but science today denies God, because God is even more unknowable today than he was then. The Jews, in fact, had faith. They believed because they still experienced. Science does not believe, because science has to know. Science is almost tautological: since God is unknowable, science does not study to know Spirit. And it's the same with the breath, or spirit, for science; since they can't weigh the breath—although they can measure it—they believe in biology and biotechnology. Life, however, is still a mystery despite DNA and the double helix and the genome. Science does not care for mystery, so life and its origins have traditionally been less interesting to science than, say, a corpse. A corpse can be measured and weighed. That was how anatomy and physiology began in modern times with autopsies about six hundred years ago. But you cannot perform an autopsy on spirit. Science preferred to talk about clocks and mechanics, and now the genome. These things can be known. You don't have to believe in them anymore. They are proven. They aren't mysteries. But life and its origin remain a mystery. Breath itself is, in a way, still a mystery. Maybe old Egyptian science could weigh a breath, but not Western science. And that's what Spirit and soul originally meant—weightlessness and breath.

Back to the Arabs. The Holy Ghost, a person, is anathema to the Arabs, because they believe in only one God: Allah. Not three: the Father, Son, and the Holy Ghost. Besides, none can worship a spirit. So an Arab who flies into the Trade Towers, naturally, becomes a body—a dead body. In Islam, it is the dead bodies that get the rewards. This is one reason why the famous Islamic school for assassins and suicide is so big. A lot of Arabs, it seems, want to be dead. In a strange way, this is because much of Islam is so spiritual, in a materialistic way. Moreover, they pray a lot; they are spiritual in the Western sense—that is, prayerful and religious. It seems this life on earth is not as good for them. Things don't work here. The Arabs don't seem to get enough material goods here, or the right politics. The Holy Ghost is democratic by tradition, too—another reason, perhaps, why they would prefer to become bodies and live with Allah and the virgins.

America, instead, is part of the West. Here is where Christendom has been for almost two thousand years. Here we have learned that, when we become spirits in the world of the afterlife, we will then get our rewards. The afterworld is not material, however, though doomsday is. This may be why many Americans, who think they have a good life here in this world are scared of the afterlife. They don't want to go there—not yet anyway. Like the Greeks, they don't want to become shades or spirits. They want to be materialists, and stay right here—eat, drink, and watch TV. They want to prolong life, not shorten it.

The Holy Ghost is not material either. Nevertheless, Billy Graham, the most famous Christian in America today, said, "Heaven is like driving around in a gold Cadillac." Some Americans, in fact, have more in common with the Koran and the Arabs than they think—namely, pleasure. The difference is that they don't believe Allah makes gold Cadillacs anymore than Jesus does, and anyway gold Cadillacs are not as plentiful here as they might be. A lot of Americans who think that the Holy Ghost is a spook want heaven on earth; they want to drive around in the gold Cadillac while they are still alive and breathing, not when they are dead and gone to heaven.

The Arabs who do not think America is paradise prefer to be dead, because they actually believe in real paradise—and they want earth in heaven—that is where one gets to drive a gold Cadillac. They know (except for oil sheiks) they will never have one on earth. Americans, on the other hand, usually believe in America, and less often in the Holy Ghost. Americans, in this material way, are smarter than the Arabs. They can't pray as well, but they know that, if they make enough money, they can get a gold Cadillac here and now and drive around Hollywood—and not just in a Chevy or a Volkswagen Bug.

But some Christians are into something else. Many Christians, particularly Europeans and Russians, do not want to drive in a gold Cadillac at all, anymore than those Arabs do. Since the days of the early martyrs in Rome, there have been Christians, too, who want to renounce worldly life, be done with the passions, and have nothing more to do with sex. Some people think this is what the Spirit means. It reminds me of the American Episcopalian minister who officiated a wedding and a funeral on the same day. "I'm afraid that I buried the bridegroom and married the corpse," he said afterwards in his confession.

Some Christians even think that being a Spirit means not to marry. Some early Christian martyrs, like Arabs, wanted to become spirits not in the sense of breathing and living, but in the sense of being dead, immaterial, and enjoying the spiritual afterworld. This was at a time when early Christians were against Rome, and Rome was against Christians; many were like the Arabs today, except that the Christians wanted to enter heaven without a body, while the Arabs want bodies in heaven.

Among the nonreligious, a lot of people today think of the Holy Spirit as some sort of religious taboo that will take away their fun, their liquor, their sex, and their songs. They think you have to be a materialist to have any pleasure in life. But this is not the whole story. Those often responsible for this negative image were the pilgrims, the Puritans, the Catholic Inquisition, Luther, Calvin, and others—sometimes even in the churches themselves—as well as ascetic sects, religious cults, some forms of monasticism, and secular writers and scientists who have a bugaboo about the mention of spirit in any form. For some of them it is simply not real.

Others think of the Holy Spirit as part of the other world—kingdom come after death and the afterlife. For them, the Holy Ghost is aptly named. It lives in the dead if at all, in the cemeteries and graveyards. Others, in churches, nevertheless forget that the Holy Ghost lives in the congregation and think that the Holy Spirit is an ineffable something that transforms the bread into body, the wine into blood—and that the faithful person should not look, not see, but turn their eyes downward. Above all, they should not look the Holy Spirit in the eye—but let the priest consult it in books, in formulas, and in the Sistine Chapel.

Still others, secularists, think of the Holy Ghost as a superstition and a joke. Among some of the faithful they think of the Holy Spirit as the mover of history and the guide of redemption. A lot of people talk about spirit or matter, about dualism, mind and body, but never ask or know how the Holy Ghost is different from God or what it, she, or he is actually all about—whether it has any relevance to actual life, science, or culture, much less life in the churches. East and West, North and South, all think differently about the Holy Spirit, yet, strangely, even the theologians and clergy seldom discuss who and what the Holy Ghost represents.

Spirit is for many often the neglected dimension of the Godhead, even in Church itself—not to mention on Madison Avenue, Hollywood, and Washington.

## Chapter 4

# The Presence: Being

This book on the Holy Ghost, whose story is the least told in tradition, is not a history of the Church or of theology; rather, it is a biography. This means a life story of the word *spirit* and *Spirit,* a relation of the Holy Spirit in and out of world history. Ideally, it should include folk talk as well as definitions and invocations. Naturally, much of the official talk took place at council in the Church—but not all. We can call all this presence—within but also sometimes out of the Church—by the name of the Holy Ghost. We can trace the biography of the name itself: and who said what about it and when. This would not necessarily be Church history, and we don't mean to limit the Holy Ghost just to church. The spirit also lives in the tradition, say, of Hegel the philosopher—spirit outside the church landing where it will and connecting the spirit of philosophy to the spirit of the Holy Ghost. This being, or Being, this indwelling, has nevertheless been with us from time immemorial, in peasants as well as in prophets, popes, and kings. Inside the church, yes, and outside. In the Godhead, but also on Earth. In Jesus Christ and in the Apostles, but also in words of John Glenn and Jimmy Carter.

There is an old saying that it is one thing to believe in creed, and another to believe the Creed. Such a caveat is also true of the presence—this beingness of the Holy Ghost. This is harder to talk about than merely naming the name. It gives gifts; it appears in signs. Lindbergh and the Spirit of St. Louis may have flown with it, and the men at Normandy may have felt it. It may be on the global Internet. The beingness in the history of the Holy Ghost does not talk a lot about itself. We can't prove much, either, or even say all that much. But we can surmise and sample, as when Einstein says, "God does not play dice," or when Bach writes a chorale, or Beethoven writes "Ode To Joy."

People and things allude in action, too, to what others feel in church, or speculate over it in theology. People of action do not proclaim their creed of the Holy Ghost in a Papal Bull, but actions speak louder than words. Others try to experience consciousness as in the New Age culture, or Hegel writes about the phenomenology of spirit in philosophy. Then, too, a picture is worth a thousand words and Leonardo, Michelangelo, and Raphael may have tried to paint this being indirectly; there have been very few paintings of Pentecost and the dove, and no direct illustrations of the Holy Ghost. Nor are there any photographs.

All this we can only sample. But we can talk in some detail about the narrower history of the name, the "conceptology," the philosophy and the theology—and the history. For example, were the visions and voices of Joan of Arc attributed by her to the Holy Spirit? How did the Ghost itself come to be named, where did the idea come from, what was the spirit that inspired the prophets, or the Bible? What is the voice of the spirit when modern Pentecostals talk in tongues today in assemblies in the United States—and is it the same as the Holy Ghost of the Anglicans? Holy Spirit of the Roman Church, or spiritual inspiration invoked by Mormons, Christian Scientists, and others may differ—may not work the same way. What is the difference, we might ask, between the Spirit of the Ghost, indeed, and our modern day secular spirit? But more important than this: We can discuss and clarify what this Holy Ghost—a lofty name or person—is to personal existence, to our own being as body, soul, and spirit. And to "the Ghost in the Machine." Does the dimension of the Spirit, even in the Bible, relate to questions of whether our own struggles over whether we are inert matter or accidents of chemistry, and whether our own mind is just the brain? All we can do in a short journalistic book is to make a dent on such a huge subject; in itself, in the widest sense, it is an inexhaustible subject. Nor is this a scholarly tract or an academic exercise. There is not much elaborate apparatus here or footnotes. It is talk. Yet we can establish whether Thomas Jefferson wrote the Declaration of Independence in the name of the Holy Ghost, or not. But we can probably never establish scientifically, beyond much doubt, that the being of the Holy Spirit moved his hand. Yet we can ask; we can probe. The inspiration, for example, that moved Jefferson is very different than the inspiration that moved Hitler and Stalin. It may have been just atoms. It may have been the Enlightenment in one case and Arab sources in another. Or demons.

A demon, too, is a spirit. Even science, which does not study demons because they are immaterial and "do not exist," will admit that demons are spirits. The New Age talks about angels all the time, and angels are spirits, too. But none of these people talk about the Holy Ghost anymore. But wasn't the Holy Ghost the spirit of spirits—the grandaddy of them all?

In 1264 the new Pope Urban IV, once the archdeacon of Liege, ordained the Bull *Transiturus*—a decree establishing the feast of Corpus Christi. This is different than Pentecost. In 1964, after some seven hundred years, I traveled with Pope John XXIII to a small Italian town to celebrate the memory of this Bull and Feast Day. Pope John had been the first Pope to leave the Vatican and visit a jail in Rome, Regina Coeli, and then go to Assisi.

Pentecost celebrates the descent of the Spirit. In some ways, Corpus Christi is an opposite mystery; it celebrates the co-inherence of matter with the Deity. Corpus Christi brings the intellectual splendor of doctrine and a glory of liturgy together in a show—the show of the sacrament. There were Processions. Banners. Finery. Robes. Jewels. Things of this world.

Traveling with the Pope (who is now in the process of being made a Saint) and reading the *Transiturus* on the seven-hundredth anniversary of its promulgation, I felt that the spirit, in a very theatrical way, was getting special attention here, as though the priests were assuring us that matter got its due. Incidentally, I did not get the same feeling of reverence at all when, thirty six years after the *Transiturus*, Pope Boniface issued a new Bull, *Unam Sanctum*, declaring that the salvation of every human creature depends on his or her obedience to the Pope. The Corpus Christi teaching has to do with the relation of matter to spirit; *Unam Sanctum* is about the Pope in relation to authority, control, and power. There was a time when the Popes—no longer interested in the democracy of the Holy Ghost—took away the cathedral chapters rights of appointing bishops, taking for themselves the rights to dispense all offices and benefices. Even the King of England, returning from exile, started confiscating benefices. These are the kinds of quarrels we can ignore here; they have to do not with the Holy Spirit but with earthly power.

The Holy Office, too, sometimes becomes a kind of long shadow. A Corpus Christi, the feast, is one thing—a matter of Christ's body and the transubstantiation in a new feast and doctrine; but when the Holy Office needs not only to correct the spirits of heretics but to kill their bodies as well, something wrong is happening. Getting rid of bad thoughts in a material way is different than getting rid of noxious doctrine. The clerics in the Inquisition, for example, begin to actually go for the body—burning, hanging, and torturing. Since co-inherence is of the body, not just the spirit, the Church—much like the Romans and later the Nazis—went overboard and started to disinherit the bodies, not just the spirit. It was no longer just mind control. This passage in spiritual life does not offer much to commend itself, in my mind, but it proves a point: that what people think about spirit and matter can lead to action and consequences. I would not personally call those actions spiritual—though some church and religious historians consider them part of the history of spiritual life.

Another attitude toward the Holy Sprit and the Holy Ghost would have led to a different history. In my mind, the doctrine of *Ad Extirpanda* (1252 and the Inquisition) was not written under the inspiration of the Holy Ghost. Canon Law—like the withholding of the right of *ius morendi* by the Romans in Jerusalem that denied Jews the right of putting to death—forbids clerics to shed blood. The Inquisition, true, handed heretics over to the law and magistrates. The secular arm did it for them. Was this any different from the Jews handing Jesus over to the Roman authorities?

I prefer, as a song of the spirit, Saint Francis "Canticle to the Creatures," his song to Brother Sun and Sister Moon. Here is something that one can believe is infused by the Holy Spirit.

With the revival of Aristotelianism in the thirteenth century with St. Thomas Aquinas, though, a new conflict arises, or at least reblazes as a tyranny of reason against common sense and human spirit. St. Thomas has been accused of absolutist thought, and, in a word, the antidote would have been to start the *Summa Theologica* with the words, "The Holy Ghost supposes," or "The Spirit guesses." Instead, in Scholasticism, some claim, reason dictates order as absolutely as does faith. Others compare Scholasticism, despite its sometimes-sublime intellectual beauty, to making a bureaucracy out of belief. The antidote here would have been the spirit of the Holy Ghost, perhaps, and, as a poet, so would Dante. For one thing, Thomas Aquinas does not need women except for reproduction, while Dante requires women for salvation. Poetry, unlike theology, turns formulas into experience and tests them there, in the realm of metaphors, diction, and lyrics. I don't know whether the Holy Ghost reads poetry, or writes it, but it would be better than the Inquisition.

When I was in Rome, I had a lot of trouble accepting Canon Law. For one thing, I wasn't a lawyer. Canon Law, the letter of it, was promulgated in 1234 by Gregory IX. It remained in force practically unchanged until 1918. The spirit of the Holy Ghost is needed to interpret Scripture, but a lawyer is needed to interpret Canon Law.

Even Romance and sex, not just usury and torts and the sacraments, was controlled by Canon Law. Before the Council of Trent in 1645, however, marriage was valid without a priest. The two parties were themselves the authors of the sacrament. Canon Law then applied the letter of the law and even said not only how Romance could be conducted, it also dictated how to understand the male and female organs, turning marital relations into a contract and handing it over to the Sacred Roman Rotary.

The Spirit of the law is different than the letter of the law.

Though I should know whether the Holy Ghost reads poetry, because I write poetry, I do not know if the Holy Ghost ever read law; Jesus did not think so.

Sometimes historians are tempted to accuse the Holy Ghost of inspiring the Children's Crusade. But the children of Europe, blessed by the Pope, went innocently, enthusiastically, and well intentioned enough, indeed, in the Spirit—to redeem Jerusalem. The crusade ended, of course, in political doom, betrayals, and sale into slavery. Many died of hunger and cold.

Some people think that all this activity of the Spirit led to the Templars in France. The role of the Holy Ghost is very obscure here, because the Inquistors accused this spiritual order of strange idols, obscene kissing, spitting on the Cross, renouncing Christ, and black Masses. The King of France arrested them all in 1307 in the name of the Spirit. Exactly what their sacrilege and blasphemy were—if there was any—is unclear. The claims of the Templars to spirit and virtue have been lost in ghoulish reminders of Halloween, Vampires, black cats, and witches on brooms.

We know the Bible and the Koran are in different languages. God wrote the Bible; Allah dictated the Koran. The spirit spoke or mediated to St. John; the spirit spoke or mediated to Muhammad. No one seems to know how this was done, however. Gabriel delivered the message to the Virgin Mary that the Holy Ghost would visit her. Is there anything in common here—anything that touches the grounds of our own self-awareness and being? Was the spirit invoked here in any way connected with the spirit that moved Christian martyrs to be torn apart and eaten in the Roman Coliseum? Or was this spirit the same as the Arab spirit in the School of Assassins, which promises paradise to the Arab martyrs and pilots who flew into the New York Trade Towers? Can knowledge, theology, and science of the spirit be developed, just like, say, biotechnology? Or is that what Freud did in psychology—concluding that most of spirit was unconscious wishing. Can we discriminate consciously or objectively between the spirit of martyrs in Rome and the martyrs of those in Baghdad and Palestine?

Faith and religion often tried over time and the centuries to temper, to control, and to moderate the human being. The Holy Ghost is called the "Comforter." At other times, movements sprang up that stirred fundamentalist passions, sometimes in the name of religion, and almost never in the name of the Holy Ghost; but in the name of God or Allah, riots, disorder, and mayhem follow. In some quarters, enthusiasm is a mark of the spirit in some senses; to others it is a mark of insubordination, heresy, and rebelliousness.

In this book, we take a look at this, inasmuch as we can pin anything down journalistically about something as immaterial as the Holy Ghost. Historically, there has been a great deal more interest in God, Allah, Moses, Jesus, Muhammad, and the Buddha than in the Holy Ghost. That helps our task enormously, because there is much less to read and write than about, say, the presidents of America or about the czars of Russia. Most science deals in bodies, not ghosts, so there isn't much there either. History prefers to talk about wars and heavy metal rather than spirits, so there isn't a lot about the Holy Ghost in *The Rise and Fall of the Roman Empire* or by Toynbee or in encyclopedias or, for that matter, in recent books from Yale University about the end of American civilization. There may only be a few telltale traces. Often the Holy Ghost is like a trace element.

When it comes to the Holy Ghost, we are on a frontier again—the frontier of the past sure, a few outposts, a few scraps, a few signs. It is, when it comes to the Holy Ghost, a frontier between death and eternal life, too—a frontier between the material and immaterial. And traditionally, the Holy Ghost has to do with the future, so the frontier is the future as well. But journalists don't look only to heaven for their sources; they do "dirt time"—time on the trail reading the leaves, the footprints, the moss on the trees, the sticks and stones, and the direction of the breeze. A praying mantis, traditionally the insect of the Holy Ghost, may tell the way. An eagle may soar above as an augury. The broad wings of the Holy Ghost brood on all things, however, according to the poet Gerard Manley Hopkins.

Clear explanations need not kill the mystery and wonder and reverence. Knowing that a pain in your arm is there because it is broken does not reduce that pain, but it helps focus your attitude toward it. The same is true of spirit for the poet William Blake. Knowing that a grain of sand is from the beach, that it is a granite crystalline silicate, does not mean you need wonder less—but more. It is still a whole world. An explanation need not spoil the attitude—it can fulfill the attitude. The affective side—not just the cerebral side—of the attitude needs cultivation; the grain of sand remains the same. It may be that what you think and feel about a grain of sand, or about the Holy Spirit, will determine what you do—indeed, what governments do, what cultures develop, and what and where wars will be fought.

Spirit, in history, has been abstracted and often eviscerated. Sometimes it has been materialized, as in spiritualism of the table tapping kind. So what does spiritualism have to do with the Holy Ghost? The answer is: maybe not much. The Holy Ghost is not a medium for communicating with the dead. It is not even a ghost in that sense. It is not a "haunted" person. Spiritualism in America instead got its modern impetus in 1848 in Hydeville, New York, when the Fox family heard noises in the attic. The noises became loud and were heard often, even by neighbors. One of the Fox girls, Katie, named the ghost Mr. Splitfoot and tried to talk with it. The Holy Ghost did not answer, however. It was Mr. Splitfoot who answered. Katie devised a method of tapping and querying, and found out that Mr. Splitfoot had been a traveling salesman who was murdered in the house. He said he was buried in the cellar. When the family dug there, they found the bones of Mr. Splitfoot. A new rage for spiritualism was born in America and Europe. The Victorians, straight-laced in their propriety and prudery, tuned in to tables and held séances.

Finally, in 1888, the Vatican publicly condemned spiritualism and communications with "spirits" as false. Faith and science intervened. As with many actions of the Church, this dampened popular enthusiasm and favored institutionalism—later, "controlled" research into spiritistic phenomena was carried further by the Society for Psychical Research and later on in this country at Duke University. In the sense of this research, the Holy Ghost and anything it does would be a "paranormal" phenomena. The Church had its point; it did not want a revival of witchcraft, mediumship, and hobnobbing with dead spirits, the remarkable, and the fantastic. It did not want an alternative consciousness; in fact, the Church speaks instead for a life-based, family oriented, communion, based on a churchified spirit. Church is, in fact, supposed to be a community of the Holy Spirit.

There were others who wanted to combat nineteenth-century materialism and what they viewed as materialism and ossified doctrine in the Catholic Church itself by latching on to the fad of spiritualism and linking it with intellectual pursuits and ancient wisdoms and secret teachings of the East. In this spirit, the Russian Madame Helena Petrovna Blavatsky, along with Colonel Henry Steel Olcott, founded the Theosophical Society—the wisdom of God—in New York in 1875. Theosophy was more interested in the old wisdom of the spirit—in the sense of esoteric tradition—than it was in the Holy Ghost as an incorporation or spirit of Christianity. Later, the Pentecostals would try to revive the original spirit and enthusiasm of early church and Pentecost. All this is not an empty dispute and is still relevant today in the aftermath of the permissive culture and as post-liberal America seeks to pursue its values in the twenty-first century. Truth, supposedly the province of the Holy Spirit, needs research and protection, whether in journalism, science, or religion. So does *being*—that is, behavior.

The news that the spirit blows where it will has always been used not only to enable new ideas and new actions, but also by almost everyone promoting a new cult, new sexual standards, new practices, new morality, new drugs, new art, and even perversion and license to behave in anyway anyone wants, from Nazidom to hippiedom. Academic, university, and secular scoffing at the Holy Spirit, however, does not appreciate the legitimate purposes of the Church or others who cultivate the defense of truth and the observance of the spirit as a method of sorting out the values of history and the culture wars.

Many people think the Holy Spirit is some kind of superstition, not a matter of theological science and the fruit of a method and an existential guideline for researching truth, culture, and history. In this sense, history is the story of a trial—the great trial of Kafka. The advocate is the Paraclete, the Holy Spirit. The Judge is God. The defense witness is Jesus. In the dock is Satan, the devil. It is a trial in two senses—a trial by fire, of being and life, and a trial of truth by the intellect: guilty or not guilty. Culture itself, and human evolution, may be the crime. Was it crimes against humanity or original sin that constituted the sin against the Holy Ghost—the one unforgivable sin? Or was it some other blasphemy?

Many people prefer to view the Holy Spirit in real being, in life—in the swaying black ladies dancing and singing Gospel songs. In singing the spirituals—"Old Man River." They suspect, instead, the incarnation of the Holy Spirit as doctrine, dogma, or even truth, because, according to political correctness, truth is relative. There has been too much intolerance already in the name of truth. The truth can never incarnate, they say, even if it has already incarnated, as Christianity claimed and as John and Paul witnessed.

What people forget, and what the Holy Ghost tries to remind us of, is that truth and being—thinking and life—are interconnected. What you think and what you do—what, when, and how—are related. And in just such a way the Holy Spirit and matter, the Holy Spirit and life, are related too. The quality of truth one holds, what one thinks and believes, may effect the quality and fullness of being one lives: *the presence.*

# Chapter 5

# Spirit — What Is It?

This book breaks journalistic ground in several ways. It is alone, as far as I know, in dealing solely with the lineage of the Holy Ghost and its relation to the word spirit—that is, spirit with a small "s," Spirit with a capital "S," and Holy Ghost as a person. Here, spirit, the concept as well as the devotional soul, or Spirit, receives a short, concise history in broad brush, and "spirit" is not always the same as "Spirit." Many people who do not talk of or believe in the Holy Ghost nevertheless talk of spirit and cite Spirit, or even the secular spirit. For instance, a cruise ship sails in Boston Harbor: the *Spirit of Boston.* "Spirit of America" is on the Massachusetts license plates. It was a plane, the Spirit of St. Louis, that first flew across the Atlantic nearly a century ago. There is a patriotic spirit. *The Spirit of '76* is claimed in Marblehead, Massachusetts, in Abbott Hall to be the most famous picture in America. In the nineteenth century, the philosopher Friedrich Hegel defined the abstract concept "spirit" for the world and for German idealism. In Germany, to this day the fine arts are called *Geisteswissenshaften*—the sciences of the spirit. These terms, these things, may even have a relationship that we can treat with the Holy Spirit.

What is the difference, if any, between spirit and soul? Is soul, in the sense of *psyche* (Greek for soul, as in psychology) any different that the word *spirit?*

As much as possible, the story of Spirit, as in the Holy Spirit, is separated here from a more mundane bread-and-butter history of the Church. For instance, the Holy Ghost is usually dealt with in connection with the history of the Trinity, but here we try to avoid the disputes about Father and Son and substance, and focus instead on the experience of spirit, Spirit, and the Holy Ghost. For instance, too, we will deal with appearances and citations of the Holy Spirit in history, without going into all the Church wars, Church politics, founding of orders, or all the heresies and conflicts. Everything that has to do only with Church and State, or clerical matters, or discipline, or regulation we will leave out when the spirit is not involved more broadly. This clears some underbrush from our story and focus. But we do deal, for example, with the Archangel Gabriel's announcement to the Virgin Mary that the Holy Ghost will come to her. Nor do we focus solely on spirit as in religion, but we work over the difference between Holy Spirit as in Holy Ghost—and spirit as in the secular or scientific spirit. We try, for instance, to see where the lineage of the Holy Ghost diverged into the lineage of the scientific spirit. Or where the concept of Spirit diverged from a conception even of the mind. In fact, I look to see if the words *mind* and *spirit* diverged at some point in usage—if they always mean the same thing, and if any of that touches the same area as that is devotionally referred to as Holy Spirit, both inside and outside the Church.

*Holy,* as in Holy Spirit, seems to be added only later to the descriptions of early experiences of Spirit by Jesus and the Apostles. *Holy,* from the Anglo Saxon *halig,* meant hale, perfect, or whole. It was used to translate the Roman *sanctus*—which the Church added to the word *spiritus* in later years, as it codified and installed the Ghost as the third person of the Trinity. The Romans, as we saw, used *spiritus* in a different way, connected to vigor, ardor, breath, and life. It was a natural spirit and also a Pagan spirit in classicism. The Roman medical doctor Galen (130–200 AD) distinguished between the natural spirit, the vital spirit, and the animal spirit. Natural spirit was connected to growth, nutrition, and generation, and was a vapor arising from the blood and located in the liver. Vital spirit arose in the heart and mixed with air breathed by the natural spirit supplying heat and life. The animal spirit was the power of motion and sensation, and, in the rational principle was a modification of vital spirit that affected the brain. It is a long way from this Roman view of spirit to the modern encyclopedias and dictionaries, which define *spirit* as "the supersensible, a reality that cannot be perceived by the physical senses." The distance from Galen to this view is as great as the distance from Galen's vapors to modern medicine. The word has come to mean not only a specter, but also something unknowable, nonphysical, ineffable, and immaterial. History has, in a sense, eviscerated and abstracted spirit, both the thing—*thing* is the wrong term—and the word itself. It should be essence rather than a thing. As an Irish priest at the Ecumenical Council at the Vatican (1962–1966) once joked to me, "Alcohol is the only spirit I've ever seen."

For the Romans, however, spirit—in the Pagan spirit—still means breath, courage, vigor, vivacity, animalism, ardor, temper, mood, enthusiasm, as well as "immaterial intelligence" in the Platonic sense. It was the later traditions, both in the Church and, for example, in Alchemy, that picked up the immaterial tradition of spirit—spirit as a quintessence, spirit—as in the spirit of wine and fermentation, as the volatile distillation of matter, the soul as a phoenix and butterfly.

The Hebrew tradition gave it another sense, too, than did the Romans—an earthier more immanent sense of the Spirit in the temple, Solomon's Temple. Roman Gods were anthropomorphic; they looked and felt like bodies. Statues. Idols. The Jews, with their monotheistic tradition, had the tradition of the Spirit of the one God Yahweh, who breathed on the waters of creation and on the dust to make Adam. Early views of Spirit changed, too, particularly through the story of Jesus. John and Paul related the Spirit—so often contrasted with the law—to the Spirit of Truth. The early comrades of Jesus spoke of the "Spirit being with you"—not the Holy Spirit. The Church, in large part, added the word *Holy* gradually, and for real reasons, as we shall see in the next chapter on Holy Spirit as distinct from Spirit.

Again, we are trying here to sort the heritage of the word *spirit* from its early meanings and see how it evolved into the *Holy Spirit*—and, in the next chapter, some of what that shift meant. Also, the name is one thing, and the being, or essence, of spirit—particularly as in Holy Spirit, the feel, and life of it—are different. The word and the being are not, unfortunately, always the same.

Spirits appear in the tradition of animism—the spirits of trees, for example. In the Bible, spirits are also exorcized. Demons are spirits, too. All of these uses are different in some sense, yet they have something in common, too. The philosopher George Santayana in *The Realm of Spirit* used the word *Spirit* often, but narrowly, in an almost physiological sense. But he used it in a different way in the mid-twentieth century at Harvard University than the way William James used it at the end of the nineteenth century in his landmark work *The Varieties of Religious Experiences.* And this is different than the way Massachusetts Bay uses it in the "Spirit of America," or the way Mary Baker Eddy refers to it in *Christian Science.* Some people distinguish harshly between spirit and matter, some between soul and body. Many scientists deny the spirit altogether—or, for that matter, the soul and mind. Are any of these people talking about the same thing, or the same spirit?

By focusing on the lineage of Spirit and on the story and name of the Holy Ghost, we are laser beaming into an intense land of light, narrowing and intensifying a discussion. We are not dealing exclusively with the religious matters of whether God exists or not, nor are we debating about angels or proofs of God. We are not doing a history of religions, Christianity, or the Bible, but a phenomenology. We are not recording Indulgences or reciting the names of Popes and reformers—except where they or the story touch the record of Spirit—when there is the touch of the spirit or the Holy Ghost.

We are dealing, insofar as we can—the reader and I—with the story of, or the difference between, spirituality and religion. There is a difference, yes, between spirit and religion. The Church has in fact, in some ways, often been diffident about the spirit. Consider, for example, the difference between the spirit in religion and the spirit in New Age spirituality. The history of the organization of religion, or Christendom, the First Estate—the Church, the Cathedrals, the schools, the catechism, the crusades, or, for that matter, the burnings, the tortures—does not concern us much here. Who is the Holy Ghost, or what is more the question? We separate that question out as chaff from the wheat, but when it says, "The spirit blows where it listeth," or when the Church claims inspiration from the Holy Ghost, we turn our attention on. And we try to identify, too, the signs and gifts of the Holy Spirit, as well as what Isaac Newton or Einstein or Galileo said about spirit.

What happens with this approach is that we get a narrower field, but a brush treatment of the overall subject as it effects or appears in history. We zoom in, so to speak, on the Holy Ghost wherever we can, even if there is no close-up except inside ourselves. And we hit Hegel, or what Jefferson thought of Spirit, but we don't discuss proofs of God the Father or the Son nearly as much as they are dealt with in devotional and history books or in books of theology. This way we get a broader brush treatment—and see the shift from spirit as in Rome, to spirit as in supernatural—the age of the Holy Ghost as the vibrant web of the universal spirit, or supernatural co-inherence, trying to emerge.

For Hegel, later on, all history is spirit. We cannot record all history. But we can now turn, with some sense of ancient spirit, to the emergence of the Holy Ghost—the Holy Spirit as it emerged after the age of Pontiff Augustus.

## Chapter 6

# Holy Spirit

In Rome, the Fates were Spirits; they spun and cut human life. By the time of the consul Boethius (470–525), divine purpose had replaced fate. The classical Pagan Gods, playful and spirited, were dying out, and Boethius issued a wakeup call to the Romans: "It is divine purpose that rules human beings, not fate." This is an announcement in a way of the Holy Ghost — the new Holy Spirit replacing the Pantheon of old Gods. In some ways in America, it was the reverse: the Manifest Destiny of the New World replaced the old hegemony of the Holy Ghost, and the ghost of the Roman, Hapsburg, and even British Empires. That new Holy Ghost would help change God from a harvest deity increasing the crop into one interested in faith, hope, and love — although as St. Basil said, "Who worships a spirit?" The idols fell. At least that was the original intention, until tradition, codification, and abstraction in part eviscerated the spirit.

One commentator, Leonard Shalin, describes this in *The Alphabet Versus the Goddess* as a conflict between a pre-literate and post-literate world. He refers to the "old image-oriented holistic and nonlinear Goddess" of the pre-alphabetized world as against the era of the Holy Spirit in the post-alphabet abstraction of a one living world. It almost sounds like a forerunner of the Worldwide Internet. All this is partly true, but remember that Jesus also personalized the old Gods originally with his new message of a living spirit versus dead idols and impersonal law.

Today a Google search on the Internet for "Holy Spirit" comes up with more than 4,220 results, including a fourteen-karat Holy Spirit lapel pin and a ten-karat Holy Spirit ring. There is a monastery of the Holy Spirit in Conyers, Georgia; a southern parish of the Holy Spirit that advertises Holy Spirit hymns, a Pennsylvania Ukrainian Church of the Holy Ghost; a Mormon.org Holy Ghost page; a Holy Ghost monthly service at Camp K146 in Lagor, Africa; a Holy Ghost film; a Holy Ghost Missionary College in Dublin, Ireland; a page on rites of the Holy Ghost Festival of the Portuguese, which is celebrated in Stonington, Connecticut, replete with Holy Ghost sausage and hot dogs; in Hawaii, an alpha course of the Episcopal Church of the Holy Spirit; a Holy Spirit Radio 1570 AM, WISP, out of Doylestown, Pennsylvania; and a page for the final recovery plan of the Holy Ghost: IPOMOPSIS. One would think the Holy Ghost is alive and doing well.

Back before the fourth century, however, the Holy Spirit had not yet been defined, and the Holy Ghost was not officially enshrined until the Council of Niceae in 325 AD. The Holy Spirit — *pneuma theou,* or Spirit of God — was in some ways an import from Judaism, known there as the Spirit of Yahweh, the "I am the I am," the same spirit, or *ruah,* that breathed and moved on the waters in the beginning, and that "breathed into man's nostrils the breath of life" when the human being became a living soul. Then dreams were still related to spirit. Isaiah the prophet had talked of the spirit of wisdom, too — the spirit of understanding — and already at the first temple of Solomon, the blood sacrifices had been supplanted by the sacrifice and spirit of the word.

Holy, as distinct from pagan and profane, was also an import. "Holy" rendered the Hebrew word *Kadesh,* meaning the separate, as in hallowed, or sacred ground. *Hal,* or "whole" in Anglo Saxon, also meant pure or free from sin. There was, however, originally a difference between *holy* and *sacred,* which is lower on the totem pole in Roman usage than *holy,* for the sacred is made by human institutions and rites, while holy is by the power of above and its own nature holy. God himself and his Spirit are Holy, while his commands and laws are sacred. It was also the essence of prophetic ministry in Judaism, as revived by Jesus, that spirit acts *proprio motu* (in the Latin term) by its own impulse, as distinct from contracts and laws that apply externally. This difference is the source of Jesus' saying that the Spirit "blows where it listeth — where it will." This, too, is the source of one of the greatest controversies in religious history — the tradition of selling Church offices and titles.

In Greece and Rome, the oracles had been paid for. Pagans consulted the spirit for a price. In Hebrew history, prophecy, which acted *proprio motu*, could not be paid for or controlled by contract. This was the great significance of the scene in the New Testament, when Simon the Magus asked Peter and John if he could buy the power of the Holy Ghost from them. "And when Simon saw that through the laying on of the Apostles' hands the Holy Ghost was given, he offered them money" (Acts. 8:18). Peter tells him that, for thinking that the gift of God could be bought, his money can perish with him. Simon Magus also tried to fly to heaven, incidentally, but crashed when Peter and Paul's prayers against his evil spirits brought him down. The Church's practice of selling offices and titles took its name from Simon Magus and was called "Simony." But Simon was worshipped by some as the founder of Gnosticism — the esoteric wisdom that emphasized knowledge of the spirit over faith in the unknowable. As such, of course, the Church cast him as the earliest, archetypal heretic, even though the Church adopted his practice of selling the Holy Ghost's powers.

Today the word *ghost* means wraith, specter, or someone in a white sheet. *Whitsunday*, the English term for Pentecost, comes from the word *white.* But originally *ghost* meant more of a divine, vibrant spirit. Holy madness was the shamanic possession of a body by a spirit, sometimes dancing, singing, or dervishing. Spirits were not just holy either, but also unclean or demonic, and even Jesus practiced exorcism by chasing out demons. Only later did ghostology come to be the study of dead spirits — the ghost in the attic, which is not a Holy Ghost. Incidentally, one of the keys of exorcism is to get the exact name of the possessing spirit. This, too, was a reason, in the opposite sense of enshrining the Spirit, for the Church's cultivation of the name of the Holy Ghost. In Hebrews 10:29, the Spirit is referred to as the "Spirit of Grace."

Although the Holy Ghost can be named, it cannot be pictured except by signs. The person of the Holy Ghost has never been pictured directly in art, although there is an icon of the Holy Ghost on the porch of the Basilica of St. Mark's in Venice, and there is a brush drawing by Anthony van Dyck (1620) in the Hermitage in St. Petersburg. It was a folk saying that Jesus Christ is actually seen, but it is the Spirit that actually reveals him. Iconoclasm, the smashing of images, in the East during the Middle Ages was partly a movement to keep the purity of the spirit by not making images of God, the Son, or the Saints. But the Spirit is sometimes pictured as a dove, a finger, a light, water, oil, or fire. Of course, this is partly because the Holy Ghost is not an anthropomorphic figure but an indwelling spirit. Likewise, the Holy Spirit has never become a statuary idol or even a cult object like Mary. And there are visitations of the Holy Ghost in the sense of inspiration, but no record of hallucinations or miraculous appearances of a figure.

The Holy Ghost is never pictured looking on at the crucifixion, for instance, or the deposition. It is only in the form of the dove at the baptism. The sign of peace, too, exchanged by churchgoers, is not specifically the sign of the Holy Ghost, but more the spirit of Christ and the spirit of "peace be with you." From the point of view of gender, God, or *theos,* was masculine: God the Father. But *pnuma,* Spirit, was neuter. This gender was important, because Greek and Pagan Gods had proliferated with sexuality. The distinction between creators and created had been blurred. The glorification of virginity and neuter became important. Gregory of Nyssa used the maternal metaphor for God often — both deity (*theotes*) and Trinity (*trias*) were feminine in Greek. *Logos* was masculine, but *Sophia,* the Spirit of Wisdom, was feminine. Divine nature in some traditions, particularly for the Holy Ghost, transcended gender.

Among Jesus and his comrades, the Spirit was initially democratic and even individual. That is, it spoke through anyone and didn't just run an office. Its dwelling, previously the temple, now became the community of believers, and it visited each person individually. This is one of Jesus' gifts to his followers — the worth of the individual person. Now different from the transcendent, all-powerful God, the Spirit is in each and God's temple is our own body: the temple of the Holy Spirit. Fertility and the phallus as worshipped by Pagan cults were somewhat faceless. Christianity is sometimes credited with developing an appreciation of the countenance, the face, as well as the spirit in the community, the presence. The recognition of the early Spirit in the early cells, in other words, was a score for personhood, individuation, self-actualization, inalienable rights, and even the pursuit of happiness. Whereas the great God of wrath in his fullness was beyond the person, the Spirit, in its new sense, drew the Great God down into the small heart. Even individual conscience, the awareness of choice in good and bad, was born under the spirit. For Jews, Jawveh and God were towering fathers, but the spirit brought the "unrevealed essence" of God through the Spirit to each person. And this was not the recognition of an academic or state religious system, but a personal experience and personal witness.

God, as Spinoza later said, was the prime mover, and his own. Although, even the Catholic Church recognizes that the Holy cause, or Spirit, was at work in the world before Christ and the Vatican was glorified, the Holy Ghost is not thought to be its own cause; it didn't originate itself. Maybe. This is important later in history, when the origin and procession of the Holy Ghost becomes an issue. Suffice it to say here that the Spirit was thought, when it came into focus, to originate with God and then, by the Apostles, was further experienced by them as coming from the Father through Jesus Christ, the Son.

True, Plato had said that religious insight could be apprehended by "the eye of the spirit" in *theoria,* which meant "seeing" at that time. But Plato was talking about the *nous,* the mind — mentalness or intelligence. Christianity personalized this, although discussions of the immortality of the soul hearken back to Platonic discussions about the permanence of the *nous* and intelligence over the instability and mortality of the body. For Plato, in fact, intellect was akin to spirit. Intellect needs no sense medium to operate — and is therefore not bound by necessity. As the senses are to things sensible, our intellect is to things intelligible. Moreover, the intellect can be immaterial — and immortal. Christianity adopted some of this but said only in God can His intellect be His Essence. Christianity, by upgrading the divine, tended to downgrade the human being.

As opposed to God, the Holy Ghost, through Jesus' eyes, was newly seen as the aspect of God immanent in the world; by the Church as the giver of Faith; and by Jesus called the Paraclete, the advocate "by your side," the Great Comforter, the "indwelling." It is sometimes termed, in theology, the manifestation, or infusion, of the essence of God directly into experience. Formal recognition of the Spirit came early to the followers of Jesus in Mathew's baptism formula, to baptize "in the name of the Father, and of the Son, and of the Holy Ghost" (Matthew 28:19). Paul speaks of all being "made to drink into one Spirit" (I Corinthians 12:13). This, although the Church Fathers did not extensively discuss the Holy Spirit doctrinally until the end of the third and in the fourth centuries, the source for canonical recognition of the Holy Spirit and the Holy Ghost's place in the later doctrine of the Trinity.

It says in Acts 1:5, Jesus spoke to the Apostles after his death saying, "For John truly baptized with water; but ye shall be baptized with the Holy Ghost not many days hence." This, of course, was to be Pentecost. But even in child baptism it is the action of the Holy Spirit that begets new life. John records Jesus speaking of the need to be "born of water and of the Spirit." (John 3:5). In Acts 19:2–3, the disciples complain, "We have not so much as heard whether there be any Holy Ghost," but Paul answers, "Unto what then were ye baptized?"

Jesus himself, it was said, baptized with fire. In the teaching of baptism there is a dispute about infant baptism and its authority versus adult baptism, when the person is conscious of the spirit. The Catholic position is that all Christians have received the Holy Spirit "secretly" at baptism, but most are unconscious of this presence. Nevertheless it bestows certain gifts, which we shall discuss later. Chrismation, which developed in the East, or Confirmation, in the West, was meant in part to bring the person into a conscious relation to the Spirit at a later age of development, since the baptism had taken place as an infant. Jesus himself, when the dove of the Holy Spirit descended on him, had been baptized as an adult.

The institutionalization of the name of God, the Holy Ghost, and the Trinity (the name as mantra, instead of the being of the breath) took hold in churchified tradition. Clerical and Church tradition later also emphasized the communal and public character of the Spirit — the community (read "Church") as the temple of the Spirit. The structure was God's house, the cathedral; the congregation was the dwelling of the Spirit. This developed more in the West; in the East, individual spirituality and the personal body as the temple of the spirit held faster. Hermits were more common in the East, while communal, cenobitic monasticism developed more in the West. Important to notice, too, is that on the cross it was not God or the Holy Spirit that was crucified, but Jesus, the Son of Man, the Son of God. This is also relevant in the Resurrection, when not death but the living spirit in the risen body is seen as the new spiritual reality.

Hans Küng, the liberal German theologian, says of all this, "To believe in the Holy Spirit means to believe in God's effective power in human beings and the world — this belief in God's spirit can also be common to Jews, Christians, and Muslims." Thus the Spirit and the Holy Spirit are bearers of the powers of transformation in a static world of powers that be, and this, too, is the source of the regenerative and transformation through baptism, as well as the change of heart that takes place in conversion. Even Isaiah had already said of the Spirit, "Behold, I will do a new thing" (Isaiah 43:19).

Holy Spirit is for John also the living memory itself *anamnesis* — a remembrance (John 14:26). The Holy Spirit is that faculty which recalls works of God. This is important to the development of the Mass, a memorial in remembrance. John and Paul related the spirit to the Spirit of Truth, as we shall see. The later Trinitarian doctrine of the Holy Spirit slowly got codified only later, and it challenged the Patristic Fathers to distinguish between the Father, Son, and Holy Ghost. Augustine put the "essence of God" to one side and dealt with the Trinitarian nature on another side — the relations between the three persons of God. In this important teaching, the Holy Spirit became "the mutual love by which the Father and Son love each other reciprocally." The Holy Spirit, although removed from the original energy, became the source by which the persons of the Godhead joined together in love with those from whom they proceeded. Thus the tradition of the Holy Spirit as "love" sprang up.

Chris Bamford, a friend and colleague who writes in the esoteric tradition, tried to trace certain strands of all this spirituality in his earnest book, *An Endless Trace.* In reviewing the whole spiritual passion of the West, he never mentions the Holy Ghost in more than three hundred pages, except on page 166. There, he mentions the Holy Spirit, which he equates with walking and friendship, conversation, and thinking. Spirit, otherwise, seemed in so much tradition to be associated only with incorporeality. Bamford, after a sort of conversion through the Rosary, annunciates the Holy Spirit as "the spirit of love who is also the spirit of truth." In an original interpretation, he says this spirit — presumably our ancient friend the Holy Ghost — "unveils the meaning of all things." A deep interpreter of poetry, Bamford adds that the Holy Spirit is "like a fine rain that falls forever on the garden like a heavenly dew."

Further on, he makes the important Pauline distinction between "flesh" and "body," and says that the body — not the flesh — is the temple of the Holy Ghost. By this admirable distinction St. Paul may have meant that the flesh is molecules, or matter, whereas body is the form and life principle.

According to Elaine Pagels, the Gnostic disciple "becomes a disciple of his own mind" — the gnostic disciple discovers that his own mind is the father of truths (*The Gnostic Gospels,* p. 132). Were this the full extent of early Gnosticism — perceived as the greatest threat to Christianity by the Church establishment up to the second century — the case might not have been so hard to close. Gnosticism, too, might have had a better name; it might have been an early forerunner of self-reliance and unmediated knowledge. The Holy Ghost itself might have been Gnostic. But Gnosticism was laden with too much other baggage for the Church Fathers, and the Holy Ghost became the province of mystery and Faith — rather than knowledge — by the time of the Council of Nicaea in 325.

In passing, Christopher Bamford also makes claims for an uncreated Sophia — a sort of sister wisdom to the Holy Ghost — who, beyond Mary, is "the Holy Spirit's corporeality." *Corporeality* here means a body of wisdom in the old sense of "substance revealing the Spirit." For the later Rosicrucians, then, God became the origin of birth, Christ was where we died, and the Holy Spirit was where we come to life again. In Gnosis, on the other hand, in the first century, and then made heretical by the Church Fathers, the Highest Spirit, through the Greek *nous*, or mind, still brought people true knowledge of the spark of divine spirit, just as Jesus did. The Church rejected the Gnostic doctrine that this divine spirit was alienated by matter, which an evil God of this world used to create humankind. In this way, the Church paved the way for Christian life in connection with matter and of the world, although it held to the doctrine of original sin.

By the time of John Scotus Eriugena in the medieval era, nature and grace are like two hands of the Spirit, the two wings. For St. Patrick, in the Celtic tradition, the spirit appears still and speaks in dreams. In the Celtic tradition, radical or alternate interpretations of the gifts of Spirit can be seen; that is, the spirit has bestowed upon them wholeness; earthiness; the gift of legend; visions of fairies, elves, elementals, and ghosts; a sense of homelessness and home everywhere the world over; a deep respect for study and learning; an aptitude for chaos, confusion, and mirth; and their sense of humor. Scotus added to the lore that woman is the soul or *anima*, while man, the male, is the *intellectus, animus*, or *spiritus* — the "I." The soul relies on faith; the spirit brings knowledge. The *anima* "drinks spiritual gifts" from the *animus*. Jung, in his spiritual archetypes, revived some of this theory.

Paul Williams' infamous and popular handbook of 1989 — *Everything You Always Wanted to Know About the Catholic Church, But were Afraid to Ask* (for fear of excommunication) — has long lurid passages on the "worst" Pope ever (Alexander VI — the Borgia Pope, 1492–1503), but not a single entry on the Holy Ghost or the Holy Spirit.

St. Paul, early on, was much more explicit. In one of the most famous passages on spirituality of all times, he discusses the difference between natural human and spiritual human — and between the plain wisdom of things and the Holy Spirit in things. What Spirit means gets this lengthy treatment in Paul's first famous letter to the Corinthians where he says "eye hath not seen nor ear heard ... the things which God hath prepared for them that love him" — but God "has revealed them unto us by his Spirit." Paul says, "The Spirit searcheth all things, yea, the deep things of God." You cannot know the things of a man except by "the spirit of man which is in him." Likewise, Godly things are known only by the Spirit of God (I Corinthians 2:9–11). Jesus' people have received "not the spirit of the world but the spirit which is of God." These things are known "not in the words which man's wisdom teacheth, but which the Holy Ghost teacheth; comparing spiritual things with spiritual." The natural man doesn't get the things of Spirit for to him "they are foolishness." The natural man can't know them because they are "spiritually discerned" (I Corinthians 2:12–14).

Paul contrasts this with carnal being made of envying, strife, and divisions. And what you build on, whether carnally or by the spirit, shall be proved by fire. Then Paul, as the Church later will teach too, says to the Corinthians, that they, not the stones, "are the temple of God, and that the Spirit of God dwelleth in you" (I Corinthians 3:16).

## Chapter 7

# From the Prophets to Jesus

The Jewish saga begins with the Spirit moving on the waters, but then the Spirit—at least as an ineffable, immaterial agent—fades out in favor of the strong personality of Yahweh, the Father God. God breathes the spirit into Adam, but *ruah,* or breath, is not made into a cult, an otherworldly substance. The Jews turn to this world. And God—just, righteous, and demanding—deals face-to-face, even if unseen, with the Old Testament kings, patriarchs, and prophets. The Judaic tradition, just as it reveres one God, reverences the human as a unity of soul and body—not a split. The conflict is between righteous and unrighteous, between pure and impure, between God's chosen and the idol worshippers—not between body and soul. The holy and sacred, and the law, have a more central place than spirituality, asceticism, or renunciation. The Judaic tradition refers to the Spirit and the Spirit of God, but not the Ghost. The Ghost gets imported into the tradition through the English and the Germans.

The Jewish tradition delivers belief in the Messiah—the anointed one, and the oil is a sign in Judaism, like fire and the finger of God that writes on the wall, of spirit. But when Jacob wrestles with the angel, it is a struggle for power between human and divine, not an agony of self, split between carnal and spiritual being. Job suffers tremendously in the hands of God, but it is not a torment of the spirit. He accepts his lot in this world. It is a test in the existential, human world of fate and mortality measured against the towering personality of an often very intimate God. God talks repeatedly with the patriarchs and kings and prophets; and Solomon, when asked, requests not spirituality and removal from the world, but wisdom in the ways of both God and humanity. The characters of the Old Testament are, in a word, robust, and robustness, not spirituality, is the sign of Jewish life and spirit. In fact, *spirit* almost means robustness, just as anger and wrath—as well as love—are signs of God's spirit. In sexuality there is an acceptance of the earthly spirit of love and the unity of the soul and sex in the body, but not the later Christian scorn of sexuality and the conflict between heavenly and earthly love introduced by the Manicheans and the conflicted Augustine. God himself announces the spirituality of existence, too, and the centrality of the human ego when he announces, "I am that I am" (Exodus 3:14). Christianity will later develop the renunciation of the "I am" for "the Christ in me."

In the Jewish tradition, too, the Temple—though it hardens in some ways (through Rabbinical law, for example)—also spiritualizes, even through the trials of the destruction of the temples. By Solomon's time a liturgy of the word largely replaces blood sacrifice, and with the passing of the temple, the synagogue becomes a place where God dwells in human gathering. The displacement of the Jews contributed to homelessness, which in turn produces an ethos of the wandering Jew as a kind of migrant with a soul on his back and spiritual baggage. The house and the name of God, once too holy to speak, became the preoccupation of Solomon who reminded Israel that "the Lord hath said that he would dwell in the thick darkness" (II Chronicles 6:1). Solomon instead built a dwelling for "the name of the Lord." And the ark, containing the two tablets of Moses, is put into the oracle of the dwelling, in "the most holy place, even under the wings of the cherubim." Here a strain of Jewish spirituality, the realities of the spiritual hierarchies, surfaces: "For the cherubims spread forth their wings over the place of the ark, and the cherubims covered the ark" (II Chronicles 5:8). One hundred and twenty priests with sounding trumpets, and Levites in white linen, with cymbals and psalteries and harps greet the ark with praise and thanks and "then the house was filled with a cloud ... so that the priests could not stand to minister by reason of the cloud for the glory of the Lord had filled the house of God" (II Chronicles 5:13–14). Such was the Spirit in Israel.

Solomon's famous prayer in the temple, however, is not a prayer to the Holy Spirit. It is high national and addressed "O Lord God of Israel," beseeching God not for the Spirit, but for safeguarding the temple, the ark, and the central preoccupation of Israel: requiting of the wicked and justification of the righteous. But already this was a spiritual step forward from the old propitiatory prayers and pleas for a blessing of the harvest. Jewish spirituality, the soul of Spirit, is often represented in the warmth and aliveness of poetry. "For the waters are come in unto my soul." (Psalms 69:1). King David writes: "Have mercy upon me, O God, according to thy loving kindness" (Psalms 51:1). But the Psalms are written and sung mostly to God, the Almighty—not to the Spirit—and in the name of Zion. The poetry, however, brings spirituality to earth. "The Lord is my shepherd; I shall not want. He maketh me to lie down in green pastures: he leadeth me beside the still waters. He restoreth my soul" (Psalms 23:1–3). Though these are songs "of soul," the spirit was said to be the source of the psalmist. These songs were bringing the good and comfort of the spirit into the book of wisdom.

The Old Testament renders things belonging to God as the Hebrew *kadesh*, the separate. The separate is the Holy in the good sense, apart from impurity and imperfection. But the Spirit may, though in a bad sense, also be separate from the Holy Spirit, and this, in a bad sense, is sin, or separation. Holy separateness was God's. The Pentateuch, the Jewish books of the Bible, was thought in its entirety to have been dictated by the Spirit for the Jews.

King David himself wrote some of the Psalms, as did his successor Solomon, who, asking for wisdom from God, refers in the Psalms to "cymbals breathing the spirit." Even for the Old Testament prophets, the Spirit was the divine, active power of God—the Spirit of God—in humankind, the universe, history, and nature. Later, the Church, canonizing the Spirit of God instead as their Holy Spirit, combats spirit in nature in an attempt to hold back animism and later pantheism—the heresy that the Spirit could be found in the natural world, not just through the Church. But the Jews had not yet alienated themselves in this way from the natural world and the creation.

The Lord, according to Ezekiel, the greatest of the Jewish Prophets—greater than Jeremiah or Joel—spoke in the desert with the bones. He was told to do so. He heard this: "And say unto them, O ye dry bones, hear the word of the Lord" (Ezekiel 37:4). Then he was told to prophecy to the Spirit and to say to the Spirit, "Spirit, blow on these dead." There had been a rattling sound. Then Ezekiel prophesied. A breeze sprang up. Voices said, "The bones are dry. Hope is gone. We are doomed." Then Ezekiel was told that the graves would be opened. Later, the expression "give up the Ghost" in the English Bible would be the translation of the Hebrew "he gave up the Spirit."

In a way, Yahweh, the almighty God, had not achieved spirit status. He was, though unknown, almost a material presence—very much a real actor like the Zeus of Olympians, only more personal. Yahweh, of course, enters the intimate soul life of the Jews. Hebrew, although it spoke of the *ruah*, or breath, treated it as a vital life principle; as such, it had not been divinized as the Holy Spirit. God's activity as creator was the focus. The Sadducees—an upper class order from which the priesthood came, and with whom Jesus had trouble—even tended to dampen the prophetic tradition of the spirit despite its base in scripture. Judaism on the whole rejects a split between mind and body in favor of a biopsychic unity of mind, body—and soul. This biopsychic unity in humankind is, moreover, "in God's image." Often, then, Jewish spirituality does not split ascetically away from the world into angelic realms, but remains connected. The unity of mind, body, and soul (read "spirit") means the unity of worship, ethics, and social action. Spirit means business practices more than it does any rejection of the world or even sexuality. Ritual is important for addressing the soul in the right direction, but so is behavior and social justice. The spiritual task is not asceticism but *tikkun olam*, to repair the world.

An early conflict, dating from the first century, was between the Law of Moses and moral commandments to be kept "in the spirit" only. Malachi and Jeremiah (Jeremiah 31:31–34) had promised a new covenant to supersede the Law of Moses in the literal sense. Pork and unleavened bread were issues here—indications of belief. Also images. The Egyptians had "worshipped animals." The Jews had moved on. Early Christians were then "freed" of such rules. The Holy Ghost, in Christian terms, was meant to free in a sense the Jews from literalistic food prohibitions, and even from superstitious fear of images—idolatry, in Jewish tradition.

The Shekinah, a divine female indwelling spirit of "the dwelling" in humankind—the womb place of God's spirit—was important to the Jews as the spirit of Jerusalem, of this home as the chosen people. Their doctrines ran deep: the later Zohar describes the Elohim, the highest principle of God's Spirit, as the syllable *Mi,* the hidden subject, combined with *Eloha,* the hidden object. Elohim was then the spirit of their union—subject and object. *Ain soph* was, instead, the endless, ever-creating aspect of God. The dwelling of Spirit in the Temple, after the Temple's destruction, became the moveable synagogue where the dwelling was "in spirit and truth," not necessarily in a fixed natural place. And, of course, the Temple itself, as we have seen, was seen as the symbol of Spirit in mankind. In contrast with the female Shekinah, Aor was the principle of "intellectual light" in the Hebrew tradition. The Shekinah was pictured, too, in the Sefiroth as an upside down tree with roots in En Sof, or heaven, and the crown summit in the world—another aspect of the Jewish tradition of bringing the divine into the world. According to some sources, this female manifestation of God may have been one reason for the skullcap, the yarmulke—not being seen bare by the divine. The Shekinah, now dwelling in Zion, the Temple Mount where King Josiah (639–609) was renovating the Temple of Solomon. This was where, according to Deuteronomy (purported to be Moses' last message to his people), the Lord made "his name to dwell." So this, like the Holy of Holies, was a vessel of the powerfully present emanation of the Spirit of God—a *mysterium tremendum et facinorum*: a dangerous place.

The beautiful poetry, as in the Song of Solomon, was supposedly inspired directly by the Spirit. As Ezekiel said, in the passage that inspired our song, "Swing Low, Sweet Chariot": "Then the spirit took me up, and I heard behind me a voice of a great rushing, saying, Blessed be the glory of the Lord from his place. I heard also the noise of the wings of the living creatures that touched one another, and the noise of the wheels over against them, and a noise of a great rushing" (Ezekiel 3:12–13). Ezekiel, in warning of spiritual deadness, also attributes to the spirit the forgiveness of guilt, the renewal of the heart, and the bestowing of the gift itself. At one point in Jewish tradition, the Rabbis said that, with the deaths of the prophets Haggai, Zechariah, and Malachi, the Spirit had departed from Israel.

*Logos* was *Memra* in Aramaic, and in Hebrew, *ma-amar*—God's activity in the world when a group of Jews studied Torah together; the Shekinah came and sat among them. The Spirit was thought to mediate between the God we experience and the unknowable essence of God. The transcendent Yahweh had been brought close by the prophets and rabbis, too, as a temple, a physical phenomenon in the Talmud—and a brooding Spirit. In fact, the Spirit for Jews was almost physical.

Jesus, in later times, tries to recapture the prophetic strain and the wisdom tradition to revivify the Spirit. Isaiah had said, "There shall come forth a rod out of the stem of Jesse, and a Branch shall grow out of his roots: And the spirit of the Lord shall rest upon him, the spirit of wisdom and understanding, the spirit of counsel and might, the spirit of knowledge and of the fear of the Lord" (Isaiah 11:1–2). This was a prophecy of not only of Jesus' coming, but also of an outpouring of gifts of the Spirit (which we look at in another chapter). So the greatest story ever told segues into Jesus' tale. Originally, the Holy Spirit according to Jesus and his followers was democratic, then newly viewed as if it resided in all the Jews who gathered around Jesus. The feeling among the Jews around Jesus was that all the followers were endowed with the wisdom, insight, maturity, and holiness needed to contribute to the pursuit of truth—not just Rabbis, or as later in the Church, the hierarchy. The Jesus story is a new chapter in the history of the Jews, and the beginning of the chapter of the Holy Ghost, though embedded in Hebrew tradition. First of all, Jesus was conceived in the Virgin Mary by the coming of the Holy Spirit. We will examine this event and its meaning more closely in a later chapter on the Virgin Birth and the Immaculate Conception. Then, Jesus begins the three years of his ministry in the last years after the descent of the Holy Ghost came down on him in the form of a dove at the baptism at the River Jordan. But the crucial talk by Jesus about the Holy Ghost—that is, before the Last Supper—comes in his extraordinary conversation with the Samaritan woman at Jacob's well.

Some fourteen hundred years after Jacob's Shechem schism—separation of the tribe of Jacob and Rachel from the other tribes of Israel—Jesus returns to Jacob's well. He stops. Lo and behold, there stands not Rachel, but the Samaritan woman, possibly a descendant of Rachel. Here, in the longest recorded conversation between Jesus and a woman in the Bible, they converse about the spirit and the truth. The well itself needs some documentation. The under-appreciated encounter of the Samaritan woman at the well in John's gospel tells simply, perhaps for the first time, "the news," the announcement of the Holy Ghost's revelation. This took place at Shechem, North of Jerusalem and South of Galilee. (Shechem, incidentally, may be a key even in our day to the dilemma of the Israelite presence in Palestine.) This mystery woman went to Jacob's same old well—the original Patriarch who married Rachel, the comely one. Rachel's son, Joseph, of course, went to Egypt, and only with Moses' return, the Exodus, did Joseph's bones return to Shechem. Abraham, the first Patriarch, had originally touched this land and passed it on through Isaac.

Also this well was where Jacob first met and first kissed Rachel, his first cousin. A great stone sealed the well's mouth, Jacob removed it, and they fed some sheep together at an unusual hour of the day. Rachel was, in turn, daughter of Laban, and she is the one who steals the images from her father. These were the tribal Gods. And nearby, at Bethel, God called Jacob "Israel" for the first time. This is, in fact, where Jacob had the original dream of the ladder to heaven, when God promised him the land. Near here, too, Rachel died in hard labor. Jacob had a new young son on his hands, whom he called Benjamin, the youngest brother of Joseph, who as noted had fled to Egypt and whose bones Moses eventually brought back to Shechem.

Rachel's well is thus sacred ground, and the woman of Samaria is introduced to us at the famous well in the Gospel of John (4:6–42). The meeting is rich in import. It was afternoon, and Jesus, weary from his journey to Galilee, stopped by the well, too. The woman comes with her jar to draw water, and Jesus says, "Give me to drink." Surprised, she reminds him that Jews do not deal with Samaritans. Jesus rebukes her and says that if she knew the "gift of God" she would have asked him for a drink—a drink of "living water." In fact, they are not only trading barbs and witticisms but, according to some sources, almost flirting. She tells him that the well, the sacred well, is deep, and reminds him he has nothing to draw water with. She asks him if he is greater than Jacob. He tells her that whoever drinks of her well water will thirst again soon. "But whosoever drinketh of the water that I shall give him shall never thirst; but the water that I shall give him shall be in him a well of water springing up into everlasting life." The woman asks for this water, but then Jesus tells her to call her husband, and she says, "I perceive that thou art a prophet" because Jesus guesses or knows that she has been married. Then he tells her that the new worship takes place not just in the place of the Jews, in Jerusalem, but that "the hour cometh" when "the true worshippers shall worship the Father in spirit and in truth." The place, even the temple, is no longer the important place. "God is the Spirit," Jesus says. The woman says that when the Messiah comes, he will tell us this and all things. Then Jesus says, "I that speak unto thee am he." It is the first and only time he reveals himself.

When the disciples return, they scold him for talking to a woman, and urge him to eat. "I have meat to eat that ye know not of," he says. He tells them his meat, the Spirit, is to do with the will of God, and that "the fields are white already with harvest." He tells of sowing and reaping life eternal and the Samaritan woman testifies to the townspeople, "He told me all that I ever did."

Jesus' talk with the Samaritan woman reminds us that St. Basil spoke of a tradition handed down from the Apostles—that Jesus had, in addition to his public ministry, a "private and secret" teaching "which our holy fathers have passed on." The silence on this private teaching "safeguards the sacred character of the mystery.... The uninitiated are not permitted to behold these things: their meaning is not to be divulged by writing it down." This esoteric tradition is said also to be an oral tradition of secrets and wisdom from the Holy Ghost. Yet, when interrogated before his death by the High Priest Caiphas, Jesus denies having said anything "in secret." As death approaches, however, he refers more frequently to the Holy Ghost. "I have yet many things to say unto you, but ye cannot bear them now," he tells the frightened Apostles. "When he, the Spirit of truth, is come, he will guide you into all truth: for he shall not speak of himself; but whatsoever he shall hear, that shall he speak: and he will shew you things to come" (John 16:12–13). Jesus prophesies this descending "Spirit of Truth" several times, along with his own death. This revelation of the Holy Ghost will happen in part at Pentecost, as we see in the next chapter, and then the acts of the Apostles begin—and the Acts are sometimes known as the Gospel of the Holy Spirit.

Before Jesus' capture in Jerusalem, Nicodemus, the Pharisee, visits Jesus by night. Jesus, telling his visitor that no one can enter the realm of God without water and Spirit, reveals something to him about the risen flesh and Spirit. Nicodemus, a learned Israelite, says, "How is this possible?" Because, according to one modern commentator, Hebrew *ruah* (or in Greek, breeze, breath or spirit) means "vivifying power."

Finally, at the Last Supper, Jesus speaks of the Holy Spirit when prophesying and comforting the disciples. "These things have I spoken unto you, being yet present with you. But the Comforter, which is the Holy Ghost, whom the Father will send in my name, he shall teach you all things, and bring all things to your remembrance, whatsoever I have said unto you" (John 14:25–26).

Perhaps Jesus' most famous words are said to Nicodemus:

> Except a man be born of water and of the Spirit, he cannot enter into the kingdom of God. That which is born of the flesh is flesh; and that which is born of the Spirit is spirit. Marvel not that I said unto thee, Ye must be born again. The wind bloweth where it listeth, and thou hearest the sound thereof, but canst not tell whence it cometh, and whither it goeth: so is every one that is born of the Spirit. (John 3:5–8)

# Chapter Eight

# Pentecost

Passover, or *Pesakh*—liberation day—was on a Thursday evening in March that year, also the start of Mazzot, the festival week of unleavened bread. There were celebrations of the Jewish liberation from Egypt, but also remembrances of the nomadic shepherds who went from winter pasture to summer grazing lands on the first full moon of the vernal equinox.

The bread of affliction, unleavened bread of the Seder—the feast—was originally a remembrance of the unleavened bread that the Jews scurried to bake for their trip to the Promised Land as they fled Egypt in a hurry. But it was also a reminder of the passage from the old harvest of last year to the new harvest to come when the old grain was cleaned out and the people waited for the new grain.

The Passover Seder (*Seder* meaning "order") had the elements itself of the wine, the washing of hands, the breaking of the bread, and eating the bitter herb. All this was part of the paschal mystery before Jesus. The Pasch was fused with celebrations for freedom from Egypt, part of the background of Passover, commemorating the salvation given the Jews when the avenging angel bypassed their homes and struck down only the firstborn of the Egyptians (Exodus 11). By tradition a lamb was sacrificed for Pasch, roasted, and eaten with bitter herbs and the unleavened bread. The feast, by the way, is a joyous occasion moving from the solemnities of the Seder plate and prayers to a happy family dinner and feast that often lasts till after midnight.

The Jewish time frame for Jesus' passion thus was the Passover starting Mazzot, then, counting seven weeks (forty-nine days) one came to Shavuot, the Feast of Jewish weeks, which was an agricultural feast for the first fruits. The agricultural feast was then turned by the

Jews into the celebration of the giving of Torah, the law, to Moses in the Sinai. This then came to be Pentecost (meaning the fiftieth day) in some ways the original birthday of the Holy Ghost in the Western tradition after Jesus' death. Whitsunday, in English, is named later after the white robes, liturgical color for Pentecost, white often being taken as the color for spirit.

Against this time frame, Jesus plays out his story, going to Bethany six days before Passover, entering Jerusalem on Palm Sunday, then praying on the Mount of Olives, and back and forth from Bethany, preparing for the Passover, the Last Supper, on Thursday night. He is betrayed that night in the Garden of Gethsemane, across the Cedron River (East Jerusalem), then his trial, passion, and crucifixion take place on Friday. But it was before this week, leading up to Passover, that Jesus, after telling his disciples, "I am the true vine," (John 15:1), first speaks openly of the Holy Spirit, as if prophesying the future Pentecost. Remember, on Thursday night he tells Caiaphas, the High Priest of the Sanhedrin, "And in secret have I said nothing" (John 18:20). In the weeks before, he told the disciples, "But this cometh to pass, that the word might be fulfilled that is written in their law: They hated me without a cause" (John 15:25). He then predicts the Pentecost, to come some fifty days later: "But when the Comforter is come, whom I will send unto you from the Father, even the Spirit of truth, which proceedeth from the Father, he shall testify of me" (John 15:26). It is as if Jesus sees the body leaving him, his coming death, and then the detached Spirit—the Holy Ghost—to come. Then he says that he is saying these things now so that, when the time shall come, "ye may remember that I told you of them" (John 16:4).

In the last fifty days after Easter, in fact, he appears at least five recorded times, including in the sepulcher garden; Easter evening in the Upper Room; eight days later again; and then on Mount Tabor at the Ascension at Lake Tiberias in Galilee. Lest this all seem overly supernatural, one should remember that the ancients had seen Greek Gods appear to human beings before in phantasms as forms of light. The real difference with Jesus was that, unlike Greek Gods, he had died a human death. Having been interwoven with death and the material world, when the risen God now speaks as a spirit it is with knowledge not just of the Gods but also of life and humankind.

In the Upper Room after his death, that evening was when he showed his wounds and said to them, "Peace be unto you," and then still before Pentecost, actually on Easter evening "he breathed on them, and saith unto them, Receive ye the Holy Ghost." The appearance eight days later was when Thomas touched his wounds and reached a hand into the wound on his side (John 20:21–22, 26). John says that in those fifty days Jesus showed himself alive after his passion by many infallible proofs and that in those days he was seen and spoke of the things pertaining to the Kingdom of God. In one of these deliveries to them after death, he told them—again prophesying the coming Pentecost—"For John [the Baptist] truly baptized with water; but ye shall be baptized with the Holy Ghost not many days hence" (Acts 1:5).

The idea of the "outpouring" of the Spirit is associated with the ancient roots of the word God itself, which in the Indo-European language base is *gheu* or *ghu,* which means to invoke or pour. The sense of *to pour* came from the ancient practice of libations. This was the pouring out of water or oil, mediums for the spirit.

Now, without prejudicing the record, some commentators have suggested that when the disciples in the fifty days after his "death" hear Jesus speaking, they are actually, as Jesus had himself predicted, remembering what many things he said in the hectic days leading up to the Passion. These "remembrances" may have been more or less visual and auditory hallucinations. Given the confused, bereaved state that the disciples were in, their remembrances may have been extraordinarily vivid. They may have come back to them as if he were alive—otherwise they would be the supernatural uttering of a ghost of light. This for what it is worth.

The Upper Room, where the Last Supper took place, and the Pentecost fifty days later, was in the Old City, probably not far from the houses of Joseph of Arithmaea and Nicodemus. It was a hall, maybe forty by sixty feet. It was owned by "the good man of the house," and

Jesus had directed the disciples to it before Passover, originally when they had asked where they would be eating the feast. It was called a guest chamber, and Jesus said that "a man bearing a water pitcher" would bring them there and that it would be furnished and set out for the feast. It was in this Upper Room, fifty days after the Last Supper (in the Jewish time frame) that Pentecost took place. Pentecost, the birthday of the Spirit, became—after the Jews threw the Christians out of the synagogue—the second most important Christian feast day after Easter. Christmas gained predominance only later. The day of Pentecost was the day predicted by the prophet Joel as the day of "the outpouring of the Spirit."

Some 120 disciples were gathered in the space. "And when the day of Pentecost was fully come, they were all with one accord in one place." Then the remarkable moment came that Jesus had told the disciples about: "And suddenly there came a sound from heaven as of a rushing mighty wind, and it filled all the house where they were sitting" (Acts. 2:1–2). Next appeared, in hallucinatory reality in the air, cloven tongues like as of fire, and they sat each upon each of them. "And they were all filled with the Holy Ghost," The account says that, upon this visitation from the Holy Ghost, they all began to speak "with other tongues" as the Spirit inspired them to give utterance (Acts. 2:4).

Both Ashkenazi and Sephardic Jews from all corners of the world were living or visiting in Jerusalem, and, as they celebrated the Shavuot, news got around that something remarkable was going on in the Old City. A crowd including Persians, Romans, Libyans, Turks, and Egyptians gathered, and they were startled because "every man heard them speak in his own language." The account said they were amazed because all the disciples were Galilaeans themselves and "how hear we everyman in our own tongue wherein we were born?... We do hear them speak in our tongues the wonderful works of God" Marveling, they turned in the crowd to each other and asked what it all meant. There were protesters there too and they scoffed at what was happening, saying, "These men are full of new wine" (Acts 2:6–13). In other words, drunk.

Peter the fisherman—Simon the Rock—came out and spoke to the crowd and said, "These men are not drunk, as ye suppose, for it is still morning." Then he told them Joel's words were coming true. "And it shall come to pass in the last days, saith God, I will pour out of my Spirit upon all flesh; and your sons and your daughters shall prophecy, and your young men shall see visions, and your old men shall dream dreams." Peter says to them that the spirit will not pour out just on Rabbis, the Sanhedrin, the priests, the Roman aristocrats and the upper classes but on the servants and handmaidens, too—and the women—of the Lord. He says that "wonders in heaven" will be shown and "signs in the earth" and "blood, and fire, and vapour of smoke. The sun shall be turned into darkness and the moon into blood." And then he goes on to give a loud, vigorous, and outstanding exhortatory sermon on many of the things that Jesus had told them. At the end, the crowd "pricked in their heart" asks, "What shall we do?" Peter says, "Repent!" He urges them to take baptism and promises them "ye shall receive the gifts of the Holy Ghost" if they do. About three thousand souls converted on the spot and the ministry of the Apostles—the Gospel of the Spirit—was begun. Some of them began to sell their possessions and goods and divide them with the needy. Good days followed and "breaking bread from house to house, they did eat their meat with gladness and singleness of heart." Fear, it is said, came on every soul but also, they were having a party. The fellowship of the Holy Spirit had begun (Acts 2:14–47).

Earlier, before his death, as the days of Passion approach, Jesus had described this Spirit after telling Thomas, "I am the way, the truth, and the life." (John 14:6). Philip and Thomas had trouble understanding and questioned him, saying they didn't know where he was going and how could they know the way. Jesus had predicted his death and then added, "I will pray the Father, and he shall give you another Comforter, that he may abide with you for ever. Even the Spirit of Truth, whom the world cannot receive, because it seeth him not." (John 14;16–17). This is a source for the invisibility of the Holy Ghost—the supersensible. Jesus himself is seen and touched; Christ is seen. The Spirit is unseen, and the world does not receive truth.

"You know him," Jesus told Philip and Thomas. "For he dwelleth with you, and shall be in you" (John 14:17). He says he will not leave them "comfortless." Either he will come back to them; in a word, as Holy Spirit, or the Holy Ghost, in his stead, will visit and be with them. The Spirit, then, has a deep relation to the risen Christ beyond its relationship to wisdom. The Spirit is what testifies to the Resurrection of Jesus, but it is also the empty tomb and rising of the Christ that testifies to the Spirit. A tautology for some, a profound revelation for others, the arising from the dead is almost a metaphor for the Spirit itself. The Pentecost is thus a sort of intersection of time with eternity.

In Acts 5, there is a strange story of how the Spirit of Truth worked in those times in the episode of Ananias and his wife Sapphira. People were selling their houses and lands and bringing the proceeds to the Apostles, but Ananias, with the connivance of his wife, held back part of the sale price from Peter for himself. Peter said to him, "Why hath Satan filled thy heart to lie to the Holy Ghost?" Peter's concern was that Ananias had lied "not unto men" but unto the Spirit. When Peter rebuked Ananias, the man "gave up the ghost"—he died on him. Three hours later, Sapphira, not knowing what had happened, burst in and Peter asked her what the price had been. She lied, too, and Peter said, "How is it that ye have agreed together to tempt the Spirit of the Lord?" She, too, died and "yielded up the ghost." This episode scared everybody and showed how the Spirit of Truth was a living reality—which is fine, but frankly I personally don't see what business it was of Peter, and it sounds to me like the start of political correctness, which is not in the Spirit's character. Not long after those first days, in fact, the Church began to codify the Spirit and dampen it down. The enthusiasm of the early days was soon over, and the "outpouring"—so democratic and universal—became of concern only to the Apostles themselves, their followers, the Church Fathers, and the authorities. The heretic, Montanus, as we shall see, soon learned this and died for it.

The twelve Apostles, like "refigurations" of the twelve tribes of Israel, set up the new Assembly of God, a new covenant of the Spirit. This, of course, was then rejected by the Jews themselves and the

Spirit, in the new form, went over with Paul and John to the Greeks and the gentiles.

Two features of Pentecost—after the Ascension, and after the "rushing of the mighty wind"—were universalism and timelessness, as well as democracy, and the disciples now saw into the future. Commentators point out that, before Christian times, blood and tribe were very strong and almost the only forces—individualism and personality were weaker. Through the mother, a person identified with the blood, tribe, race, and folk; through the paternal side came what there was of individuality and personhood. The sense of common humanity was relatively scarce in ancient times, but it is this sense, the sense of universality, that the Holy Ghost, the new Spirit, brought. The Holy Spirit was in contrast to tribal spirits, folk spirits, and animistic spirits. This same spirit appeared as a descending dove at the baptism on Jordan by John the Baptist. This dove, at Pentecost, becomes many separate tongues of fire. The Spirit—one in Christ at the Ascension—becomes manifold in every single individual at Pentecost.

All these forces have relevance for today, an age of United Nations and globalism. For humanity, the common divinity of the Holy Ghost individualizes, in each new heart, a freeing force from race, tribe, folk, body, and blood. The new common, universal humanity is individualized in each single free soul; it is the mystery of Pentecost, and this explains its importance. This same spirit also explains the import of the words Christ left behind, "I am with you unto the end of the world" (Matthew 28:20).

The spirit of universality is also behind the sense of speaking in tongues and being able to understand strange tongues, which we examine more closely in the next chapter. This may be the Holy Ghost's antidote to the fracture of language at the Tower of Babel. The Holy Spirit as tongues of fire also had the force of renewal and constant outpouring and was not stuck, as some religions are, on a single tradition at one place and time. This side of Pentecost is what some evangelicals embrace in the outpouring of Spirit: an annunciation that speaks in new tones and ever renews. And this sense of Pentecost is meant to bring freedom through the awakening of the individualized spirit, while arousing the infinity of the spiritual by its sense of universal common humanity. Ideally the mysteries of Pentecost may thus be one mixing wisdom and eternity—quite different in import from the feasts of Christmas and Easter. At Christmas one may feel the mother and father elements; at Easter the son; at Pentecost, the Holy Ghost.

During the first century, the early Church was, after all, a group of Jews talking among themselves under the inspiration of a new impulse— indeed, an impulse of the Holy Spirit rather than rabbinical law and just the book. To them, the new assumption was that all believers, not just Rabbis, were endowed with the wisdom and might have the maturity to interpret the truth. This was precisely because the new discovery was that the Holy Spirit was not just revealed through an ordained hierarchy but through all. Even the Catholic catechism—on the whole a conservative document—admits that "communion of the Spirit" transcends racial, cultural, social, and all human affinities. Pentecost becomes the manifest of the Church to the world and "dispensation of the mystery."

The Holy Spirit graduates from Pentecost, apart from establishmentarianism, into being "the living memory of the Church" (John 14:26). Remembrance. The Holy Spirit recalls the work of God. This remembrance, rather than active intervention, was supposed to slowly become more and more the call word of the Church. St. John the Damascene later says, "I shall tell you the Holy Spirit comes upon them [the Faithful] and accomplishes what surpasses word and thought." Of course, possession of the so-called true Spirit almost immediately began to become a *shibboleth,* dividing Christians from Jews and Christians from pagans. I suggest that this was no longer just the true Spirit, however, but sometimes the politically correct observance of the name of the Spirit—membership cards. What had been universal and democratic in impulse became a divisive word—no longer the Spirit itself.

In an unusual book on the three years of Jesus' life on earth as the Christ, one commentator calls the descent of the true spirit at Whitsuntide the "indwelling" and compares the tongues of fire to the light of growth around seeds, after the plant has passed from blossom to the slow formation of fruit. This spirit, the light of Spring, then hardened with institutionalism into a divisive word. Another commentator says that the Church was "made immortal for all time by the infusion of God's breath, the Holy Ghost, on the day of Pentecost." So perhaps it was meant to be.

By the fourth century, after the Holy Ghost was officially elevated to the Trinity by proclamation at the Council of Nicaea in 325, the story begins to change. Without putting a further moral on the story, let us give the final word to St. Leo the Great, the Pope from 440 to 461, who secured stable rulership for the new Christian Pontiffs. St. Leo was less concerned about the Holy Ghost than keeping Attila the Hun out of Rome and persuading Gaiseric the Vandal to spare the lives of Romans. He said (in Sermon 76), "When the Holy Spirit filled the Lord's disciples on the day of Pentecost, this was not the first exercise of his role but an extension of his bounty, because the patriarchs, prophets, priests, and all the holy men of previous ages were nourished by the same sancitifying spirit." In other words, the Holy Ghost had officially come of age, but had been with all, even the Jews, from all time.

# Chapter 9

# Gifts, Signs, and Fruit

The Holy Ghost gives the *charismata,* or gifts, but the Holy Spirit also delivers fruit. These are different. Nor are the gifts or fruit the same as moral virtues. Besides that, the Holy Spirit is known by its actions; for instance, it is the Holy Spirit that raised Jesus from the dead. Furthermore, the Holy Spirit reveals and inspires, as in its work with scripture and prayer and inspiration in general. Then, there are signs of the Holy Ghost—some visible in actions, gifts, symbols, or the dove, for instance. These are not exactly the gifts, which show up in people through the presence of the Holy Ghost, but symbols and visible presences that figurate the otherwise invisible Holy Ghost.

The dove from above breaks into the brain, giving a vertical option to the mind. The circle of earthly totality—the world of five sense, stimuli, and science—is a closed circle. The dove breaks this serpentine circle. It is an opening in the closed circuit of thinking, providing an upward option, in contrast to the horizontal. This option is the opening for spiritual evolution in the closed circle of deterministic, biological evolution. It gives the option, too, for freedom from the wheel of fortune—from the line of the genome.

Note that the original the appearance of the dove at the Jordan River and at Pentecost is seen later as the descent of the dove, not the ascent; the bird comes to humankind. The light comes down. The Holy Spirit, in this view, is not a bird flying away that the human follows; it is not streaming upward or outward or in soaring flight. And besides the dove, there is oil—the symbol of anointing, the medium between the body of the chosen and the spirit of the choosing. Water, too, is a sign of the Holy Ghost, and symbolizes birth. When Christ's side was pierced as he hung on the cross, blood flowed forth (a symbol of humanity) as well as water (a symbol of the spirit).

Fire, cloud, and light were also signs of the Holy Ghost, the Spirit. The seal, emblem of authentication, was also a sign of Spirit, as were the hand and the finger. When the writing on the wall appears in the Old Testament, it is the disembodied hand or finger that writes. Michelangelo pictures the hand of God and the finger of Adam touching in the Sistine Chapel. Sometimes the flower—the lily, or fleur-de-lis—represents the Holy Spirit.

The virtues are not the same as the gifts. The sins are pride, covetousness, lust, anger, gluttony, envy, and sloth, or laziness. These are the traditional bugaboos of medieval culture, and even today they are listed as line items of basic teachings of the Catholic Church in the 1973 Catechetical Office of the Holy See. The Holy Spirit is seen as incorporating into the Church and the life—the new person in the spirit—of the individual Christian. There are, then, deadly, mortal, or capital sins, as opposed to mere venial sins, or mere facts of vice. Controverted to these vices are the virtues: humility to pride; generosity or liberality to covetousness; chastity or continence to lust; meekness to anger; moderation to gluttony; solidarity to error; and industriousness to sloth. As said, these are not the gifts or fruit. In contrast, too, are Plato's four cardinal virtues in the classical world: prudence, justice, fortitude, and temperance. Hardness of the heart, a worried state of mind, dishonesty, and unjust practices block the virtues; but the virtues are gained and are not, in themselves, the gifts of the Holy Ghost. People achieve them. A virtue is a habit that perfects the powers of the soul, the powers of the soul being intellect, will, and memory. The virtues are natural—that is, acquired by human activity. These virtues are achieved through a person's efforts.

Further, virtues are either moral or divine. Natural virtues are moral; supernatural virtues are infused by God and are closer to gifts. They are virtues, moral or divine according to their object; divine virtues have God as their object. Moral virtues have something to do with that which is created by God—the creation, society, or the environment. Divine virtues can be like monastic chastity, poverty, and obedience, but are more often to do with the theological virtues like faith, hope, and charity. Virtues have something to do with a higher sense of values and skills to do the good.

As said, these virtues are not the charismata, the gifts of the Holy Spirit, though the Holy Spirit may abet them. Moses, incidentally, experienced theophanies of God while receiving the commandments, but not the Spirit directly. His were *appearances* of God, as in the burning bush, but this is God himself, not the Holy Ghost. Instead, the seven gifts of the Holy Spirit, the charismata, are infused, according to St. Paul in the first letter to the Corinthians (12:4–11). They are sometimes called signs of the Holy Spirit, not to be confused with symbols, as, for instance, the dove and water. Paul calls these gifts "qualities" (*qualia*) of the Holy Spirit—the gifts: counsel, fear of the Lord, fortitude, piety, understanding, wisdom, and knowledge. They are superior to the intellectual and moral virtues—honesty, for instance—and their function is to perfect the exercise of the virtues. They are thought of as special graces of the Holy Spirit. They are not earned, but infused. Humankind seeks them by prayer, meditation, contemplation, and control of the will. These gifts are habits by which the soul responds to the inspiration of the Holy Spirit, and their function, as said, is to perfect the exercise of the lesser moral and intellectual virtues that belong to humankind. The even higher theological virtues—faith, hope, and charity—instead inform the moral virtues. Examined more closely they are:

> Wisdom: Knowledge strives for wisdom. Wisdom is insight arrived at beyond thought. It is knowledge fulfilled, but insight still strives—while truth is wisdom or insight already arrived at.
>
> Understanding: Understanding is not intellect, but intelligence of things or of God. Understanding is the mode of intelligence most necessary to people outside the church when they wish to grasp the truths that church people otherwise receive in faith, dogma, and sacrament. It includes faculties like openness of mind, discrimination, sound judgment, and inquiry.

Knowledge: An intellectual virtue associated with information and understanding. In a more religious sense, knowledge is the faculty by which we know the spiritual value and utility of things and upon which we make a judgment. Knowledge is either infused, coming from above, or it is based on sensing, perceiving, and experimenting. Humankind's knowledge is of God or of the created world. Knowledge can know divinity through reason. Revelation can bring knowledge directly by Faith.

Counsel: The ability to advise persons in religious or other matters, to give guidance. But it may also be social, psychological, or physiological. It may be about the sacraments, or alcoholism, or marriage—or spiritual guidance. Counsel includes the ability to refer persons to competent specialists.

Piety: Piety is not the usual picture of downcast eyes and folded hands. It is a sense of duty raised to awareness; it is charity applied to loving duty. It is not, as popularly portrayed, the response only to things religious but a preparation for prayer.

Fortitude: Both a cardinal virtue and a gift of the Holy Spirit. As a virtue it is a strength that fearlessly acts to do right. It is the effort behind the good deed, bypasses fear of criticism, and strengthens the will to perform good acts. As a gift of the Holy Spirit, it is the infused impulse to act rightly. It reinforces other virtues by its steadfastness.

Fear of God: Servile fear is mental anxiety or emotion arising from fear of punishment—from God or authorities or others. Filial fear is the fear of loss of grace or well being by separation from God. Filial fear is a gift of the Holy Spirit and is called "the beginning of wisdom" (Proverbs 1:7). Fear is a warning, a guidepost that gives way to confidence and love when attended to and listened to.

These gifts are, in Christian tradition, *gratis datae,* freely bestowed for the benefit of others. In other words, some people are endowed with them for the benefit of others. They are, as said, superior to the intellectual and moral virtues, but less perfect than the theological virtues: faith, hope, and charity, which have God for their object. Further, gifts of the Holy Spirit are either preternatural, such as freedom from suffering and death, supreme knowledge, and perfect control—all beyond human nature—or supernatural, such as prophecy and miracles. These cannot be merited or achieved by nature either but are God's endowments.

Prophecy and miracles may also be seen as actions of the Holy Ghost rather than as gifts, like some further qualities that Paul extends to the list: powers of exhortation, and shows of mercy. Aquinas grouped these extended gifts in relation to knowledge, speech, or miracles. The gifts, however, after pertaining to the cognitive faculties, like counsel, wisdom, and knowledge, are seen as special living, infused, and immanent signs in the actual life of the presence of Spirit.

Note, for instance, by way of contrast, that the *trivium* (grammar, rhetoric, and dialectic) and the *quadrivium* (mathematics, geometry, astronomy, and music) of Scholasticism, and the basis of the modern Liberal Arts, are not gifts in this sense of the Holy Spirit, nor did the Holy Spirit ever claim a relation to the Muses of antiquity, or memory. And, indeed, in our day, the cognitive sciences, although deeply committed to mental faculties, do not make any room, mention, or allowances for the Holy Spirit, much less the Holy Ghost. The gifts of the Holy Spirit instead sustain moral life in the best sense of the word—in the sense of righteousness—not just as politically correct right or wrong. They are not only cognitive but also affective faculties—that is, not just of the head, but also of the heart. They are permanent dispositions that form humankind's attitudes in response to the promptings of the Holy Spirit.

The gifts of the Holy Ghost are reminiscent of the Jewish Sephiroth—the ten spiritual emanations of the Kabbalah. These were, in Judaic tradition, Wisdom (*Chokmah*), Reason (*Binah*), Knowledge (*Daath*), Greatness (*Gedulah*), Strength (*Guburah*), Beauty (*Tephereth*), Eternity (*Nitzach*), Majesty (*Hod*), Principle (*Yerod*), and Sovreignty (*Malkuth*). The Jews could lift the curtain of the Great Unknown and lift themselves into the realm of blessed spirit by *Chabad* (Wisdom, Reason, and Knowledge).

The Ecumenical Council, Vatican II (1962–1966), addressed itself to the gifts in a decree (*De Ecclesia*) on the renewal of the Church. The Holy Spirit, the decree said, "sanctifies the People of God through the ministry and sacraments," but also by giving the faithful special gifts as well. The Council was, by the way, called a "new Pentecost" by the Vatican and by some press. Though the gifts are divine and some are called to serve heaven, others are called to "the earthly service of man." Each, according to his or her individual gifts, administers to one another, and the distribution of grace builds up "the body of charity."

The decree stated further that believers "need to enjoy the freedom of the Holy Spirit," who breathes "where it will"—a concession from the Church that claims "stewardship" of these gifts. St. Thomas Aquinas had said the gifts are needed for salvation, but not in their absolute fullness, and likened them to the beatitudes. In the decree on the Apostolate of the Laity (*Apostolicam Aeternitatem*), the Council urged laymen "to make use of the gifts which they have received from the Holy Spirit."

The gifts are not the fruit. The gifts are distinguished from the fruit of the Holy Spirit—fruit, incidentally, in the singular. The gifts are the "inward unction" of the Holy Spirit, but the fruit is even more inward—and closer to grace itself. The fruit, in fact, is a perfection—or the plural, perfections—that the Holy Spirit forms in people as first hints of eternal glory. In his letter to the Galatians, Paul says, "Walk in the Spirit." This is contrasted with fulfilling the lust of the flesh. Paul, as you may remember, distinguishes between "flesh," the lower element of the body, and "the body," more a form principle of the body as the "image of man." Paul says that the fruit comes forth through the struggle of overcoming the flesh—not necessarily the body—and that the Holy Ghost thereby does another remarkable thing: it illuminates the crucifixion. For Paul, crucifixion was the remedy for the flesh. The Holy Ghost illuminates the crucifixion with wisdom and glory otherwise unobtainable, because without the Holy Spirit the crucifixion would otherwise be a repulsive riddle to the worldly, just as it was a lowly, mean, nasty and scandalous death in Jewish and Roman times.

Similarly, St. Basil (329–379), who was associated with the oriental Cappadocian fathers who solidified the Holy Ghost's place in doctrine, argued that the work of the Spirit is hidden, witnessed to by the unwritten tradition (oral tradition) and liturgy, and that the Spirit in fact is what makes it possible to see the Son in the image of the Father. St. Basil said participating in the liturgy helps "understanding of the spiritual gifts." He named eight other gifts: tranquility (*hesuchia*); solitude (*eremia*); leisure for reason to sever passion from the soul (*schole*); angelic choiring (*pietas*); reading and meditation (*lectio* and *meditatio*); life together (cenobitical life)—memory (becoming the temple); and continence (*enhiateia*). The gifts are further extended by other actions of the Holy Ghost—for instance, in baptism and the laying on of hands, as well as prophecy, healing, and miracles.

The flesh, Paul says, "lusteth against the Spirit, and the Spirit against the flesh" (Galatians 5:17). They are contrary, in his view. The conflict prevents you from doing what you would. He then gives a stinging list of works of the flesh: adultery, fornication, uncleanness, lasciviousness, idolatry, witchcraft, hatred, avarice, emulations, wrath, strife, seditions, heresy, envy, murder, drunkenness, and revelry. But, Paul says, if you are led "of the Spirit, ye are not under the law" (Galatians 5:18).

Fruit of the Spirit comes in to the picture as a foretaste of Grace, a foretaste of reward in Heaven, a foretaste of the glory of eternity—but it indwells already here and now on earth. In human beings, in life, it is a sign of the touch of the Spirit. Fruit of the Spirit then is love, joy, peace, longsuffering, gentleness, goodness, faith, meekness, temperance, and patience. Paul names them in Galatians. The Church traditionally names twelve such qualities as the fruit: charity, joy, peace, patience, kindness, goodness, generosity, gentleness, faithfulness, modesty, self-control, and chastity. The fruit differs mostly from the virtues—both theological and moral, although there is some overlap—and from the gifts. The virtues are something you can help yourself to; you can achieve them. The gifts are given but touch on service in this world; the fruit is really between you, God, and eternity.

Besides distribution of the charismata, the gifts, also attributed to the Holy Ghost were inspiration of scripture, its interpretation, sanctification of Christ's mystical body, and sanctification of the faithful—the People of God. The community as a whole is the temple of the Spirit, as is the individual. The Holy Spirit, in a word, is the great sanctifier. Whereas grace is come of by God, love is come of through Jesus Christ, but by the Holy Ghost comes "the fellowship of the Spirit" (II Corinthians 13:13). In Church this means that the congregation itself is a living offering.

Just as in baptism, in the laying on of hands it is supposed to be the Spirit that is passed—this power coming from the Holy Ghost itself. In Church tradition, it is even the root of the tradition itself, ensuring the apostolic succession of the clergy. The passing down of the Holy Spirit is supposed to ensure this (Acts 19:1–7). Although there is no canonical literature to this effect, it stands to reason that in marriage it is accession to the Spirit that makes marriage one of the "states of perfection," separating it from civil union and coupling. Likewise, with last rites and last unction, the dying and dead are probably seen as communing with the Holy Spirit at last.

Miracles, although their action or the power to do them is sometimes attributed to the Holy Ghost, they are usually credited to Mary, Jesus, or the Saints. The gift of doing them may come as special powers from the Holy Spirit—as in prophecy and healing—but the Holy Ghost itself does not usually get the credit or veneration. In fact, there is no cult of the Holy Ghost, as there are Marian and other cults, and there are no visions of the Holy Ghost that I found. Instead, at issue in miracles are usually faith and degrees of divine intervention and, unfortunately, sometimes pseudo-mysticism and even fakes. Local bishops and then, on up to the Sacred Congregation of the Causes for Saints at the Vatican, are involved in investigating such incidents and claims, and sometimes even the Holy Office, which is the office of spiritual police who watch over the authenticity of the Holy Spirit.

A word about prayer as a gift: Prayer is not listed as one of the gifts, but as God's speech "it is a spiritual echo of his voice sounding in the human heart," according to tradition. "We do not know how to pray as we ought," says Paul, ": but the Spirit itself maketh intercession for us with groanings which cannot be uttered" (Romans 8:26). So we can say, without bending the sense, that Spirit is the master of prayer. When we pray, it is the Spirit praying within us. The Spirit, in prayer tradition, is known as the searcher of hearts (Rom. 8:27).

In a tract called the *De Oratione*, the early Christian apologist Tertullian, a Roman in Carthage, says the movement of prayer comes forth from the Holy Spirit. As such, it ought to be free from anger and perturbation of mind because "a defiled spirit cannot be acknowledged by the Holy Spirit, nor a sad spirit by the joyful, nor a hardened spirit by the free." In *De Cultu Feminorum*, he says modesty, is the "sacristan and high priest" of the Holy Spirit, who makes us into God's temples.

In hesychasm, the silent prayer tradition of the East, the Jesus prayer was seen as a special action to "reveal" the baptism by the Holy Ghost, whose secret presence from infant baptism is unconscious in most persons. Through the Abba prayer, "Our Father," Paul says one is taken into the "sonship" by the spirit of adoption—which is the same as the spirit of the resurrection, itself an action of the Holy Ghost. And finally, the Holy Spirit's gift—from baptism on—is seen not as uncertainty, but as assurance and discernment. This is true about the faculty of discernment of spirits, too, which Loyola talks so much of in the *Spiritual Exercises.* The Holy Ghost's action, in baptism and conversion, is one of transformation. Thus the Holy Ghost became the principle of transformation in some of the tradition—the agent of change and inspiration.

Spirit issues, teleologically (that is, in its aims), from "justification toward glorification," and God's creative power, from the origins in history and the story of salvation, is "diffused in his Spirit."

The ancient Sareem Missal prayed for a twofold spiritual blessing, distinguishing the two modes of Spirit: a blessing for the mind, the light for right judgment of truth; and a blessing for the heart, comfort and joy in Grace. As Romans 5:5 says, "The love of God is shed abroad in our hearts by the Holy Ghost which is given unto us." For the Holy Spirit, the key word is not something made, but something *given.*

## Chapter 10

# Tongues of Fire

Speaking in tongues is the name for one of the most outwardly sensational of the Holy Ghost's gifts, known technically as *glossolalia*. *Gloss* came from tongue; *lalia* was Greek for voice or speech—thus, literally, tongue speech. The gift of tongues descends in the form of tongues of fire upon the heads of the disciples in the Upper Room in the Old City after Jesus' death. The gospel account is in Acts and is specific about what happened. After they were filled with the Holy Ghost, they began to speak with "other tongues." A crowd of people from all corners of the city and indeed the world gathered around the house and "were confounded, because that everyman heard them speak in his own language" (Acts 2:6). The disciples themselves, from Galilee, were native speakers of Aramaic, but Persians, Syrians, Egyptians, Turks, Asians, and North Africans, as well as Greeks, Romans, and Jews of course, heard this all, as if, as it were, in their own tongues.

The crowd asked what it all meant, and some scorners suggested that they were all drunk. It was still morning, though, and Peter gets up and delivers a long and famous speech, saying that these men were not drunk but touched by the Spirit (Acts 14–36). He cites Joel's prophecy when God said, "I will pour out of my Spirit upon all flesh" and sons, daughters, slaves, and old men shall "dream dreams." From this moment on, speaking tongues has a long history and goes on today as part of the Pentecostal movement. But what is it all about?

The Greeks, in the orphic oracles and even Delphi, were aware of speaking in tongues: the pythoness and the oracles, when consulted, often answered in a higher language of riddles, and gnomic rhythmic, exalted verses. The priest of the temple then interpreted the meaning of the pronouncements. The oracles themselves, the Pythonesses, was usually in an altered state of consciousness, often under the influence of smoking laurel leaves (hydrocyanic acid plus alkaloids).

In our own experience, we know thc sense of wisdom and inspiration that nonsense can sometimes deliver—even skat singing or hip hop. Take Lewis Carrol's famous line in *Alice in Wonderland:* "The slithy toads did gyre and gimbol." This is phonetic, phonemic, morphemic, and syntactical. It simply doesn't make any sense—and yet it does. Although modeled on English, it is really an unknown language. But it seems to make sense—a lot of sense, in fact. In thinking of the communicability of nonsense language, and glossolalia, too, we need to remember the creativity of baby talk, reggae, and hip hop.

Another aspect of glossolalia is the slip of the tongue. Today, this is a mere joke. Someone at the Holiday Inn says, by mistake, "I'm at the Hollywood Inn." But in ancient times, these slips were very important—even dramatic. They were omens. Sometimes they even prophesied death or assassination. For instance, someone says the room was painted "with guilt"—meaning, of course, the gilt trim in gold. Freud revived the omenology of ancient times and employed this aspect of tongues in interpreting dreams and the unconscious. Theologians do not deal with this kind of linguistic trivia, but it has a big undertow in the global village, where on a day-to-day basis people deal commercially with many languages. It also has currency for speakers of primitive languages, slang, jargon, and other areas of what one might call an underground Pentecostalism. This is sometimes a phenomenon of cross-hearing—sometimes shorthand code, sometimes unconscious and sometimes, yes, even a joke. "That is a spiritous witticism, on a low or high level. But as Einstein might have said, "The Holy Ghost doesn't make jokes."

Linguists avoid glossolalia and the study of speaking in tongues. It is not even mentioned in the *Blackwell Companion to Philosophy* series on the Philosophy of Language, edited by Bob Hale and Crispin Wright. This seems a grave oversight, since glossolalia, with its challenging phenomena—generation of a foreign or private language by a native speaker of another language; cross-understanding of a given language in another tongue; or thought transference across a linguistic barrier—would seem to be a challenging language laboratory and a theoretical playground and testing lab for linguists. But linguists, if they do mention glossolalia, usually dismiss it as a pseudo-phenomenon.

George Steiner, the eminent philologist and linguist, says in *After Babel:* "In the genesis of the human spirit, all nations traverse the same stages of linguistic usage, from the immediate and sensory to the abstract." And so it may have been with the Holy Ghost. The original Tower of Babel, incidentally, where all language was fractured into many tongues, was apparently Nimrod's ziggurat, and Steiner *does not* cite Pentecost once. But he does cite the story of the lunatic tower launched at the stars. He simply does not discuss Pentecost. He has pages and pages on the dismemberment of language, and how the Titans smashed each other—their broken bones being the splinters of different languages. Eavesdropping on the Gods, human beings were struck mononic and lost the universal tongue. Steiner goes on to briefly mention, after the citation of Jacob Böhme (1575–1628), Pentecostal language as "the speech of instinctual untutored immediacy." He likens it to the speech of natural humankind; savages, he seems to think, echo nature.

In *The Language Instinct,* Harvard linguist Stephen Pinker's only remark on glossolalia is, "The linguist Sarah G. Thomason has found that people who claim to be channeling back to past lives or speaking in tongues are really producing gibberish that conforms to a sound pattern vaguely reminiscent of the claims of language"—in other words, a phonemic transfer. He calls this kind of cross-phonemic talk "generic pseudo-language gobbledygook." He likens it to talking a foreign language with the sound pattern of another language—in other words, with an accent, as in Franglais.

But, taking tongues more seriously—and though a journalist, I also hold an advanced degree in linguistics—glossolalia, of course, is translated as "speaking in tongues." It is supposed to be the ability to speak—to produce discourse, a language sample—that is understood by listeners of another language, listeners who speak different languages than the speaker. In glossolalia, a person who "speaks in tongues" produces discourse that is supposed to be understood by another person—or by groups of listeners who themselves speak different languages from each other—as if they are hearing the discourse in their own language.

It is in a sense the first recorded example of the kind of simultaneous translation that goes on at the UN, without transference into the actual foreign language—as if Mr. Putin from Russia spoke in Russian or semblance thereof, or a token language, and through the earphones you understood as if hearing English. Except that in speaking in tongues, in glossolalia, there is no translator and no machines. It happens somehow in your head. Often this kind of speaking is a primary kind of utterance, though whether it was so at Pentecost is not clear.

What happens, too, is not quite clear. That is, the listener hears and supposedly understands the speaker, but there is a difference. A listener might hear a tongue and, not knowing the language, still understands. The speaker would be producing, say, a primary utterance, or, if the Pentecostal testimony is to be believed, say, in Russian, and I, a native English speaker who knew no Russian, would understand—although we will differentiate glossolalia later from *xolalia.* It is as if I were dropped into Africa, having never studied any African languages, and Swahili suddenly made sense. This is at least the biblical version. A person would say in Swahili, "The new life is the truth"—and I would understand that. It would be different if I heard an actual voice, either inside or outside, that said in English: "The new life is the truth." I might then understand the Swahili, that is, without actually hearing it in English. That is, in one scenario, I would hear Swahili—but would understand that "the new life is the truth" without physically hearing an English translation. If I actually heard the English from the mouth of the person talking Swahili, or if I heard the English phrase in my head, it would be what is sometimes called "audition," or better, an *audiocination,* or auditory hallucination. Actually hearing a language that a person is not speaking, or hearing—that is, *understanding*—a language that they are speaking that I do not know would be a sort of miracle, in the sense that it would be an inexplicable phenomenon beyond the bounds of natural law. This is what is claimed by religion and the Acts as happening at Pentecost on the fifth day after Easter in the year 34.

Xolalia is different from glossolalia. This is when a speaker produces discourse in a language that he or she does not know. Having never studied or heard them, I suddenly start speaking Russian or Swahili. This phenomenon is reported to happen, usually from speakers in special circumstances: persons under stress, under hypnosis, in coma, in their sleep, under emotional exaltation, or in trance. This is also somewhat miraculous, but it is not normally called a miracle. Xolalia is not necessarily reported as what happened at Pentecost. Jesus' disciples did not come out and talk in various different languages necessarily that they did not know—Chinese, Swahili and so forth—although this is what readers of the Bible or churchgoers often think happened. They came out and "spoke in tongues," some kind of language—that is, they generated discourse that wasn't English or Togalog. But the listeners, who were variously Greek, Syrian, Egyptian, and Persian, most all of them Jewish, are reported to have understood. And the speakers, the disciples, were not necessarily speaking Hebrew either, though they may have been. They were mostly native speakers of Aramaic.

When I go to a foreign country and a person passes me the sugar and they say, "Here. This is sugar," I understand. The Pentecost mood was exalted and this kind of understanding may have taken place; something may have been happening in the crowd, that they had heard about, or in the mood, and when the speaker said, "the new life is the truth," it may have been clear from the context, just as in passing the sugar. Also, since many of the listeners were Jews, though from different communities, they may—as Ashkenazis and Sephards in Israel do today— have understood a common language or communal communication or feeling, just as foreign Jews in Israel today begin to understand Hebrew.

In the Old Testament, the Bible tells another language story—the story of Babel. In this story, God punished the speakers—who were all building a tower, the ziggurat of Nimrod—for their pride. As a result, they were forced to speak in different languages. This may also be a story based in part on fact: that many workers from different countries came together at the tower but, as they went along, couldn't understand one another. This would be a sort of parable. The New Testament story of Pentecost would be a reverse parable—the solution to Babel.

Both stories are about the origins and future of language, and they are both about the unifying nature of language. This is also a possibility at Pentecost—that whatever the speakers were doing, the crowd—the listeners—were having a unitive experience. The Holy Ghost might produce primary utterance, but it is not likely that the Holy Ghost produced gibberish. They understood something together and had a higher, alternate experience of some sort related to language. To scoff at claims that something miraculous was going on is just as foolish as being gullible or misinformed about what was actually going on. Whatever was happening linguistically, there was some kind of cross-hearing, communication, and cultural event at hand. Pentecost is considered to be the actual birthday of the Church, and, as we know, it was a Jewish first harvest feast day—Shavuot, the fiftieth day after Passover. And the glossolalia—the speaking in tongues of fire—was experienced as a primary gift, or sign, of the Holy Ghost, along with prophecy and the power to heal.

The term implies that the speakers, like gifted orators, were endowed with a special faculty and ability at the time, and the primitive glossolalia of today may be very different after all. The phenomenon also seems to be one of listening; the listener has the experience of communication and understanding—whatever the language. In other words, some authorities claim that it should be called "listening in tongues." But it may be that writers of the New Testament, themselves inspired, were taking liberties, too—for instance, describing a psychological state of the crowd. Many politicians, demagogues, and rabble-rousers also seem to speak in tongues, and many audiences claim to understand what is going on. Very elegant crowds at the Metropolitan Opera spend hours listening to language that is gibberish to them, yet they come away exalted and claim to have understood and been delighted by what was happening on stage.

A lot of people listen to lectures, too, and sometimes it could be called a miracle, too—either that people understand or that they think they do. Glossolalia doesn't get much attention from the experts, but then again, its opposite—everybody talking and nobody understanding anything—doesn't get the attention it deserves either. Although some theologians claim the Holy Ghost left the Church shortly after it began, Glossolalia, the gift of tongues, is still experienced today, though sometimes in primitive forms, and actually practiced widely in some religious movements. Speaking in tongues, as presented in the biblical account of Pentecost, challenges science, linguistics, and our understanding of languages as a system of contrasting known signals and signs that contribute to communication. It challenges our understanding of communication itself. But the lofty linguistic fellows of Cambridge and the University of Geneva, Oxford, and Harvard, and master theoreticians of translation all totally ignore the origins of simultaneous translation—that first Whitsunday.

In Benjamin Lee Whorf, however, linguistics has something very essential to contribute to understanding not only language, obviously, but also the spirit. For Whorf, what translates the underlying metaphysics of a language into surface grammar is the "cryptotype." It is a semantic level related to the mysteries of thought. Of note here is the Whorfian qualitative phenomenological description of these levels of meaning—such as submerged, subtle, elusive—corresponding to no actual word, but functionally important. And, as categories of semantic organization, these levels work by "dispersion without boundaries, oscillation without agitation, impact without duration, directed motion."

I submit that these two descriptions mentioned here are about the finest definition of "spirit," and maybe "tongues," as we will ever get—unless we simply revert to the one used earlier: breath, and *vox, ruah,* and *lalia,* voice and speech. All this Whorf refers to as "the inner music of meaning."

So "pure speech"—the logos, the divine speech—is a no-man's land between language *A* and language *B,* and pure speech may be the Holy Ghost's idiom. At least if we look at it this way, we can remember what the theorist of translation, Walter Benjamin (in 1923) says: "If there is a language of truth, in which the final secrets that draw the effort of all thinking are held in silent repose, then this language of truth is—true language."

David Crystal, in *Linguists, Language, and Religion,* contrasts genesis and Adam's naming of things with Babel, when "the language of the whole earth was confounded." He contrasts this further with Jesus' linguistic action as a healer of divisions, and the charism of tongues; in those times, remember, there were no grammar books.

It is fairly clear from the gospels that Paul himself did not always understand what the speakers in tongues were saying—it is better to prophecy and be understood, he says, than to speak in tongues, and more useful" (I Corinthians 12–14). He was wary, as a good Jew and an intellectual, as the Church itself still is, of possession by a supernatural spirit—as opposed to, as in the delivery of scripture, the channelling of divine proclamation. Paul's testimony may mean that it was a primitive, primary utterance. But Paul also claimed the gift for himself in Corinthians 14:18.

"Follow after charity and desire spiritual gifts, but rather that ye may prophesy. For he that speaketh in an unknown tongue speaketh not unto men but unto God; for no man understandeth him, howbeit in the spirit he speaks mysteries" (I Corinthians 14:1–2). Thus Paul says that speaking in tongues is the spirit wrapped itself in talking to God, but that prophesy is clear and communicative: edifying, exhorting, and comforting. Speaking in tongues may be an edification of the speaker, but it may be that, at Pentecost, the others, the listeners, also had the veil lifted and joined in the message, as sometimes today still happens at Pentecostal gatherings.

Giorgio Agamben, the Italian linguist critic, in an article on glossolalia in Daniel Heller Roazen's *Speaking in Tongues* (25:2, July 2002), argues that "to speak with tongues is to speak without definite meaning and without speaking oneself." Tracing of the forms in which the figure of speaking in tongues refers throughout the work of Giorgio Agamben, the structure and philosophical implications of glossolalia as a speech act calls into question the very concept of language and its ends. This represents the best of the thinking on glossolalia, which is sometimes examined by behavioral psychologists and by missionaries interested in language transmission. Pentacostalism still practices it (we cover this in a later chapter). To say that hymns, psalms, or other such texts are the speech of tongues is wide of the mark, however, and stretches the meaning of speaking in tongues.

In 1960, *Time* and other magazines reported that, with Episcopalian Rector Dennis Bennett claiming to speak in tongues in Van Nuys, California, tongues had "broken out of the Pentacostal ghetto." H. Newton Malony and A. Adam Lavakin, both behavioral scientists, then reported that the phenomenon had been poorly covered by the sciences. They published with Oxford University Press in 1985. Many behaviorists, said Malony and Lovakin, "have simply inferred that those who express themselves in this manner were either abnormal or mentally deranged." This bias is to be expected in educated quarters, and those who actually practice glossolalia don't care. It is largely, in this context, class prejudice. One concern of the researchers was to note claims of value and health changes in glossolalists, which were usually for the better. The phenomenon is sometimes associated, too, with the counterculture. These researchers noted a relationship between glossolalia and mysticism.

Again Paul is very sharp on the phenomenon, saying, "Tongues are for a sign, not to them that believe, but to them that believe not: but prophesying serveth not for them that believe not, but for them which believe" (I Corinthians 14:22).

Speech, because it is on the breath, is anyway akin to spirit—*geist* in German, a cognate of ghost. The nineteenth-century German philologist Wilhelm von Humboldt claimed that "the diffusing Spirit of language thus hovers, like a silent breath, over the whole culture." Even George Steiner says that it is in "the nature of spirit to seek to realize, to energize, into conscious being, all modes of possible experience." Language is seen as life-determining and life-giving—but it should be noted that the Holy Ghost does not "speak" traditionally as God sometimes does, but "infuses" itself.

Other outbreaks of glossolalia have been noted historically among the French Camisards; children, speaking in eloquent French; Mother Ann Lee of the Shakers in Lancashire, Pennsylvania, spoke (xolalia) in a number of recognizable tongues; in 1830 a Scottish woman broke into unknown tongues and recovered her health, prompting the Presbyterian preacher Edward Irving to found his own Catholic and Apostolic church featuring glossolalia; and in Tibet there is still the tradition of maintaining trance-like oracles, often using epileptics as mouthpieces.

The South American author Jorge Luis Borges developed the trope that we are all existences that are dreamed elsewhere—that we are mere figures of a divine speech. In the poet laureate Richard Wilbur's translation of "Compass,' Borges writes essentially of tongues of fire when he says, "All things are words of some strange tongue in thrall to Someone, Something, who both day and night proceeds in endless gibberish to write the history of the world." *

From the Church's point of view, according to the Patristic Fathers, Pentecost ushered in a new post-Babel period when the Church itself (using Latin) speaks every language and understands all tongues in charity, thus, ideally, overcoming the dispersion of Babel.

* Quoted in George Steiner, *After Babel: Aspects of Language and Translation*. Oxford: Oxford UP, 1975.

## Chapter 11

# Truth

Another early name for the Holy Ghost was the "Spirit of Truth." Why is this? It is partly because the Greeks, Romans, and Jews — and other pagans — viewed truth in such a different way. In our time, truth has been nominalized and relativized, and it is often viewed differently in the universities, in the press, in Washington, in the rest of the world, by common sense, or by religion and Rome. These differences can be traced through a long lineage back to before the Medieval split between realists and nominalists, and to differing views that came out of the Greek Academies, or the sophists, the Roman Pantheon, the Hebrew Rabbinical tradition, and Jesus' new witness as embraced by John and Paul. This can be summed up in the question put by Pilate, who was asked to pass judgment on Jesus after the chief Jewish priest Caiaphas turned him over to the Romans. Hearing that Jesus had said that he came to be a witness to the truth, Pilate asks him, probably rather scornfully, even sneering, "What is truth?"

A new experience of the truth, as distinct from the dictations of Mosaic law and Rabbinical regulation was, during the three years of his ministry, a cornerstone of Jesus' message. And the conflict for the Greeks and Romans is between truth in the abstract — the truths of the academies — and the truth of being — intellectual truth versus being, the truth of witness. And the conflict is germane not only to universities today, but to journalists, who must always distinguish between the veracity of their sources and fact, opinion, norms, and accepted universal truths. In what way is the news true? This should be a relevant question even to judges.

In Jerusalem, in the year 34, this was not just about the "truth" of Jewish laws or the relative truths of Greek sophists, but about the "Good News" brought by the Holy Ghost. Later, it will again be important when we flash forward to Muhammad, who says that *Al-Haqq*, the Truth, is one of the names of Allah. And Pilate's question to Jesus is about whether truth is an objective condition or a subjective state. Pilate and Jesus have this same argument on the night before Good Friday in Jerusalem, when the Roman asked him scoffingly, "What is truth?" To Pilate, truth was a relative—speculative skepticism. He had been taught by the academies, intellectually, by sophist philosophers. To Jesus, truth was witness—what you live and what you experience directly. It was a form of existentialism, not an academic discussion. And he would die for it the next day.

But is the reality of experience itself and witness subjective? Do all eyes see the same thing? Or are the sophisms, models, and paradigms of university philosophers and professors "objective?" John and Paul try to explain this in the New Testament when they equate the Holy Spirit to the Spirit of Truth. Journalists might take note. Doctors all over the world swear by the Hippocratic oath, but journalists take no oaths. They try to protect their sources, yet theirs is the mission and mirror of truth; they are themselves witnesses. Does this mean merely that they should not lie? Should not tell falsehood? Should honor their sources? Facts do not lie. But they need both understanding and interpretation—stories spun from facts. The story is supposed to represent what actually happened, but is the story merely subjective and made up? Or does it correspond to reality and to experience? Ask a journalist. Ask Mark, Mathew, Luke, or John. They were journalists, too. They "reported" the life of Jesus Christ. Jesus had taught them the "new journalism," to see with one's own eyes. How does a modern journalist measure truth? Get the gist of a story? Is it a faculty of the spirit, dedication to reality, or good faith?

Jesus, in custody that night, said to Pilate on the steps of the Praetorium: "To this end was I born, and for this cause came I into the world, that I should bear witness unto the truth. Every one that is of the truth heareth my voice." Pilate answered him: "What is truth?" Jesus was silent. Pilate told the Jews: "I find in him no fault at all" (John 18:37–38). The Jews cried, "Crucify him. Crucify him" (John 19:6).

The chief Jewish priests, at the height of speciousness and hypocrisy—in contrast to Jesus' testimony that, " I have spoken openly to the world" (viz. the free press)—cried, "We have no king but Caesar" (John 19:15). The Holy Ghost meant nothing at this moment to them.

Paul, talking to the Greeks, reports, "It is written, I will destroy the wisdom of the wise, and will bring to nothing the understanding of the prudent" (I Corinthians 1:19). This doesn't seem like the action of a Holy Ghost either, but at stake is rabbinical and academic tradition. Paul's position is a symptom of how radical the new Spirit of Truth was. He asks where the wise ones are. He asks: Where are the scribes (read "journalists")? He suggests that God has made the wisdom of the world foolish. "For the Jews require a sign," he says, "and the Greeks seek after wisdom." He then tells them that God, in the new spirit of truth, has confounded the wise and with common and lowly things, and has chosen weak things to confound the might. Conscience was supposed to have become the new Greek truth and the new judge of reason regarding morality and goodness or the badness of an act. But even the new Greek conscience was not "the still small voice." Rather it was the hallmark judgment of each person, governing personal life according to one's own principles, usually stoic. Even this conscience, unlike the still small voice, does not yet appeal to the Holy Ghost. The small still voice of Jesus' was greater than even the burgeoning conscience of the Greeks.

Vatican II in 1962 decreed: "Conscience is the most secret core and sanctuary of man." But it is not just that people impose on themselves (an inner voice) but their relationship to a law outside themselves, or a principle that people must observe (a standard). Even for Vatican II, it was not the same as an inspiration.

For Jesus, rather than truth being an objectively codified standard, the Spirit was seen to be a matter of witness, by any or all, and remained a mystery rather than the dictum of tablets. St. Paul, in fact, asks, "What then has Athens to do with Jerusalem?" The Spirit of

Truth brought something like conscience, but more—conscience having been partly a Greek contribution to the evolution of consciousness. The Jews deferred here to the law—the righteous were observers of the law not arbiters. Jesus, John, and Paul, when they talk about truth, are talking about living it. Spirit, in this relation, is true witness—Greek conscience and more.

This new mystery is confirmed by the Holy Spirit, the Spirit of Truth, "whom the Son sends from the Father, and the Father sends in the name of the Son" (John 15:26). Truth in Greek philosophy was related to factual content on one hand, and then to the more elusive aspects of truth. It is a guidepost to opinion. *Aletheia* meant that which is not hidden, but made open; *mathein* meant to learn; *pathein* meant to experience. *True* in early English meant loyal, steadfast, or faithful—to be trusted. It was only in the 1500s that it came to mean that which corresponds literally to fact, or reality. In this discussion, the line of reason goes from the Greeks through to Abelard and the beginning of nominalism, and the line of experience runs through to the mystics.

The Holy Ghost has another incarnation than just in truth, and that is being. The early Apostles and the Church Fathers were concerned with the Holy Spirit in the guise of truth, and this continued through the ages into the times of Luther and Calvin and beyond. The Inquisition and the Holy Office at the Vatican that polices doctrine and thought were arms of this interest. Error, for them, was the opposite of truth. The nineteenth-century promulgation of the Infallibility dogma was another outcome of this line of interest. But the Holy Spirit's second appearance was truth in the sense of being—rather than the truth in the sense of the academy—also held fast through the ages. This is the aspect of the Holy Ghost that is sometimes dearer to evangelicals and to Pentecostals, and it was dealt with, too, by some of the Patristic Fathers, who changed the nature of the Holy Ghost's being from truth to the tradition of love.

James Carroll, a former Paulist father and priest, also argues in *Constantine's Sword* that Pilate's question, "What is truth?" is important. If truth is totalitarian, the exclusive province of authority, then the duty of people is to conform. But if truth is partial—an analogy rather than a syllogism—then "our knowledge is imperfect and our prophecy is imperfect," as St. Paul said. It then behooves people to bring their own thought and experience to the community—to converse, revise, criticize, and honor the position of others. The Vatican called this "Americanism," and we look at it in a later chapter. "The mutuality, in this community, has a name," Carroll says, "the Holy Spirit." The Holy See sometimes viewed this relative mutuality as the heresy "Americanism."

The Spirit of Truth, in its codified form, leads to the doctrine of Infallibility promulgated in 1870, when the Vatican was under siege from the *Risorgimento* (the liberation movement) in Italy, and the new growing wave of relativism and materialistic positivism. Infallibility is widely misunderstood. It does not mean that the Vatican is always right about everything or has a monopoly on knowledge, but that, as inheritor of the Spirit of Truth through apostolic succession, the Pope is without error in matters of faith and morals.

Talking of this one day, I asked my wife, "If you had to choose, would you take 'truth' or 'being?'

She said, "How do you mean?"

"I mean if truth is the purity—the rightness. 'Being,' instead, is like when we were down in St. Martin's and went to the Black Church. The folk got not the doctrine of the Holy Spirit, but the 'being.' They swayed, they clapped, they shouted, they sang."

"I prefer the being," my wife says.

Okay, but truth has been given a bum rap, too. Truth has been equated with correctness, with political correction, instead of the original trustworthiness and faithfulness. Straightening people out. For a while, truth in America under McCarthyism meant simply being against any kind of communism. At other times it has meant the Inquisition. The law. Even science.

As a journalist, that was not what truth meant to me. Truth was more of an attitude: facts, information, and an open mind. Truth in my mind was more like *kosher* or pure or righteous—without prejudice, without blindness, with fairness. There was reportorial truth, the facts—who, how, what, when, where, and editorial truth—fairness, both sides of an issue, and balanced, experienced judgment. Truth of this kind is far different than absolute truth dictated by authority—a fixed standard principle, or convention. In the name of this kind of truth, very often made by men, people have been burned, tortured, tyrannized, and politically corrected and wars made.

St. Paul, John, and Jesus testified to truth as an enlightened experience—a personal testimony. Some argue that this, as opposed to Rabbinical law and revelation, is more subjective—relativism. Pilate asked Jesus, who had said he came to witness the truth, "What is truth?" He too was weary perhaps of sophists and lawyers. The Spirit—not the letter—Paul argued, was the truth. It was a truth proved by being—not by the law books or letters or disputations.

"Do you promise to tell the truth, the whole truth, and nothing but the truth?" The answer is not always in the head. The experts do not always have all the answers. There was a reason people swore on the Bible. It was because the spirit—the truth—was being tested. The witness of being. And as anyone who has ever been on the stand and taken that oath knows, the answer lies in your heart. You become a witness to your own words, your own veracity, by consulting your heart as much as your knowledge.

In the end John, a great witness to the Spirit of Truth, modified his view. Being, as witness, was the truth of Jesus, and he lived it—in the ministry and then in the Passion. Truth as being, John came to say, is love.

# Chapter 12

# Scripture

Scripture raises the question: did the Holy Ghost write the Bible? The Jewish Pentateuch, the Old Testament, is said to have been written by God—not necessarily by the Holy Ghost—but the voice of the Father, the Almighty. Moses brought the Torah back from the Sinai where the great God dictated it to him to put in stone. John, in the Gospels, says he is the disciple who "testifieth" of these things and that "his testimony is true." If they should be written, everyone and everything, "I suppose," says John, "that even the world itself could not contain the books that should be written" (John 21:24–25). After Jesus was taken up, John reminds Theophilus, "The Holy Ghost had given commandments unto the apostles whom he had chosen" (Acts 1:2). In his first epistle, John says he reports what "we have heard, which we have seen with our eyes, which we have looked upon, and our hands have handled, of the Word of life" (I John 1:1). Thus the Word of Life becomes another name for the Holy Ghost. And the question arises: Does the Holy Ghost not only write the Bible, but also history itself?

Finally, John says the Revelation was "sent and signified ... by his angel unto his servant John" (Revelation 1:1). Yet the Holy Ghost is not portrayed itself in the Bible as a writer or a speaker. The Holy Ghost acts by "infusion"; it is an "inward unction," a presence, a being, an inspiration. God's own voice is different, more transcendent, and mightier, and the angel by which John is given gospel is not named.

Obviously, there is a figurative sense to the "writing" of the Holy Ghost. In the Old Testament the most famous example of direct writing is the finger of God that writes on the wall—the invisible hand writing on the wall. But the Holy Ghost does not write in visions, hallucinations, or actuality in this sense.

St. John and the Apostles, the Gospel writers, were inspired by God and received the Revelation from the Son, though they often received the Holy Ghost through Him. Not even the Church or Biblical scholars agree exactly how this inspiration from God was done — that is, how inspiration works. The Churches and Protestantism agree that the Bible is a book of revelation and that scripture is divine revelation. Some people can agree on how God created the world, because in Genesis it says He breathed upon the waters. But inspiration of the scriptural kind is not so easy and the Bible is clear about when it happens, but not how — not even in the Prophets. Not even Biblical scholars can agree on all this, but argue all the time about human versus divine inspiration, textual relativity, historicity, and social contexts. Writing is not one of the Gifts of the Holy Spirit — one of the charismata — though prophecy is. The gifts of the Holy Spirit are sometimes for the good of the person receiving them, but the more special gifts are for use by the receiver toward the common good. Inspiration from the Holy Spirit is usually talked of as being infused — that is, it is both immanent, coming from above down to earth, and incarnating. You don't go up, as it were, to get it.

Some forms of meditation, mysticism, and spirituality, of course, do this. But the Holy Ghost is generally not transcendent in the way that people think of transcendentalism, going up to some ideal, some Platonic form world of spiritual furniture; you don't necessarily go to heaven or out of your body or mind to get it. It comes to you. It is experienced not just by individuals, but also by congregations. After all, that is one of the points of church service. The gifts come the same way, under the Christmas tree, so to speak, not on top of it. Since all these forms — writings, sayings, speeches, and revelations — affect the way we live and what we think, the whole subject of inspiration is a great deal more important than the jokers, scientists, and news reporters let on or what people generally believe.

But not even the Vatican, although it has dealt profoundly and extensively with revelation and scripture, has never issued a Bull or

Encyclical—except for *Divino Afflante Spiritus*—on how to write or on the mechanics of inspiration. The Vatican has often said what to say, as in the catechism, and the Holy Office has often said what not to write. That's about it. Whether it's the help of the Ghost that writes a poem or a speech in a book is never discussed much—except in the case of the Bible, where the Holy Spirit gets some credit sometimes, yet how it gets channeled receives much less attention. Most of the time, however, it is the first person of the Godhead who gets the by-line: God the Father.

In the 1953 new edition of the Catholic Bible—the Douuay and Challoner Rheims version, approved by Pope Pius XII and with the imprimatur of Francis Cardinal Spellman—the introduction said that "inspired by the Divine Spirit, the Sacred writers composed these books, which God, in His paternal charity towards the human race, deigned to bestow on them." Again, the Divine Spirit is another word for Holy Ghost. In an encyclical letter, *Divino Afflante Spiritus,* (By Divine Inspiration), the Pope urged Bibilical scholars to scrutinize, explain, propose, and defend "the very word of God, communicated to men under the inspiration of the Holy Ghost."

Two prayers were cited, one for before reading, and one for after—to help with interpretation. Before reading scripture, the prayer was: "Come, Holy Spirit, fill the hearts of thy faithful and enkindle them with the fire of love." This was to set the attitude in which reading might take place, and then, after, that the interpretations might be sound, the prayer was: "O God, who didst instruct the hearts of the faithful by the light of the Holy Spirit, grant us by the same Spirit to have a right judgment in all things." Also for right interpretation the prayer of the Venerable St. Bede was suggested for after scripture: "Let me not, O Lord, be puffed up with worldly wisdom." Wisdom passes away, but love—or being—never abates. And this rather than "truth" in the sense of political correction is what infuses the word when it is thought to be the inspiration of the Holy Ghost, not the literal fundamentalist truth of absolutism.

In Scriptural tradition, it was the Spirit that dictated the Scriptures sometimes to the prophets—not the physical words in their mouths, but the spirit. The spirit was the intention of a passage as distinct from the literal and historical meaning. The writings were not the reflections merely of the authors themselves, but something transmitted to them. The traditional claim, indeed, is sometimes that the Holy Ghost inspired the writers of the Bible—not only that God dictated the Word of God or the words himself. Indeed, the Holy Ghost also inspires the interpretation of scripture—the hermeneutics. What scripture means becomes clear with the right attitude, understanding, and wisdom of the Holy Ghost—not by an authoritarian fundamentalist or punitive literalism.

Subsequent to this revised Bible, the Ecumenical Council of 1962 to 1966 at the Vatican—Vatican II—dealt with scripture in a decree, "On Divine Revelation." The decree repeated the tradition that scripture has been written "under the inspiration of the Holy Spirit" and said that this means "they have God as their author." In addressing the age old problem of whether a human hand or God's hand wrote scripture, the Council said that God works like this: "To compose the sacred books, God chose certain men, who, all the while He employed them in the task, made full use of their powers and faculties so that, though he acted in them and by them, it was as true authors that they consigned to writing whatever he wanted written and no more." St. Augustine, indeed, had said, "God speaks through men in human fashion" (De. Civ. Dei XVIII, 6,2).

In interpretation then, in hermeneutics—telling what is meant—scholars and lay people alike need to "carefully search out the meaning which the sacred writers really had in mind" and respect "that meaning which God thought well to manifest through the medium of their words." Not just the divine source needs to be respected, then, but also the inspiration of the Holy Ghost in literary forms: the historical, prophetical, and poetical forms. The Holy Ghost here is a kind of genius of language. Beside literary forms, the customs, patterns of perception, speech, and narrative mode of the age need to be sifted. Finally, the conventions of the people at the time need to be regarded.

This answers in large part to the Biblical reforms that came in the nineteenth century through the so-called Higher Criticism, which humanized and relativized the sources. But the conflict has been painful to many, and only recently, in 1996, conservative scholar James B. de Young, out of the Evangelical Theological Society meeting in Jackson, Mississippi, summed things up by saying, "When it comes to scholarly methods of interpreting the Bible, the Holy Spirit may as well be dead."

The polarity rises and is a hot issue in evangelical circles today, on the one hand because the Church tried to hold to oral and traditional views on the Word of God against the historical and relativistic views of Higher Criticism, and because fundamentalists still hold to the literalist tradition, and on the other hand because populist tradition today, according to some commentators, means merely a pooling of ignorance—"what this verse means to me"—and a merely pietistic approach to Scripture dictating interpretation.

Other factors are impinging on the Holy Ghost's role, too—postmodernism, which stresses experience over logic or rationalism; evangelical stress on rationalism over historicity; and ironically, a post-conservative politically correct tolerance, which accepts every view as equal and jettisons both conviction and hard scholarly work. We are not concerning ourselves with the technicalities of hermeneutics and interpretation. What we are focused on is the broader issue of whether scripture is divine or human, and whether and how the Holy Spirit inspires writers. In any one interpretation, or reading, for example, does the Holy Spirit add more value to the written word?

In the sixteenth century, the conflict between Protestantism and the Church also centered around the role of the Holy Spirit in interpreting scripture and inspiring the Church. The Church claimed that oral tradition had given as much authority for doctrine and rites as the scripture—the written word—and that the Holy Ghost had worked through the oral tradition passed down as well as the written word. The Protestants went back strictly to the scriptural sources, but allowed that individuals could interpret the scripture for themselves, not just under the guidance of the Church, which had in effect monopolized the Holy Ghost.

Take an example: on the way into Jerusalem just before Passion Week, Jesus blasts a fig tree near Bethany. When informed by history and custom, on the one hand, and anagogic or figurative interpretation on the other hand, this may be a parable about reforming old atavistic ways of meditation and clairvoyance rather than the mere narration of the killing of a cursed fruit tree. "Sitting under the fig tree" was an expression for old atavistic meditation—as contrasted with the freedom of the new individual ego in witnessing the Spirit.

Daniel B. Wallace of the Dallas Theological Seminary has listed a number of ways the Holy Spirit relates to reading or meaning:

> The Spirit's work adds more conviction than cognition—more heart than head.
>
> Experience and intellectual witness often conflict when dealing with the Holy Ghost; sympathy with the author's spirit helps unveil meaning; belief in the supernatural as a disposition, given by the Holy Ghost, helps with understanding miracles and prophecy; the Spirit is an act of inner witness.
>
> General illumination as a function of the Holy Ghost.
>
> Historical illumination in a wider sense, the Holy Ghost as actor throughout history, is important to a generous and liberal reading of scripture.

Wallace closes with some wise caveats for persons dealing with the truth of texts: transformation not rationalist interpretation is the goal—the Holy Spirit is seen as a transformer; study and critical faculties are as important to the Spirit as prayer and spirituality; a merely cognitive approach to the Spirit without worship and heart qualities will be cold and fruitless.

In an earlier chapter we mentioned the question of whether the Word, or Logos, and Holy Spirit are the same, or whether, as here seems to be the case with scripture, the Holy Ghost is the great brooder of language, the inspiration, the medium of the word. It is odd in the Bible that the direct voice of the Holy Ghost, a person, after all, is not heard. The Spirit works by infusion, immanence, inspiration, and incorporation, not by speaking directly itself. The theology of the Holy Spirit in this regard is more crucial than is commonly supposed and has more to do with everyday life than people often suspect. This is because the view you hold as to the origin of the word, whether literal or inspired, and the origin of all our texts—not scripture alone, but the Constitution, the Declaration of Independence, and all our texts, even the news—is a key to the views, respect, and understanding in which we will hold the truths of our society.

The Holy Ghost, if not dead and gone, is, in a word, a sort of patron saint of readers and writers.

## Chapter 13

# The Sin Against the Holy Ghost

A small venial sin can be forgiven — a Hail Mary, or two, and it's gone. A mortal sin can be indulged, paid off, or worked off in Purgatory. But the sin against the Holy Ghost can never be indulged, worked off, or ever, ever forgiven. This sin lurked in the background and in cathedral shadows during the Middle Ages, as well as in the niches and corridors of power. It was the unspeakable, never-to-be-forgiven sin, even unto the ends of time. It was even worse than pride.

The seven deadly sins are tame in contrast to the sin against the Holy Ghost. The deadly sins, you will remember, are pride, wrath, envy, lust, gluttony, avarice, and sloth. Modernity has lost the sense of sin, which originally meant separation. Theologically, sin was sometimes viewed as the loss of remembrance of God, loss of self, loss of the ability to recollect one's origins.

Milton, the blind genius of poetry in Cromwellian England, a Puritan sympathizer, described sin as a keeper with death of the gates of hell who sprang full blown from the head of Satan.

> Woman to the waist, and fair,
> But ending foul in many a scaly fold
> Voluminous and vast, a serpent armed
> With mortal sting. (*Paradise Lost,* ii, 650–653)

Nor is the sin against the Holy Ghost the same as original sin — the doctrine that corruption is born in us, and that it is the inheritance of all as the offspring of Adam. When the angels of Lucifer fell from heaven, the sin was pride. When Adam fell it was disobedience. As founder of the race, Adam's transgression and its punishment fell to his posterity. Pelagianism advanced the heresy that, because of some inherent good, human beings could achieve salvation through their own efforts. It was fiercely opposed by St. Augustine around 400 AD and was quashed once and for all by Pope Zosimus in 418. Original sin again became a keystone of the Reformation doctrine when Luther challenged humankind's relation to scripture, the role of one's native understanding, the doctrine of Justification by Faith, and the choosing of the Elect. Original sin is overcome only through Jesus Christ, and by Grace we can be redeemed from it at the end of time. Not so with the sin against the Holy Ghost.

In the Gospel, Mathew has described how Jesus cast out devils by the Spirit of God (Matthew 12:22ff). The Pharisees object that Jesus does it through the power of Beelzebub—the prince of devils. But Jesus replies that to drive out devils with devils would be to split oneself and divide the house. Rather, he drives out devils with the Spirit of God so that the kingdom comes unto itself. Then Jesus says, "He that is not with me is against me" (Matthew 12:30). "Wherefore I say unto you, all manner of sin and blasphemy shall be forgiven unto men: but the blasphemy against the Holy Ghost shall not be forgiven unto men" (Matthew 12:32). Mark and Luke record the same incident. Some people think this means that intention is sacred. Jesus says that whosoever speaks against the Holy Ghost will not be forgiven "neither in this world, neither in the world to come," and then he condemns "idle words" and warns the Scribes (the journalists) and the Pharisees that idle words will see a day of judgment and, meanwhile, there shall be no signs or vain miracles.

A curious fact of this story is that Jesus had enemies; God even has enemies; the Apostles and Prophets had enemies. But nominally, the Holy Ghost has no enemies. There are no cults or villains or movements against the Holy Ghost—except the Macedonians. People swear by God, by Jesus Christ, and by the "F" word all the time, and by excrement, of course, but not even "Gadzooks"—the closest I can think of—is swearing by the Holy Ghost. Nor, in the witness box, is truth sworn in the name of the Holy Spirit, but "so help me

God." A Google Internet search, however, turned up 4,530 hits for "sin against the Holy Ghost," so someone is paying attention.

In the 1184 Edict of Verona, Frederick Barbarossa and Pope Lucius III teamed up to search out heresy and hand the guilty over to the secular power—to the police. This started the great witch-hunts and burnings and the Inquisition of the Middle Ages. None of this, strangely enough, really has to do with the Holy Spirit and the accused were not held for the sin against the Holy Ghost, but for "error."

A heresy like the early Montanist views concern us later, because it is related directly to the Holy Ghost. But Montanus was reviled early on for promoting the Holy Ghost, not for being against it. By 1184, we are dealing largely with Church politics, which we can skip over. The Inquisition is established in 1233, but there we are dealing with power struggles among society, organization, orders, and an aberration of political correction—not about views or inspiration of the Holy Spirit. Sin, discipline, disobedience, and political correction are at stake—not issues of the Holy Ghost. The whole thing—torture, death, and execution—may fascinate the masses, but from this perspective the entire affair, which lasted into the sixteenth century and involved Galileo and the burning of Giordano Bruno, is pretty much a big bore to the Holy Ghost, whose interest is life.

Girolamo Savonarola (1452–1498) was also burned at the stake in Florence for his reformist zeal, but it was mostly a story of the enthusiastic Puritan movement and its fate. There were zealots, rigorists, and others, but these were battles among purists, conformists, and rebellious souls. In a way, the Holy Ghost is absent from almost all of it—doing retreat, penance, or a vanishing act. Important as it is to Church history, it is like war, bloodshed, and pestilence—not the Holy Ghost's thing.

Theodicy is the study of how, if God exists, evil comes to be in the world. The old joke, of course, is that what I do is sin; what others do is evil. Whether the Holy Ghost enjoys this kind of joke is up to theologians—a serious question. But, except for the sin against the Holy Ghost, there seems to be no *Ghosticy,* or *Spiriticy*—any theology concerning the procession of sin beyond its relation to God's commandments or Jesus' atonement. The last full treatment of the sin against the Holy Ghost I could find (except for Google) was a rare 1578 book in the archives of the New York Public Library, although, if I could get to the Vatican again, I would undoubtedly find much more on the subject.

The Holy Office inveighs still—although not nearly as harshly as it did for centuries—against a host of heresies and abuses. The abuses are not directed, in our view, so much against the Holy Ghost as against humanity, including those committed outside or against the church and committed by the Church itself. Today we read about such abuses all the time, even in newspapers, but they are not sins against the Holy Ghost, although they might not have been committed if there had been a better or different understanding of the Holy Ghost. Heresy and doctrine, as far as they impinge on the Holy Spirit, probably do interest the Holy Ghost, but not the torture, death, and politics. The Church, in fighting error, has probably tended to ignore the Holy Spirit or even rebuke it, though it has also had one eye cocked on the Holy Spirit while going about its business. After all, the Holy Ghost is the Spirit of Truth, and error is opposed to truth.

A prime example of this was the Macedonian heresy of 360. Outside of outright satanic cults, this is the closest we get to an officially composed cult fighting the Spirit. Its adherents were called Pneumatomachians—the "spirit fighters," or "those against the spirit." What they said was that the Holy Ghost was not a full personality or deity, but something merely created by the Son—Jesus Christ. Macedonius, a bishop of Constantinople with Arian leanings, was seen as the instigator of Macedonianism. (Around 250, Arius had proposed a neo-Platonist and literal rationalist view that Christ was a created finite being, not fully divine.) The Macedonians were formally condemned at the second Ecumenical Council of Constantinople in 381, and the emperor, Theodosius, tried to wipe them out.

Technically, however, the sin against the Holy Ghost is blasphemy—blasphemy directly, willfully, and maliciously at the Holy Spirit. But, in a broad sense, it is closer to a hardening of the heart. Blasphemy, in the sense of speaking evil of God, is found as a word in

Psalms, Isaiah, Romans, and Revelation—and, of course, in Jesus' speech to the Pharisees after casting out the devils. Blasphemy denotes a kind of calumny or abuse. Of course, the irony is that Jesus, too, was accused of blasphemy when he claims to be the Son of God (Math. 26:65)—not such an extreme statement if one understands that it refers to divine inheritance and that, in a certain sense, we are all sons and daughters of God. But to the Pharisees and Sadducees it was something to pounce on.

By extension, blasphemy is the denial of the divine character of manifestly divine works—as when the Pharisees denied that Jesus threw out the demons in the name of God. In this sense, almost all of modernity and science commits the sin against the Holy Ghost almost daily, and both Nazism and Communism were guilty of it on a secular level. More narrowly, howevere, the sin against the Holy Ghost is the malice of sin for its own sake, including hardening of the heart. Both Communism and Nazism, in this sense, exhibited signs of the sin against the Holy Ghost, as well as other overtly Satanic cults and some movements and aspects of our own general culture, in politics, science, and the media. The willful denial of the Holy Spirit's activities leads to the opposite of being born again; it leads to a second spiritual death, first in this life, of course, and then in the life beyond after death, to eternal damnation. Modern science might like to take note.

Commentators generally associate spiritual death with such signs as loss of hope, or despair; the assumption that God will have mercy or that one is saved without effort; denial of the truths of faith; envy of the spiritual progress of another; complete lack of penitence; lack of remorse at the close of life when close to death; and personal resistance to Grace. In short: despair, presumption, impenitence, obstinacy, resisting truth, and envy—a different set of vices than mortal sins—are associated with the sin against the Holy Ghost. The emphasis, too, is somewhat on intellectual vices rather than on corporeal vices.

An 1851, *Levengro,* a novel by George Borrow (1830–1881), describing its hero hobnobbing with gypsies and depicted the sin against the Holy Ghost as denial of Roman Catholic doctrine—at least according to Roman Catholic critics. Borrow portrayed his scurrilous character as a picaresque hero.

The Thomist position in the fourteenth century pictured evil as the suspension of intellectual activity. I would think that the suspension of intellectual activity, *ligamentum rationis,* would, by omission, be a sin against the Holy Ghost as well. But often the Holy Ghost seems to opt away from "absolute truth" toward heart and action.

The worst kind of sin, according to the great poet Dante of the *Divine Comedy,* was the "betrayal of essence by itself," which the Holy Ghost certainly would not like if that essence were its own. Dante, too, in *The Inferno,* was very hard on "those who followed their own mental choice against known authority—those who have petrified their minds into themselves and their own desires." That was the poet speaking.

As to the sin against the Holy Ghost, in the sense of science and culture denying the divinity of the creation and human works, the modern world commits the sin—the unpardonable sin—almost every day.

## Chapter 14

# Other Traditions

The Indians of British Columbia called the beautiful Lake Louise in which Spirit Isle nestles "the smile of the Great Spirit." The North American Indians' sense of the Great Spirit was still a concrete world—not abstract. The Apache saw a dripping spring, like spirit, as "whiteness moving downward." Spook Rock, too, juts upward on the Paramus Trail into Paramus, New Jersey, and then into Rockland County, New York. Where the Paramus crosses Highview Road from Monsey to Suffern, we find the great council rock, called Spook Rock. The word for it was also *Chappa,* or "separate place." The Dutch called it "Rock of Spirit" or "Breath of Life." Rounded off like a huge fireplace, it originally stood on a mound with a cave below, now filled with stone. A bronze plaque marks the spot, the most important Indian site remaining in greater Metropolitan New York. A holy place, it was "the abode of spirit force," which lived in plants, trees, animals, and nature. Originally, it was probably consecrated by a vision, then others brought tobacco, buckskin, herbs, and hemp, seeking wisdom and guidance there. As the white people overran Manhattan and built New York City, the native Algonquin people were beaten back. They were the "real people," the original native New Yorkers. As Chief Teedyuskung used to say: "I am a man. Nee Lenni. I am a man."

The Indian spirit meant several things then: first was "respect." The medicine man taught respect 1) for feeling and suffering; 2) for individual space; 3) for weaknesses as well as strengths; 4) for boundaries and individual differences; 5) for truth; 6) for the earth and the paths and the animals; and 7) for self. In other words, he taught people "to walk gently on the Earth." Indian spirituality had no place for dead, inert matter, or materialism. Even inanimate objects had spirit. The so-called natural world was a book of spirit signs. Even wampum, money based on natural objects such as shells, was spirit-based. "Wampum is our heart," the original Algonquians used to say. Like the sweat lodge, wampum, was sacred.

For the Munsee, in New York, *Muniktoh* was the word for creator. The missionaries, with their black bible, said that the ways of forest were evil, and they adopted the word *Muniktoh* to name the devil. They told the Munsee that their word, *Muniktoh*—the great Creator—meant devil in English. Thus the new authorities could query the Munsee: "Who created the world?" The Indians would answer, "The Devil." The new authorities would then, according to the missionaries be justified in punishing the Indians, stripping them of their land, or killing them. The new religions had arrived.

The Indians had no word for *the*—the definite article—as in "the spirit." They used the indefinite article, *a* (or *an*). This is noteworthy, because language is a gift of the spirit. For the Indians, there was *A* Great Spirit; the missionaries spoke, instead, of *The* Great Spirit. The Church spoke of "the way, the truth, and the light," but Indian parlance had no category or concept for this. They spoke of "a truth" or "a light" or of "my way" or "my truth." Their languages were experiential and qualitative. In this sense, according to linguists, the definite article *the* blocks intimacy and emotion; it eviscerates experience, generalizes, conceptualizes, and abstracts. For Indians, *a spirit* is real, but *the spirit* is some heady generality that no one can locate or identify. *The* is also exclusive and arrogant, according to the Indians. If one talked about "the society," it meant to exclude all others. An Indian would either refer to "society" or "a society."

Gitchee Manitou was Great Spirit. Great Spirit provided food for all and each Indian, and each Indian said, "Ooneewch"—thank you in Mohican—before pulling aside a bowl from the food plate. Big House was a center. Inside was fire. Great Spirit cared little for prayers, but liked singing and dancing—especially dancing. Shamanic meaning was akin to "dreamtime"—the conviction that all earth is alive and conscious. All life is inside the dream of Gitchee Manitou. If a Mohican took farewell of Gitchee Manitou, they never said goodbye;

they said, "Kumpanazxen," or, "See you again." Gitchee Manitou was "kausckhoiyek": holy, or sacred. Next to Gitchee Manitou were dreams. Dreams were "onoquaam," the same word as vision. *Ghost* in Mohican was "in'chuch'cheek," which included what English calls soul or spirit. M'chuch-cheek was like a clay pot; to be spiritual was to dip the clay pot into a river. The vessel, the soul, was filled with the water, the spirit. Whether Gitchee Manitou was inside the pot or outside the pot, Great Spirit was the same. This was "wnaumau-wauk-un": truth.

By the way, pots were painted with red ochre as a way of covering or protecting the pot spiritually. Every pot had a spirit within, but the departed spirit could not use the vessel in the afterworld unless the pot spirit was released by its own death. Pots were thus "killed," or smashed, at burial so that the spirit would be useful to the dead.

Life was ritual; rites were not separate from life or stored in Church. Big House was where Indians came to "live up." This is why when Indian life changed; the religion, or spiritual part—insofar as it was ever ceremonially separate from life—died. But it died from the actual lifestyle, too, which, like hunting, was so essential to Indians. Great Spirit had no more way of being.

Incidentally, near the Wall of Manitou, North of New York, and overlooking the spot where Rip Van Winkle slept, was the site of another sleeper—an Indian maiden—at Garden Rock. She was a Manitouceskwa, a female Manitowoc, and something of a shape shifter. Among her magical powers, she able to weave clouds for Great Spirit to rest his head on. The Catskills, of course, became famous for jokes; after the laughs, the place died; nobody went there anymore because of the stale jokes. But Manitowoc, as I call her, still lives there at Garden Rock. A New Yorker came to see her, it is said, and snooped around her lair, finding a gourd. Annoyed, she sent magic; the gourd flooded and shot a torrent of water at him, toppling him down the cliff to his death on the rocks. Afterward, smitten with curiosity, she clambered down to see what happened. He was dead. When she looked at his face, she fell in love. Not being able to bring him back to life, she climbed the cliff and to this day stays at Garden Rock, forever in hiding and crying tears that spill down the cliff in gushing torrents. Today the place is known as Kaaterskill Falls. The rainbow on the waters at the foot of the cliff is a protecting spirit that warns unwary travelers that they are not immortal. Gitchee Manitou, the Great Spirit, overlooks it all — an Indian precursor of the Holy Ghost.

The Egyptians, about the same time before Christ, had many gods — like the Goddess Astarte in Sumerian Mesopotamia, guardian of war, sex, rain, and thunderstorms (also prostitutes, who were considered sacred). Their gods were petitionary; you asked them for things, and they increased the harvest and prevented plague and disaster. Even Isis, the great magician, was not a spirit in the later sense, but a goddess. Horus represented "intelligence of the heart." Set was thought to be associated with static perception and cerebral consciousness, granulating divine consciousness into time and space. Harpocrates was a lord of silence.

The Jews and Christians later considered all these idols and false gods. But the Egyptian God Ka represented breath; Ka remained near the body after death, while Ba went into the realm of the dead. The soul was the immaterial aspect, or essence, of a human being, conjoined with the body but separable at death. Aristotle later reduced this aspect of the human being to the rational soul and said that the sentient soul, along with the body, is stripped away at death. But the natural theology of the Greeks was still able to approach the *pneuma theou* (divine breath or spirit) by intuition, for example, about the mind of the universe. Socrates, incidentally, before Aristotle, was possessed by a *daimon* (a spirit of genius) that was like a voice, an urge, and an inspirer. And an Assyrian tyrant, Tukutti (1230 BC) in a certain way prefigures the coming of the age of Spirit — or the non-figuration of God — when he kneels before an empty throne instead of an idol.

In Rome, spirit was gradually swallowed by formal religion and the State. In first-century Rome during the time of Cicero, the great orator and statesman, the sacred act was more important than the sacred thought. This sacral quality (and *sacer* meant "priest") was a source of the later sacraments of baptism, marriage, confirmation, confession, and last rites. For example, the city's perimeter — before walls were in place — was plowed by a white ox heifer, the *pomoerium*.

It was sacramental, making the invisible visible; it was holy and inviolable, and no one was allowed to cross the furrow. The plow was lifted at one place, the *ianua,* which was the entrance. No burials were allowed inside the boundary, and soldiers were not allowed in—they lost their status and rank and became civilians inside the compound.

The Forum was the political and legal heart of the city, but it was also the commercial hub as well as a sacred place; business and religion were not separate. The temples were places of exchange and part of everyday life. There was no "Sunday."

At the South end of the Forum stood the circular temple of Vesta, where six freeborn vestal virgins tended an eternal flame. They were symbolically married to the Pontifex Maximus, or the Chief Pontiff—the term later appropriated for the Catholic Pope. *Pontiff* meant "bridge builder"—in this case a bridge builder to the Gods—and the Pontiff oversaw state religion, the calendar, festivals, and public holidays. He also kept the records,: the Annals. The *Mos Maiorum,* or ancestral customs, dictated morals. Religion was not so much a system of personal beliefs than it was precise rules, rites, and procedures about how to live in accord with the gods. Predictions, omens, auguries, and divinations from the Sibylline books were common. Divine sanction was needed. Official augurs read bird signs in a small rectangular space marked off—the *templum,* origin of the word *temple. Haruspices,* or soothsayers, gave judgment by examining the entrails of sacrificed animals.

This was Cicero's world. In the spirit of oratory, Cicero opted for the Attic school of grammatical correctness: simplicity of expression and restraint from Bacchanal frenzy, inspired flights, and enthusiasm. Here we seem to be on familiar ground again: correctness versus spontaneity and tongues of prudence versus tongues of fire. Some began to criticize the Attics of boredom, convention, propriety—and lack of spirit.

Remember, this was a world where *spiritus* still meant breath, ardor, vitality, and vigor. Breath, moreover, was the major resource of a speaker. But the real forum of the spirit for Romans was the state, the

Forum, and politics. Only when Cicero was banned from public life in 58 BC did he turn to books and writing. Philosophy became a substitute for politics. He coined the words *quality, morality,* and *essence,* for instance. He wrote three books on religious and theological questions: *The Nature of the Gods* (*De deorum natura*), *Foretelling the Future* (*De diviniatione*), and *Destiny* (*De fato*). In a world of statues, Cicero began a heavy attack on anthropomorphic gods—gods in human shape who act and live like human beings. God is, or was, made in the image of humankind. This, from our perspective, is noteworthy because soon Christianity would sweep forward the opposite Jewish conception that humankind is made in the image of God.

In a sense, Cicero began clearing the field of idols and clutter and superstition and taboo for the grand public entrance of the Holy Ghost—the Holy Spirit. He made the point that divination—which Christianity later degraded entirely, and which Catholicism prohibits—is bunk: either the future is a matter of chance, in which case no omens can say what will be, or it is predetermined, in which event no amount of omens can prevent it. Dreams, portents, and astrology are soon out; free will and the polity are in. Like John Adams in America, whose favorite book was Cicero, he saw that the state and the government are where the *spiritus* plays out. The temples regulate and sanctify. Virtue is the result of spirit, not an apparition, or otherworldly presence. The four cardinal Roman virtues are wisdom, fortitude, justice, and temperance.

Later, Seneca, the Roman stoic, said that all the tug and scuffle for dominion and wealth of our wars "is but a wretched point of Earth, whereas the dominions of the soul above are boundless." Although he did not talk of the Spirit, he wrote that contemplation of the soul's dominion gives us "force, liberty, and nourishment," and he enshrined the mind as that which "takes delight in its own divinity" and contemplates "the rise and fall of stars, the admirable harmony of order even in their various motions." The mind learns there the end of its proper being, which is knowledge of God. "And what is God?" Seneca asks, using the singular. "An oncoming and almighty power—and great without limits." The Almighty is all Mind, all Reason. It is folly and madness for people to arrogate to themselves the faculties of Providence or believe that the world is merely fortuitous or the work of chance.

We have seen what the Jewish prophets delivered, but as Rome dies and Christianity arises, we see another stream emerging: that of Islam. In both Judaism and Islam, the Holy Ghost is more or less absent. In fact, both religions saw God as more of a moral inspiration than as a theological or "spiritual" concept. The Jews and Muslims had more in common then than now—rejection of new scriptures, rejection of the nature of Christ, rejection of the Trinity, outrage at the worship of Mary, outrage at the Christian mixing of God and humanity, and a fanaticism about the awful otherness of the Deity. On the other hand, both accepted spirit as the mediator between God and humankind.

It was not the Spirit, however, that called Muhammad when he was forty-three in Mecca; it was an archangel. In Islam, however, the archangel Gabriel is often identified with the Holy Spirit of Revelation—the means by whom God communicates with humanity. The Qu'ran (or Koran) was the original prophetic message, which is replaced by *Shari'a,* or law, after Muhammad, much as in the Catholic tradition. Yet the golden letters of the noble Qu'ran that embellish the Qua'ba (or Kaaba) in Mecca, are the evident manifestation of the Divine Essence, from which the word originates in the colors of the sun, itself the symbol of the Divine Intellect. Though the Qua'ba is the house of God, it is also a symbol, not of the spirit, but of the heart of God's slave, the human being. When purified, the heart is the Throne of the Compassionate One, al-Rabman, the name of the Divine Essence.

The lamp in the niche of Arab shrines represents the relationship of God to human; God is the light in the niche (or heart). But even its light is not God himself; it is the enlightenment that God bestows. This seems to be the message instead of Holy Spirit as comforter, advocate, and intercessor. Spirit, in a degraded sense, is that old nemesis, enthusiasm, which fires fanaticism. Jihad, in the true sense, was the struggle not against the infidel and America, but the struggle for righteousness within the individuals themselves. This spirit was co-opted by Arabian nationalism for Islamic Holy Wars.

The validity of prophecy is the closest thing to the Holy Spirit in Islam, as in Judaism. Later, after contact with Hellenism and philosophy, for instance, al Ghazzali recognized "the prophetic spirit," which is something higher than reason and enters a mystic path where the self recognizes the creator and becomes absorbed in God. This insight recognizes the Face of God, but not the person—the mediator—of the Holy Spirit. Islam, however, had been made in the Koran by Muhammad to recognize natural human faculties of reason and observation of the face of the world, which left Islam more open to the study of science than was Christianity, which depreciated natural human faculties. Ordinary poets in Islam are possessed by jinni (or genie), the capricious spirits that lead to error. On Mount Hira, on the seventeenth night of Ramadan, an angel visited Muhammad and squeezed the breath out of him three times in a forceful embrace until Muhammad began to recite the Koran. He rushed from the cave in despair thinking he had been taken by jinni, but before he could throw himself to his death he saw Gabriel. Islam, rather than being an infusion of the Holy Ghost or Holy Spirit, emphasizes the existential act of surrender to Allah, expected of each Muslim.

*The Satanic Verses* got the writer Salmon Rushdie into such trouble because the "verses" were supposed to be apocryphal concoctions of Muhammad that allowed followers to worship various spirits as angels—the traditional goddesses of the Arabs at Hizaz: al-Lat, the Goddess, al-Uzza (the mighty one), and Manat (the fateful one). Gabriel, however, told the Prophet to keep these verses out of the Koran. On the whole, the Arabs were to abjure the Goddesses and besides, *shirk* idolatry—becomes a sin. Allah's knowable past, *wash al-Lah,* is the Face of the World, which stands in for the Holy Ghost.

Another name for Allah is Al-Haqq (the Truth). This is *absolute* Truth, not the Spirit of Truth. Sufi 'fana is the annihilation of self, a method of the "drunken Sufis" to destroy the ego and be absorbed into the ineffable reality of God. But this is a return to God, not the immanence of Holy Spirit visiting in the soul. The sober Sufis practice *baqa* (revival), in which the goal is to enhance the self—'fana came first—but the goal is reintegration of the self with enhanced self-realization and control. This is a reuniting with the creator in an original state of fullness. God is the object not a Holy Spirit.

During the tenth century, incidentally, the sufi Husain ihn Mansar, known as al-Hallaj, achieved mystic reunion through 'fana and baga, but instead of keeping it to himself, he roamed Persia calling for the overthrow of the caliphate and the establishment of a new social order. The conservative *ulema,* like Christian priests, accepted this kind of visitation of God in the past—but not in the present. Al-Hallj was taken into custody by the authorities, imprisoned, and accused of blasphemy for claiming to have united with Allah. Al-Hallaj's answer was, "I am the Truth (ana al-Haqq)." The result: he was crucified. The moral, according to the Arab commentator Al-Ghazzali: don't mistake your inner state for outer reality, and don't proclaim esoteric truth in the exoteric forum.Finally, note that Ibn Arabi (1165–1240), the most prolific Sufi writer, claimed the Divine Spirit had inspired his writing. He proclaimed oneness of being and said that a book was the way out of the fire of inspiration that threatened to burn him up.

The Hindu world *atman* (or breath) means soul. The preexistent soul is thought to be trapped at birth in a body and released at death, after which it passes into a new body according to the fate determined by karma (destiny). Eventually, if perfected, it merges with the absolute—which stands in for spirit. Buddhism and Hinduism are not generally personal and do not view God as an objective or personal reality, but as an absolute. Spiritual presence is often seen in terms of the complex depths of the self, not as the Holy Ghost. The Chinese distinguish between a lower sensitive soul and *hun,* a rational principle that is sometimes the spirit of an ancestor.

For Japanese Zen, spirit is translated often as *ch'I,* or energy. This is said by Westerners to be achieved by "spiritual identity," a kind of tranquility. But spiritual identity and tranquility are both still concepts, and Zen eschews the medium of concepts. This is the origin, too, of "one spirit," the concept behind tranquility. Even "one spirit," however, is a conceptualism for Zen. In matters of the spirit, from the Zen standpoint, the Greeks taught reason, and Christianity teaches faith. Both depend on a dualism of subject and object. Apprehension, however, occurs outside of logic and faith. And faith further splits the seen from the unseen. Ch'i instead provides a flash of insight without deliberation, which only removes the object; it is no longer there, seen or unseen, while you deliberate about it.

Furthermore, for the Chinese, Ch'i, as opposed to the *Li,* or reason, is formless. The spirit is free of mind, while the psyche is self-willed. Through formlessness, or "mindlessness," the spirit has an immediate embracing identity with primal energy and being. Again, there is no hint of a spirit as a personality, such as the identity of the Holy Ghost, or the elevation of the spirit by Western religion into the Holy Spirit.

From a Japanese perspective, one of the most advanced treatments of the evolution of spirituality that I know of is *The Golden Laws* by Ryuho Okawa. He speaks of the "high spirits" of the West, East, and Japan. Those from Shinto are less known in the West, such as the ancient goddess Amaterasu Omikami, the sun goddess and first female monarch in Japan. Levels of truth have a high priority in Shinto, and truth is sometimes akin to Spirit. Amaterasu Omikami represented the "spirit of Japan": generosity, delicacy, tranquility, elegance, and beauty. Another Japanese goddess and spirit is Himiko. Her name means "looking toward the sun." The sun was a source of spirit.

In the sixth century, Prince Shotoku codified the spiritual principles of Confucianism and Buddhism into ranking orders called "cap ranks." Note here that a civil order code of behavior and rank had a spiritual source. These ranks were not levels of authority such as corporal or sergeant, but ranks of virtue: benevolence, propriety, faith, justice, and knowledge. In the West, these were among the gifts or fruit of the Holy Spirit.

In Japan, teachings transmitted down through the ages are synonymous with spirituality, as in the study of sutras and the sects of Saicho (767–822) and Kakai (774–835). Saicho's Tendai sect in Japan is known as Dengyo Daishi, "The master who transmitted the teaching." These came from the "real world" as distinct from our everyday world. This real world goes up to the ninth dimension, but

Saicho grasped only half of it: the wisdom of equality. His rival Kukai started by meditating under a waterfall, but he was told he needed access to the sea and sky. Gaining clairvoyance and clairaudience, he brought esoteric Buddhism (Shingon) to a peak after communicating with spirits of the real world. Again, spirituality is tantamount to enlightenment and truth. Other "high spirits" of Japanese traditions are Genshin (942–1017) of the Pure Land sect, who pray to the Amitabha Buddha; Eisai (1141–1215) of Rinzai Zen; Dogen Zenji (1200–1253) Eisai's student and founder of Soto Zen; and Nichiren (1222–1282) of Nichiren Buddhism. The lives of these masters illustrate episodes of spirituality and incidents that lead to enlightenment. Although priceless for their relation to the Spirit, these schools have no concept of the personal Holy Ghost; they are related, rather, to Truth. In Buddhist spirituality and in the teachings of Shakyamuni Buddha (c.566 BC), the spirit lives in the real world in the upper dimensions, while we live in the three-dimensional world, the shadow world of time and space. With light, The Noble Eightfold Path starts the seeker onto the way of true consciousness: inspiration.

Sources of Chinese spirituality also include Lao Tsu, Chuang-tzu, and Confucius. The guiding principle is The Way (Tao), in which all beings are subject to creation, destruction, and change according to rules of earth and nature. The Way is the path to transcending such restrictions, and, for Confucius, was based on improving the soul.

Other great guiding "spirits of light" in Eastern traditions come from India—for example, Vishnu, Shiva, and Krishna. For Krishna, spirit was tantamount to trust, love, and affection. The ultimate reality of the universe, the oneness of all, or Brahma, was taught in the seventh-century-BC book called the Rig Veda.

Nevertheless, even the Japanese consider Western figures such as Moses, Solomon, and Jesus to be the guiding "high spirits" of the West.

## Chapter 15

# Early Heresy

Gnosticism, the early view that the Spirit can be obtained and reached through knowledge and wisdom instead of only by faith, was the earliest troublesome heresy, but then came the upstart heresy of the Holy Ghost itself as viewed by a second-century firebrand Montanus.

During Jesus' time, and even in Old Testament times, prophecy had been the voice conveying immediate revelation. It was still practiced directly during group meetings of the early Church. But by 200, the time of Origin and Polycarp (Patristic Fathers in the more philosophical stream), prophecy had moved from the meetinghouse to the study and the closet, where it was considered an interpretive power—one that interpreted only Scripture and was guided secondhand only by the Holy Spirit. In effect, Polycarp and Origin said that prophecy was now limited to interpretation that uncovered mysteries beneath the literal sense of scripture, but did not reveal anything new. The Spirit no longer spoke so directly in public meetings, as in the speaking of tongues or in the sense of the prophets of old. Gradually, prophecy was eased from the Church.

Montanus promoted prophecy, thus striking directly into the sacrosanct realm of the Holy Ghost. He ended up excommunicated and outside the Church tradition, while the Holy Ghost he championed ended up (officially at least) inside the Church. This is the bizarre scenario: Montanus, a former priest of the pagan cult of Cybele, the goddess of fertility and grain, converted to Christianity in the second century. He began preaching in Phrygia, now in the south central plateau of Turkey. He preached that the Paraclete, or Holy Ghost—that is, the Advocate, or Spirit of Truth—still manifested itself directly in the world. He also claimed that it was manifesting itself through himself and the prophets associated with him. Concern arose when the Montanists encouraged alternate states of enthusiasm and ecstatic intensity with what the Church historian Eusabius called "a trancelike kind of passivity." In these states utterances came forth, which Montanists claimed were the voice of the Spirit. We have, of course, no recordings, but only his enemies' testimony. They charged the Montanists with everything from infanticide to cannibalizing the Eucharist.

The Montanist claims were important, however, because they suggested that revelation of the spirit—erupting at Pentecost and pretty much set down and recorded by 172—was not over. Something could apparently be added. The circle was open.

Other factors were also at play: Montanists expected an imminent end of time (the Second Coming), a new heavenly Jerusalem in the village of Pepuza on the Turkish plain, and a moral discipline of Montanist rigorism that detached them from material desires. The "illuminati," the illumined ones, were very strict and included the prophets Prisilla (known as Prisca) and Maximilla, who presented shades of the oracles. Fasting was emphasized, marriage was frowned upon, and second marriages were not allowed. All this is related by the Latins, Eusabius, Epiphanius, and Tertullian (who converted in Carthage to Montanism), all early Church Fathers. Even more dangerous for them, the Montanists seemed to override the authority of Bishops with their prophecy and oracular utterance.

In 177, the upshot was that the Asian Bishops excommunicated Montanus, but the sect hardened and set up a Church government in Pepuz. They added a higher order of patriarchs to the ministry, and the sect persevered locally. Finally, the Eastern Emperor Justinian used severe legislation to pretty much wipe them out in the sixth century. As for Montanus himself, who forbid his people to flee from martyrdom, it is not known how he died, or when. His life in any more detail is a mystery. The irony is that the Holy Spirit—as championed originally by the Montanists—was soon enshrined in the creed of the West at the First Council of Nicaea in 325. To this day, this first official formulation of the Church is called the Nicene Creed, and it was the first official codification of the Holy Ghost. The oneness of God in the Old Mosaic tradition, the Father and Son twofold nature of God in the early gospels of the New Testament, became the Trinity, adding the Holy Ghost.

The other irony is that Montanus' teaching of the Holy Spirit was not originally considered threatening, nor in fact was it a sin against the Holy Ghost. Indeed, Montanus promoted the Holy Ghost—the first to officially do so—and, ironically, the Montanists pretty much introduced the idea of the Spirit as part of the Godhead. When the question "Who worships the Spirit?" arises, the answer is "Montanus." And, at Nicaea in 325, this part of his views won a place in official doctrine at the first council, when the Holy Ghost was accepted into the creed, the Nicene Creed. But the Montanists themselves had already been condemned. Thus, ironically, the doctrine of the Holy Ghost was born from a schism and was defined by an error. This great issue had been settled; the Holy Ghost was no more at large—not dead yet, but safe in the Church.

So the Montanists in the second century possessed a special devotion to the person of the Spirit, by whom prophets spoke. They asserted his special age and that dispensation had begun. They are said to be the first who also called the Spirit God. They also declared that the Spirit showed divinity by moral scrupulousness and rigorous conduct. This was part of their downfall.

The early Church was still hammering out its attitude to ordinary people; martyrdom, rigorism, and prophecy had all taken their toll, as well as the issue of forgiveness of sins and, indeed, accommodation to the world. If the Spirit, as in Old Testament prophecy, was the ultimate guide, some elements—the Montanists, for example—believed that everything is important and matters. This is the rigorist view coupled with extreme disciplines. It is sometimes claimed that rigorism tends to lead to harshness, pride, and resentment. In the relaxed view, accommodation to the world counts more, and nothing matters that much to the Spirit or to discipline. It is said that the relaxed view leads to indulgence, falsity, and the ho-hum old boys' club. The Church has housed both views, but the Montanists never did.

The Montanists lost their battle to restore prophecy and direct utterance, and they lost in their effort to get the Church to impose tough morals and strict and rigorous ascetic behavior on the normal people. The Church increasingly played its card of accommodating worldly life and forgiving sin. The Montanists also lost on the issue of separation of Church and State; they were in favor of strict separation. Even then, the Church made its bargains with the state in Rome, and later with other kings, emperors, and republics. But, in a sense, the Montanists won on one issue: the Holy Spirit would become incorporated into the Godhead and remained there.

The Church had learned its lesson from this heresy in another way, too, as well as from the Gnostic heresy. It found that it would be best to formulize the Holy Spirit and knowledge, so that it would not break out in unruly ways and in moral extremism. The Church would deliver grace and forgiveness, though at a price. The Holy Spirit as well as knowledge would be available, but more or less on contract and under certain controls. Wherever there would be Holy Spirit, there would also be the Holy Office; confession to God would be replaced by confession to the priest.

The Holy Spirit also had (if it can be said this way) another channel: philosophy. This came through the Greeks. Tertullian, a Carthaginian Roman who converted to Montanus, had little use for it; "Wretched Aristotle," he said, "who gave them [humankind and the Gnostics] the art of dialectic." Of course, the Church had begun to value theology more than philosophy, putting gospel and scripture first. But, early on, it also rejected Tertullian's view that wretched philosophy is, as he wrote, "the theme of worldly wisdom and rash interpreter." Instead, the Church embraced the views of St. Clement, who, working in Alexandria, said that philosophy would be conducive to piety—a kind of preparatory training to faith and higher knowledge. Clement wrote, "Perhaps philosophy was given to the Greeks directly and primarily until the Lord should call the Greeks." Clement saw human beings getting once born by changing from paganism to philosophy—and then getting born again, as they say today, when they move on to faith. And by *knowledge* Clement did not mean fundamentalism or biblical literalism; he meant something more like theology, but even more like a higher mystical knowledge: love. He talked of knowledge as the "exercise of beneficence" and "the love of God." Knowledge, Clement says, passes into love.

The second- and third-century Montanist Tertullian, however, had already lost to Clement the Alexandrian on the issue of worldliness or rigorousness and on the issue of philosophy in the Church. Tertullian, incidentally, asked early on about the identity of the Holy Ghost: Is the Holy Spirit the ghost of Jesus appearing in the Christian community? Or is the Holy Spirit a manifestation of the presence of God the Father? As a riddlesome Roman analyst (he was famous for saying he believed because it was absurd), Tertullian wanted to know how the Holy Ghost was distinct from the Father and the Son. "Three what?" he asked, challenging the Trinity. But he answered his own question, saying they were of "one substance"—substance then meaning the opposite of matter: incorporeal essence. Tertullian the Montanist thus became instrumental in the later creedal formulation of the Holy Ghost and the Trinity.

The Church continued to build up theology and promote it over and through philosophy, but Clement had secured a place for what might be called Holy Spirit's lesser channel—philosophy—in the Church and in the West. Philosophy, a natural spirit, was also a way of taming the supernatural rigors and sometimes harsh streams of prophesy and direct utterances of the Spirit.

One of the interesting spiritual questions around the third century was this: Is a confession to a denial of faith (like Peter's denial of Jesus to the soldiers), even when made under torture, tantamount to the sin against the Holy Ghost? Could it be forgiven? At the time persecutions were on the rise, but in response there was also great enthusiasm for martyrdom. Christians actually demanded death from the tribunals. In the interest of sanity, Smyrna and other early Christian Churches tried to notch down the enthusiasm (*enthusiasm* being a word sometimes associated with the Spirit and prophecy) and cut the bloodshed. The need to purify enthusiasm itself cropped up, but others, Montanists included, held that flight and secrecy and shying away from bloody martyrdom was not permissible. Clement of Alexandria, for instance, fled in his day and worked from a hiding place instead of facing martyrdom.

Early Christendom also admired some of those who confessed their faith in prison or under torture, even when they escaped death. The third-century document, the Canons of Hippolytus, claims that such confessors need not be ordained to the priesthood, for the Holy Spirit has already ordained them directly. These officially unordained confessors began to give formal absolution and conduct rites. The Church authorities put their foot down pretty quickly, however, requiring confessors to be ordained, too, or to cease all priestly functions.

At Nicaea in 325, the Council added, "And in the Holy Ghost" to the creed for believing, settling the place of the Spirit in the Church; but a reaction set in, and the second big Holy Ghost heresy case arose—Macedonianism. This fourth-century heresy was also called the Pneumatomachi heresy, and it was the only case in history in which a full-fledged party formed against the Holy Spirit; its adherents were called "spirit fighters," the translation of *Pneumatomachi.*

The Macedonians named after Macedonius, denied the full personality and deity of the Holy Spirit. Macedonius, who was twice bishop of Constantinople, was apparently in the Asian stream that also denied Jesus' complete divinity. His writings and those of the of the Pneumatomachi have been lost and their doctrine is known mainly from refutations and condemnations penned by St. Athanasius of Alexandria in his *Letters to Serapion* and by St. Basil of Caesarea, who wrote the important early tract "On the Holy Spirit." St. Basil wrote a treatise On the Holy Spirit that posited the existence of an "unwritten" teaching, or oral tradition "that proved the existence of the deity of the Holy Spirit." Included in Gratian's collation of non-scriptural tradition, St. Basil's assertion about the Holy Spirit has itself been used to substantiate oral tradition.

The heresy of Macedonius denied the full personality of the Holy Ghost as part of the Godhead, as well as its divinity. They argued that the Son created the Holy Spirit through his witness, testimony, wisdom, and teaching. As a mere creation of the Son, Jesus, the Holy

Spirit was subordinate. This was another blow at prophecy, enthusiasm, and direct revelation, and as close you could come to officially committing the sin against the Holy Ghost: intentional and conscious denial of the grace of the Spirit and blasphemy.

In 381, at Constantinople, the second Council took place, and it formally condemned the Macedonians, expanding the creed of Nicaea explicitly to affirm the Orthodox belief in the Holy Spirit. The Holy Ghost, it was proclaimed, "who, with the Father and Son together, is worshipped and glorified." Under the Emperor Theodosius I, the state then stepped in and suppressed the Macedonians.

More generally, and in early times, some people asked whether the Logos, or Word, and the Holy Ghost are one and the same. A journalist, of course, deals with the word, as does a poet, but does not capitalize it. Small words, arguably, may not be the Logos; Logos is the big Word. This big Word was in the beginning, as the Evangelist John says, and it became flesh: the Son. Does the Holy Ghost, too, ever become flesh?

This business, in a way, was discussed in the second and third centuries in another heresy case called Monarchianism. The early Gnostics had been knocked back, and knowledge gave way to faith. The Montanists, promoters of the Holy Spirit, were down—the sanitized Paraclete, the Holy Spirit (and its person) had been officially adopted at the Council of Nicaea. The Manicheans, who saw matter as a dark evil, would soon fade in another huge struggle. But the answer to the question of whether the word and the spirit are the same was, more or less "No." It went this way: Theodatus and Valentinus, fugitive Gnostics—one from Asia Minor, the other from Egypt—came west. Valentinus came first from Alexandria. He was not a priest but a philosopher. Nevertheless, he studied with Theodas, a pupil of St. Paul himself, and got baptized. Then, in 136, he moved to Rome. For some twenty-five years, he taught a synthesis of Gnostic philosophy from Alexandria fused with Christianity. Next, although a layman, he wanted to be Bishop of Rome. Rejected by the community in 140, he left Roman Christianity, but stayed on teaching his philosophy. In 160, Theodas left Rome for Cyprus.

He supposedly wrote the "Gospel of Truth," fusing Pauline teachings with Gnostic wisdom. The reports on him and his teachings are various; some emphasize his contribution to a human-centered mode of spirituality—wisdom of the human. Nevertheless, he accepted from Paul the role of Christ's death and resurrection in salvation history.

Early Catholic sources emphasize a Valentinian point of view more interesting perhaps to the Holy Ghost—that is, that humankind was made of three types: material and predestined to destruction; psychic—or soul— people, who may attain salvation through redemption; and spiritual individuals destined to life eternal.

St. Irenaeus (120–203) was Bishop of Lyon, although from the East, and a pupil of Polycarp, the last known living link to the Apostles. He refuted Valentinus' wisdom of the human, but not on grounds of the Holy Spirit's presence. Instead, the question was about the Logos, which Irenaeus enthroned with the Godhead in creating the world. This doctrine found its way into the early Apostles' Creed.

Theodatus, from Asia Minor, succeded Valentinus in early Gnostic tradition. He affirmed that creation was a process of emanation, or radiation, proceeding from an ultimate principle of unconditioned being or eternal ideas. Once, this had been Platonic spirit. Theodatus said that God made matter and that Jesus redeemed it—God uniting himself with Christ to bring gnosis, or "knowledge," to humanity. Here is the clincher: salvation came when *pheuma,* spirit, was infused, or infusing, with knowledge. Theodatus also still talked of angelic intelligence.

The Bible has it in Genesis that the Father God created the heavens and earth: "And the spirit of God was stirring above the waters" (Genesis I; I–2). Saint John, in the Greek tradition, said later, "In the beginning was the Word," and the word was "with God" and things were made through him and "in him was life." So we have God, we have spirit, we have life, and we have the word. And we have wisdom. Was the Logos—sometimes translated "wisdom"—the Spirit? The Logos itself was not, remember, officially a person, but in Gnostic tradition a knowledge or wisdom. Nor had the Holy Ghost itself yet been fully installed until 325, in the second and third centuries, after Valentinus and Theodatus.

Monarchianism was in a sense on the side of the issue opposite from the Montanists. The Monarchians rejected the thought that the Logos was an independent personal subsistence. They affirmed instead that it was a part of the sole deity of God, the Father. Theodatus, who had also gotten to Rome, was, for instance, teaching that Jesus was only human—that he was divine, only in the sense that he had been filled as the son of God with wisdom and power. Pope Victor condemned Theodatus, then condemned others—Paul of Samosota—in turn for trying to teach the humanity of Jesus further. This dynamic form of Monarchianism is a basis and source for many modern American Unitarians.

To summarize, independent from God and Son, the Logos (read "wisdom") was a way of knowing God and Son; yet it also became inherent—or "cohesive," as some like to say—in both. The Logos was, however, associated with the talking tradition in the early Church, *dialogosthai,* or logical discussion and philosophy. Logos, the word and language, were the verbal and thinking part of presence, being and "infused" spirit. That much seemed secure, although the fight over whether God and Son were the same substance continued into the first millennium and later broke East and West apart. The Logos, or wisdom, was also still an issue. The East would tend to say the Logos came from the Father; the West would tend to move the Son into position.

As the Sufis, the Arabic secret thinkers, would say: The tree fell to the West. But meanwhile the Greek Logos—word and philosophy—had to be pulled together with the corpse of Gnostic wisdom and knowledge from the East. The Church, in a sense, assigned the job to the Holy Ghost.

Pagan spirits, old Biblical prophecy, speaking in tongues, and a lot else had to be brought together. The Holy Ghost—hitherto a breath of life, an ardor, an enthusiasm, an energy—would also become a person, or at least an issuance from the Father and Son: this happened officially at the Council of Nicaea in 325.

The great early Manichaean heresy, fought against by Augustine, was not about the nature or person of the Holy Ghost, but in closing we should mention the role of the Cappadocian Fathers—Cappodocia was in central south Turkey—in consolidating the doctrine of the Holy Spirit in the fourth century.

The Cappadocians—Gregory of Nyssa, Gregory Nazianus, Macrinas, and Basil of Caesarea—were early developers of dogmatics, and they largely fashioned the doctrine of the Holy Spirit. Divine theology, as opposed to natural theology, had to shake off the carnal and material to approach "the unapproachable heights." Their efforts to define the Father and Son as *of the same substance* led to their clarifying the procession of the Holy Ghost.

Gregory of Nyssa finally composed a famous statement of the Spirit that reads:

> Christ is born; the Spirit is his forerunner.
> Christ is baptized: the Spirit bears witness.
> Christ is tempted; the Spirit leads him up.
> Christ makes miracles; the Spirit accompanies him.
> Christ ascends; the Spirit takes his place.

# Chapter 16

# East and West

To those who want to get on to the pithier parts of this book, I suggest skipping this chapter, although they will lose a dimension of the doctrinal or spiritual debate about Spirit. This debate revolves around a simple Latin word—a phrase really—the addition of *filiogue,* which means, "and by the Son," to the Creed. The phrase is more about the nature and understanding of the Son, Jesus Christ, and the theology about him, than it is about the Holy Ghost; but it became the catchword of almost four hundred years of debate and conflict and lay at the heart of a tragic split between East and West.

A single, simple word—*filiogue,* meaning the Holy Spirit came "and by the Son"—was seemingly negligible grounds for war, pestilence, and the split in 1054 between East and West. But the phrase was a label for other more forceful causes of the conflict, too, including the Easter Emperor's incest, primacy disputes, economics, power, and personalities. And it was a spiritual schism as well, and still is. The West, Rome, was always more focused on the legalisms of atonement—sin and salvation—while the East was more focused on the mysticism of the incarnation and the action of the Holy Ghost.

*Filiogue* in my simple journalistic mind, too, was about Eastern patriarchal society versus a Western new sense of the linkage between father and son: the generation gap. That is, the West saw youth—the Son—as generating the future, and was not stuck just on the Father generating the past. It was a more dynamic society versus a more static society. This may be my imagination, but making sense out of the *filiogue* dispute—a word spelling the fate of two empires—is always challenging. The other issue at stake then was the role of hope and love in the life of spirit. The Father world was the creator, the first mover, and the powerful, lawful, stern world of faith and power. The Son was the channel of hope and charity, the incarnated one with a human dimension.

The Holy Ghost was not to be, therefore, just a spirit proceeding out of stern creative might and power, but a spirit coming from hope and love. The thought is of concern because can hope and love, and the heart, bring wisdom and knowledge, or is salvation only from might and power? Remember, spirit, the new Spirit, was a "model" for forming a new society or sense thereof. The *filiogue* dispute often seems monumentally ridiculous and nominal, but when seen as a search for the source of inspiration for a thousand years of culture, it becomes more sobering. Primarily, though, the dispute was less about the Holy Spirit than about the nature and elevation of the Son. And, as we said, it got lost much of the time in an imperial struggle between East and West.

The Eastern and Western traditions differ spiritually in broader ways, however, and more important really than the *filiogue* dispute is the difference between East and West over the transformation of wine and bread into the body and blood, a mystery that challenges chemistry as well as theology. In the Eastern tradition, Orthodoxy maintained that the bread and wine transformed into blood and body by "being filled with the Holy Spirit." Thus Easterners hold to the invocation of the Holy Spirit in the Mass, which is downgraded (the invocation, that is) by the Western Church. Rome stressed instead that the body and blood are made present not through the Holy Ghost but by the words of institution: "This is my blood; this is my body." Christ as source himself and then, following him, the priest, above all, did the action; the words of his institution become the essence, or *substantia,* of the sacrament; the mystery of Corpus Christi, the Body of Christ.

The model for this is the miracle. It happened first at Cana of Galilee when the water became wine. Christ did not say at the Last Supper, "This is a *sign* for my body," but "This *is* my body." The "invisible substance"—not just the accidents of physical wine and bread—are changed by the power of the divine word and by the priest.

Substance (or *substantia* in the Patristic Latin) meant what we call "essence." Thus, earthly substance—accidentally the bread and wine—was changed into an essence: divine flesh and blood. The color, taste, and smell of the wine and bread—the properties—were not themselves changed, but the substance, or essence, was. *Transubstantiation,* as a word to describe this, first came into vogue in 1140. It was a word for recognizing "the real presence" in the bread and wine. The fourth Lateran Council in 1215 first officially promulgated the term, and it was confirmed in 1551 at the Council of Trent, the counter-Reformation council.

The Orthodox in the East continued to hold that the transformation took place by the invocation to and the action of the Holy Spirit, not the priest. The words in the East were: "With thy Holy Spirit and word vouchsafe to bless and sanctify thy gifts and creatures of bread and wine, that they may be unto us the Body and Blood." The invocation of the Holy Ghost (*epiclesis*) followed the words of institution, "This is my body...." In the East, therefore, the invocation is specifically consecratory. It specifically asks that the bread and wine be made body and blood—the actual change, a *metabole,* in Greek, is attributed to the Holy Spirit. The sacramental theology of the Eastern Church sees the sacrament's effectiveness as dependent on the Holy Ghost answering the prayer rather than on the vicarious powers of the priest pronouncing the proper formula.

In the fourteenth century, the invocation, or *epiklesis,* once again became an issue between the Greeks and Latins, because the Roman Mass did not invoke the Holy Spirit. The Latins did not require the invocation or the Holy Spirit's action, because the priest was all-powerful and the transubstantiation took place when the priest pronounced the words of institution. The Roman view was endorsed again by the Council of Trent in the face of the Protestant Reformation as a central tenet of the power of the Roman Catholic priesthood.

Only in the 1960s, after the Second Vatican Council, did the liturgy of the new mass in the vernacular include an invocation, or *epiclesis,* in the canon of the Mass. The Vatican, however, placed the invocation of the Holy Spirit before the words of institution. They did this to preserve in the consecration the role of the priest, who invokes the Holy Spirit, but whose pronouncement of Jesus' words becomes, through the power of the priest—not of the Holy Ghost—still the changing agent of the transubstantiation. The importance of this and the very inclusion of the Holy Spirit in the canon of the Mass, however, was almost entirely missed by the swarming news media at the time, who were concerned almost entirely with the conflict between conservatives and liberals.

In the East, too, the other sacraments also did not work automatically, but only "in the Spirit." We can reach into the depth of this Eastern tradition by pausing a moment to examine the views of Symeon the New Theologian (949–1022), who rejected the notion that the Spirit of the original Pentecost had in any way receded from the Church. He also stressed that only conscious awareness of the Holy Spirit had power to "bind and loose." Headed for politics, at the age of fourteen, Symeon was influenced by the living, personal devotion of a monk in Constantinople at the *Studios* monastery. In this tradition, insight is passed to the novice not by book or rote learning, but by example and oral tradition from a spiritual guide or role model. At twenty, Symeon, still a layman, had the first of a series of visions of divine light. At twenty-seven, he became a monk. For twenty-five years he was the abbot of St. Manas, a busy metropolitan monastery in the heart of the imperial city. He is an urban hesychast. He was in the end canonized by the Byzantine Church, though he was controversial. Symeon recognized that the Spirit sometimes works a hidden activity at the unconscious level, but he urges advancing beyond unconscious grace to the point of explicit awareness—experiencing the Spirit "in a conscious and palpable way." He called this "the sensation of the heart."

Let us take the time to visit his remarkable hymn to noetic light and the Holy Ghost:

> Come, true light. Come, life eternal. Come, hidden mystery. Come, unnamable treasure. Come, unsayable reality. Come, untouchable person of humanity, come true hope of all who save themselves, come resurrection of the dead, come o power that acts, that transforms, and changes all with a single

> gesture, come o completely invisible, untouchable, and unexpected, come You who remain always immobile although you move everything and come into the lower depths although you live above all in the heavens, come 0 agonized name and met by all (but to say who you are and know how you are and of what nature is something denied us). Come eternal joy, come purple of the Great God and of our Lord, come transparent wrapping lie crystal and ornate like precious jewels, come refuge inaccessible, come purple kingdom, right hand of sacred majesty. Come because my poor soul has need of you, come the Aloneness to the Alone, because, as you see, I am alone. Come because you separated me and left me solitary on the earth, come because you are our necessity and make us need you whom no one can reach. Come 0 breath and life of man, come comfort of my unworthy soul, come my delight and glory and my perpetual consolation.

What is this mentality associated with the Holy Spirit? The Greek *nepsis,* meaning watchfulness, implied vigilance, attentiveness, guarding one's thoughts and heart, and practicing virtues. Watchfulness, or attentiveness, is the heart's stillness (*hesuchia*), without thoughts or images. This is the path of perpetual prayer, which means a trained attitude, not just praying incessantly, but in the sense of Evagrius of Pontus. Joy, sweetness, and light are the sensations of this "mentality" of the heat. God is a power; Jesus is an incarnated personality—the Holy Spirit is more of a mentality or attitude of the heart: cognitive state of mind or heart, in modern terms.

At the time of the Sinaite fathers, a Greek word for "luminously reflected" (a description of the Holy Spirit in the psyche or soul) was *photoeinographeisthai*—literally, "photographed," before film and cameras and snapshots. The soul was seen as a photographic plate on which is marked the noetic or divine light. This was the "light mysticism" of St. Symeon the New Theologian. This, then, could be a phenomenological description of the Holy Spirit in one regard: a state of intuitive, nondiscursive awareness in which we no longer form pictures in our mind's eye or analyze concepts with our reasoning brain, but feel and know the Holy Spirit's presence in a direct personal encounter.

Evagrius, a colleague of Symeon, called prayer (hesychast prayer) the communion of the intellect with God, and in some ways this, too, is a description of the Holy Spirit. There are echoes in all this of the Dionysian Areopagite language of ecstasy, which describes this state in which intellect becomes aware of its own splendor, and the intellect "is through ecstasy of love cloaked entirely in God alone."

By the way, doctrine at the time, as stated in the ninth century by Pope Leo III, recognized the Holy Spirit in the Father as eternity, in the Son as equality, and in the Holy Ghost as the connection between eternity and equality—something that all seems to have been largely lost but that might be relevant to America today, and the worldwide web.

In the East, objecting to the imprecision of Latin, the commentators said that the Holy Spirit "being sent" was not the same as the Holy Spirit "proceeding from." It was a question of whether the Holy Spirit was sent, imparted, or infused. The Greeks maintained that within the Godhead the Holy Spirit proceeds from the Father—that the Son only gives and shares this from outside the Godhead. In John 15:16, the Spirit is "sent." Sent, proceeding from, and "pouring out" were all competing translations. Easterners said the Father was the source, the principle, or the cause. The *filioque*—"and by the Son"—was blasphemy to them. Even Dionysius the Areopagite had taught that "the Father is the only source of the supersubstantial Godhead."

So the great *filiogue* controversy, apart from politics, is about whether the Holy Spirit proceeded from the Son as well as the Father, as the Latin Church taught, or only from the Father, as the Eastern Church taught. This controversy heated up in the ninth century and thereafter. Called the "Procession of the Ghost," deadly debates raged for three hundred years, from as early as 796 until the eleventh century, when East and West formally split for good. Already in 809, and even as early as the eighth century, King Charlemagne, the French hegemonist of the West, supported the spirit also coming from the Son. To some Westerners, denial of the Procession of the Holy Spirit from the Son was even what Jesus had taught as the sin against the Holy Ghost. Eastern Fathers labeled the *filiogue* phrase as "a wicked thing, and among the wicked things the most wicked." The kind of experienced, personal spirituality and Easter Orthodox tradition that Symeon the New Theologian advocated was slowly downgraded and distanced by Rome and the West. The office and the priest became more and more emphasized and the Spirit relegated elsewhere. About the same time that the Western Church started to deny the wine to the faithful, reserving the drink of spirit to the clergy, the Church, at the Eighth Ecumenical Council of Constantinople in 869 issued—at the request of the West—a strange canon (Canon II/eleven), apparently denying the Areopagite teaching of two souls—soul and spirit. Neither the East nor the Anglican Church accepted the conclusions of the Eighth Ecumenical Council.

This strange affair is examined in the next chapter, "Battle for the Spirit."

# Chapter 17

# Battle for the Spirit

The old legal code of Justinian, on which the Byzantine Empire was built—Byzantium, with headquarters in Constantinople, now Istanbul—started with an invocation to the Trinity, including the Holy Ghost. In contrast, one is reminded of the recent brouhaha in Europe, where a furor arose over the new European constitution then being hammered out without any reference to God or Jesus Christ—much less the Holy Spirit.

The battle for the spirit is really about the human view of self and the kind of access one has to knowledge and our relation to the Holy Spirit. So, this chapter delves into the past and discusses obscure theological battles. But don't be fooled; arcane as they seem, those battles were the real turf wars, and they have shaped our own destiny.

Theological learning was once based in Constantinople; it was there that heresies arose—and there that they were originally settled. This was the old European Union. For centuries a battle raged over whether Jesus Christ was divine and spiritual (the Monophysites) or mostly human and bodily (the Nestorians) or both together (the Orthodox). This famous dispute (which gave way to the so-called *filiogue* controversy we visited in the previous chapter) was vitiated somewhat at the Council of Nicaea in 325 and in 381 at Constantinople, but it resumed later on. But this matter, in and of itself, is not a concern here, except insofar as it affects the battle of the spirit and teaching of the Holy Ghost. An invocation to the Holy Ghost in the Catholic Mass, for example, did not enter the Roman liturgy until the 1960s. And, as mentioned, the Council of Nicaea and Constantinople officially introduced recognition—belief—in the Holy Ghost into the Creed: "and, in the name of the Holy Spirit."

After that, in the eighth century, a battle raged over icons, pictures, and worship and veneration. The place of pictures is important, as we know from TV and the Internet, because—as we find out from the eighth-century battle over icons—they affect the development of cognition and spirituality. Influenced by the Arabs, Constantinople banned icons and images in 787. Washington, DC, and the Federal Deposit Insurance Corporation could not do that very easily today. At that time, another council in 787, again at Nicaea, promoted the study of scripture. But it wasn't easy to ban pictures then either. The authorities banned pictures in favor of scripture to discourage the worship of images, which was considered to be a kind of idolatry. In promoting scripture, canon two of Nicaea in 787 said that scripture should be studied according to the views of the mysterious Dionysius the Areopagite (first century AD). The Pope set his seal to this.

Dionysius the Areopagite had taught that human nature is threefold: body, soul, *and* spirit. In the ninth century, later on, at the Eighth Ecumenical Council of 869, the religious leaders changed the official view of this teaching and distanced spirit from this picture of the human constitution, saying that humankind is made up of only a body and one soul. Spirit was withdrawn from the formula. The human being was to be a dualism of body and soul. The controversy in 787 over Dionysius the Areopagite—long a controversial spiritual figure—arose through the influence of a Syrian center at Edessa, at the time of the campaign against pictures and the Nicaean Council of 787. Edessa was under Greek and Monophysite influence—a doctrine about the pure spirituality of Jesus and Christ, denying his human dimension.

In 820, in Constantinople, after another wave of image smashing, Emperor Michael the Stammerer from Phrygia came to rule in the city. He immediately declared complete freedom of thought for all subjects. Michael the Stammerer sent a copy of Dionysius' work to the French King, Louis the Pious. There, in the School of Paris, an Irish monk, Scotus Eriugena, translated Dionysius' work. In Constantinople, however, extremist and conformist monks continued the pressure against icons. The battle over pictures continued and wreaked havoc in the capitol. A new patriarch was needed, and to avoid conflict between moderates and extremists, the Emperor named a layman—Photius—as patriarch of the entire East. Within a week, the great scholar Photius, a Greek (his name meant "the enlightened one") had been made a priest, bishop, and patriarch. Later, the West—after the split from Byzantium—always reviled Photius as the bastard child of an escaped nun and soldier of the Imperial guard, and the cause of the schism in Christendom between East and West. But the East honored him as a great saint and champion; his uncle, Tasarius, had embodied the Dionysian teaching of body, soul, *and* spirit into the canons of Nicaea in 787. Photius, however, hated to leave the calmness of university study and mystical meditation, where he had furthered the teaching of Dionysius far from civil strife and the religious conflict of Empire politics. But once he entered the fray, he championed the Patriarchate against the growing papal claims of Rome.

The Pope, meanwhile, was becoming a kingmaker, having appointed Charlemagne. He was supported in Rome by the barbarians who continued to flood into the city, and the Orthodox influence from Constantinople, Antioch, and Alexandria waned. Nicholas I, an able figure, came to the Holy Roman See as Pope, followed by the development of a political conflict between Rome and Constantinople over Bulgaria, where they collided there over secular ambitions in a kind of Vietnam-like war.

Nevertheless, a serious and much larger issue also concerned Nicholas: the spiritual unity of Western Christendom. Under the pressure of Islamic conquest and influences from the East, three streams were gaining in the West. One was a mystical interpretation of Christianity, descended from the ancient mystery wisdom, neo-Platonism, and championed by the controversial and condemned Church father Origen and Clement of Alexandria. This stream, although condemned in the sixth century, survived in Monophysite camps and was reviving in the Eastern Church under the name and teachings of Dionysius the Areopagite; it had also surfaced in the second canon of Nicaea in 787. The second stream, from Persia, was a cult of spiritual imagination centered on the traditions of the Holy Grail. It had spread along North Africa and was coming into France through Spain. And the third stream came from Constantinople itself—a cult of liturgical, forms, rites, and worship as a magical way of directly experiencing spiritual exaltations and supersensible consciousness through incense, beauty, and ceremonial protocol.

These three streams and their ideological significance remind us in our modern geopolitical and ideological conflicts of Cold War politics, the New Age, and the American promotion of or resistance to Eastern influences and various new schools of consciousness. It was a similar situation in Rome. The three streams, moreover, conflicted with the State spirit of Rome. Rome saw people as political units—citizens—rather than in the light of the Greek ideal of liberty or the "spirit of man" of Eastern Orthodoxy. To Christendom in Rome, a person was the same as the citizen had been to the Roman Empire: a bureaucratic entity. Christendom was becoming a religious empire in which the believer owed loyalty and obedience.

The Italians, however, through Anastasius the Librarian (c. 810–878), had translated the work of Dionysius into Latin—but the possession of spirit knowledge beyond the soul and body was becoming a threat to control of a religious empire. Liberty for spirit did not fit well with priestly and clerical control of the people; knowledge was for the scribes, as of old, not for the laity. Knowledge could even be dangerous.

There was a move, at the time (as in today's drafting of the European Charter) to Romanize the language and texts instead of moving to invoke the spirit of God, Christ, or liberty. Nicholas, the Pope in Rome, was an able man who tried to abolish torture and who brought St. Clement's remains to Rome, but he promoted church law to unify religion and reinforce the church's heavenly power in secular areas of earthly power. He pushed for the theocratic idea of power—and for Rome against Constantinople and against France. The Eastern Emperor was also on the move, conquering Bulgaria in 864 and calling Constantinople the New Rome. When Nicholas became ill, his deputy Anastasius sent a reply to the Eastern Emperor that claimed primacy for papal Rome—complete authority over the church, including the fate of Photius in Constantinople, and the right of the Pope to convoke General, Great, or Ecumenical Councils for policy decisions. After the Eastern emperor had conquered Bulgaria, Photius in Constantinople refused King Boris of Bulgaria a native patriarchy. The king reversed field and instead approached the Roman Pope for the same thing. Nicholas seized the opportunity; he sent two Roman Bishops to Bulgaria and expelled the Eastern Orthodox priests. Photius reacted by calling a synod and then a Council in 867, which charged the new Roman priests in Bulgaria with heresies. He condemned Pope Nicholas and demanded his overthrow, naming Louis II of France emperor of the West.

The so-called filiogue conflict that we reviewed earlier arose at this time, but had not yet become the leading theological issue; it was a disciplinary one. The Frankish priests in Bulgaria inserted the filiogue clause into the Creed. It said that the Holy Spirit proceeded from the Father—and from the Son. The Roman Bishops in Bulgaria were permitting its use, but Photius objected. He said it was not in the original creed of 325 delivered at Nicaea (in the East), which said only, "And I believe in the Holy Ghost."

In fact, Rome was not yet pushing on this one. Pope Leo III, a predecessor of Nicholas, had, as recently as the early eighth century, agreed again to the Nicene formulation without the filiogue clause, and even had it engraved on silver plates stored in Rome. Not until after the 869 Council in Constantinople—a messy affair, long after Nicholas and Photius were both gone, in the eleventh century—did a Pope in Rome (and he was a German) insert that the Holy Ghost proceeded filiogue "and through the Son" into the Western Creed. It did not become an actual formal theological issue until the Council of Florence, in 1439, and though important as to the nature of the Son and the source of the Holy Ghost, it did not relate directly to the lurking controversy at Constantinople over the Dionysian view of the human threefold makeup of body, soul, and spirit—the issue at hand here.

Events in the ninth century took a rapid turn and went against the Dionysian Photius. Photius had prematurely condemned Nicholas because, as luck would have it, Nicholas had already died by the time Photius condemned him. Hadrian—no admirer of Nicholas—had been elected Pope, but Photius' premature reply condemning Nicholas tipped Hadrian's hand; he had to push the line against Photius. Meanwhile in Constantinople in 867, Basil, an enemy of the Eastern emperor, managed to kill the emperor's uncle (a friend of Photius) and the Emperor himself and seized the throne, after which he approached Pope Hadrian in Rome. Iconoclastic extremists and Rome itself had abetted all of this; Byzantine intrigue was the world. Having seized the throne in the East, Basil said that he would accept a four-year-old decision from Rome in 863 to depose Photius. Hadrian in Rome accepted the proposal, and in a synod in Rome—not a Council—excommunicated Photius, reversed his council of 867, and in a major move declared the primacy of the Pope in Rome over the whole world. Hadrian then demanded that Basil convoke a Great General Council under Papal delegates from Rome. The emperor Basil, holding only illegitimate power, was in no position to refuse. In Constantinople, the Eighth Ecumenical Council met the next year in 869.

Basil, in his own city, tried to gain control of the Council by appointing his own man, Baanes, to preside. He insisted that Photius, who remained popular in the East, have a chance to defend himself. Basil failed. The papal legate said that the Council merely had to confirm the resolutions of the Roman Synods; nothing remained to debate. The show was then rigged, and Photius refused to defend himself. The Council excommunicated Photius and approved the canons drawn up by Anastasius the Librarian in Rome. The Council of Constantinople, held in the famous Hagia Sophia Basilica, rubber-stamped the canons without debate. One of these canons, canon eleven, said: "Certain men, given to the pursuit of evil, have reached such a pitch of impiety as to enunciate the dogma that a man has two souls." This canon inferred that these people exploited a teaching of Origen and others that had been condemned as early as 555; they said that the new interpretation of "two souls" was "an irrational exploitation of a wisdom" that had already been declared folly. This mysterious wisdom—approved only eighty years earlier at the Council of Nicaea in 787—was none other than the wisdom of Dionysius the Areopagite: the threefold nature of the human being as body, soul, and spirit.

The teachings of Origen and Dionysius had originally funneled through from Pythagoras, the Greek numbers man (355 BC). Pythagoras was an initiate of the Greek mystery centers and had learned of the human threefold nature: *nous*—thinking; *thumos*—feeling and desire; and *phrnes*—bodily instinct, or will. In this trinity from Pythagoras, which lived on in Origen and Dionysius, *phrnes* is the life sphere of the body; *thumos* is the life sphere of the passions and the soul; *nous* is the life sphere of thinking and the spirit.

Canon Shepherd of the Anglican Church took his cue to research this battle of the spirit from Rudolf Steiner, the Austrian philosopher and founder of anthroposophy (1863–1925). Shepherd claims that, in this human threefold nature, only the sphere of *nous,* or spirit, is originally sinless. If the spirit, the "second soul" of the human being, is sinless, it would be endowed with the preternatural gift of freedom and immortality. Since Augustine and the condemnation of Pelagius—who had said that humankind still was good—Rome pushed harder and harder for the concept of original sin, the corrupt nature of humankind. After all, this was also good business for a church and clergy that saves sinners. And it was good business to keep the *nous,* or spirit and thinking—and the chalice, for that matter—away from the laity and in the hands and heads of the priests.

The answer to these charges, insofar as they are credible, is that the Church had commandeered the life of the Spirit and gave back, in service to the soul life of billions of people, a rich panoply of rites, sacraments, buildings, and community services, as well as defending the Faith.

In the thirteenth century, the doctrine of the "double truth"—the notion that faith can claim truths that reason cannot understand—was petrified by the argument that thinking is in fact a soul quality that had also been tainted by the Fall. The Scholastic Thomas Aquinas, however, could not quite accept this. He wanted reason and rationality to be compatible with faith—at least up to a point.

Canon Shepard and Steiner claim that the 869 canon against two souls, canon eleven, along with the rejection of Photius and the Dionysian stream based on Pythagoras was a deliberate Roman conspiracy of the Papal legates, presumably informed by the librarian Anastasius, to downgrade the "rational and intellectual" to a mere animal soul quality tainted by sin, and thus deliberately exclude humankind's access to the third higher consciousness of "spirit." This led later, they say, to the binary thinking of the West and the tragic polarity between mind and body. Whether that is true or not, history got upended again for a while. Hadrian died, Photius was recalled from banishment, reelected Patriarch, and the Council of 869 was reversed by the East. The Council of 787, too, with its approval of Dionysius, was endorsed again. But this new move was not endorsed in the West.

From that time on, East and West diverged toward the Great Schism. Western Dionysian teachings continued in monastic studies, but concerned mainly the Being of God, not human nature. The more Aristotelian aligned dualism won the day. It demoted the soul from divinity, and the body, or sensory-based view, was tainted with original sin in the Augustinian sense.

The question, in part, is whether human thoughts arise from within the body and the animal soul of nature or are divine sparks of spirit. Analytic techniques of intellectual doubt and a kind of physicalism were already coming in from Arab sources, and St. Thomas Aquinas tried to stem these by researching the earlier, deeper sense of thought itself. But Thomas was an Aristotelian. He reconciled reason and theology up to a point, but in favor of faith. The rising wave of science, however, was winning with, as we know, thinking based on the senses, stimuli, and perceptions. In the cognitive world, higher consciousness and pure intellect—the path of direct spirit perception—had been demoted. Material science, of course, eventually leaped in to fill this void, and the scientific physicalism of today is the result.

For five hundred years in the East, however, Photius' vindication promoted a kind of spiritual renaissance of learning and spiritual culture. Images were restored but rigorously regulated; icons were allowed but treated as imaginations, and they had to be rendered two-dimensional or mosaic. They were still required to evoke the spiritual behind the physical without becoming physical, three-dimensional idols. A Greek representation of beauty was fused with a Monophysite concern for the spiritual. Outwardly, the Orthodox Easterners lost, of course, to the Turks. But through Turkish repression, as in Russia under communism, religion turned inward and maintained its spirituality despite secular culture.

This battle of the spirit is not just surface politics between East and West, between Constantinople and Rome; it is important spiritually, too, because it profoundly compromises—and comprises—our vision of ourselves. The nature of the self; is it divine? Is it human? Is it immaterial—merely matter? Is it a dualism or threefold? Is it a creation or chemistry? Is it a polarity or an integrated circuit? Along with the battle for the spirit between East and West, there was also the battle of the chalice and the Holy Spirit's place in the Mass and the mystery of the Eucharist. These issues—for instance, the Eastern belief that the Holy Spirit is the agent for transforming material bread and wine into the body and blood versus the Western belief that it happens through the priest—were related to the battle of the spirit, and they show why matters evolved differently in East and West and how they help determine our worldviews today.

# Chapter 18

## The Medievals

The medieval mind and its high religious culture spans nearly a thousand years up to 1492, the time of Columbus, and we can only take a cursory look at the Scholastic view of the spirit and soul. We are skipping over a vast block of human history, but the great Cathedrals—with their spires pointing skyward symbolizing spiritual aspiration, their stone gothic sculptures embodying the spirit—and God's house served as the foundation of Western emerging society. From the spiritual side, this was not only an age of monastic societies and Cathedrals, but it was also the time of chivalry, the romances, the Arthurian legends, and the Grail. From the institutional and social side, while the Holy Ghost perhaps is behind building the Cathedrals and the orders, Western politics is extending canon law, the bishoprics, and the parishes, and raising feudal and monarchic states.

The kings, intermittently, try to usurp divine right, and Charlemagne invokes not just military power but also religious power and the spiritual estate to direct and order souls. The Popes eventually prostrate themselves before the emperors—and vice versa—and, early on, the Church extends its crusades, domains and treasures, selling investitures and indulgences, while the Holy Ghost, perhaps, inspires more the great art that culminate in Dante's *Divine Comedy,* Botticelli's art, and finally in Raphael and Michelangelo's *Last Judgment.* The popes and clergy, who fade as they did in the Patristic age, become increasingly secular as they turn their backs on the Holy Ghost in that solidly humanistic Renaissance, which included the ascendancy of the Borgia Pope Alexander and his indulgence in splendor, wealth, power, food and drink, orgies, mistresses, illegitimate children, and political power. In 1274, the Fourteenth Council of Lyons reaffirms the doctrine of the procession of the Holy Ghost—and Aquinas, the great architect of the City of God, a sort of theocratic vision still informed by the spirit in a Scholastic—a doctrinaire school way—dies on the way to that Council. As the spirit spills over into society at large, the universities begin to rise as an alternative expression of culture.

But the Inquisition begins, and at the Fifteenth Council in Vienna, the spiritual order of the Knights Templars is anathematized. Meanwhile, the Romances popularly harvest the age of chivalry and courtly love that spills up from secular and knightly life, just as the emphasis on contrition and sanctity begin to fade.

In the East, diverging from the Western power centers, the lone voice of Symeon the New Theologian (949–1022) prophesizes that Christianity is more than formal dogmatic orthodoxy or moral rules. Each person, he pleads, should feel the indwelling of the Holy Spirit. In Hymn XXVII he says:

> Do not say: It is impossible to receive the Holy Spirit.
> Do not say: It is impossible to be saved without Him.
> Do not say: Men do not see the divine light.

Symeon allows for a real yet hidden activity of the Spirit on an unconscious level, urging people to advance spiritually and experience spirit "in a conscious and perceptible way" with "the sensation of the heart." He claimed that Spirit had not withdrawn completely from the Church, but that the power to bind and loose lay only in spiritual fathers who were consciously aware of the Holy Spirit. His voice was lost to the West.

Already in the sixth century, with St. Benedict, founder of the Benedictines, the Holy Order begins to replace the Holy Ghost and eccentricities of the Holy Spirit as the monks take on rules and vows to moderate life, and hermits and visionaries come in from the desert to buckle down to community life.

In medieval religious orders, the spiritual director takes over the role of the Holy Ghost, and the human monastic director helps control where the Spirit is leading. The novices open themselves to the Spirit, but the Director checks disordered impulses and emotions; regulates the care of the body, the study of the Bible, the life of prayer; and lays down the rules and conditions. The Spirit shall not blow where it listeth but where the hierarchical society directs.

Having lost the Pythagorean and Areopagitan tradition of the threefold body, soul, and spirit, the Council of Vienna annunciates that the soul is the immediate substantial form (essence) of the body. The chalice—the wine as spirit—is reserved for the clergy, as was the *nous,* the life of intellect and the mind in medieval life. The sense of the very word *belief* shifted from 500 to 1500, having once meant trust and loyalty, as did truth, and later gaining the meaning of accepting something on blind faith without reason. Those like Peter Abelard (1079–1147) in Paris, who are forerunners of the future age of science, object, and the Holy Ghost witnesses a battle between faith and reason. The encounter, instead, between Abelard and the Scholastic William of Champeaux in the twelfth century is exceptional.

The Holy Ghost awoke from the soporific clashes of arms and disciplinary bloodshed and political correction to debate one of the great issues of intellectual history: Does God—never mind the Holy Spirit—exist? This was the question of the twelfth century. Anselm of Canterbury backed the traditional view—"I believe, that I may understand." William of Champeaux outlined the Realist view of God as reality itself. Peter Abelard, the wave of the future, at the University of Paris, more or less reversed things, saying, "I understand, that I may believe," or even, "I doubt, that I may believe." The devout St. Bernard condemned Abelard and won at the time, but Abelard, castrated and deprived of his nun, won in the long term.

The battle was one of Nominalism against Realism in the medieval sense: the belief that universals are real. At stake was whether the Holy Ghost, for example, was a reality or just a name. In the age of theology, Lady Philosophy loses her stoic Roman roots and her tolerant Greek indifference to the plight of things, and—although Boethius saw the sparks of charity and love replacing classicism and pagan brutality—theology gradually becomes more rigid, doctrinaire, and less tolerant from early on and up to the Inquisition.

St. Francis, however, talks to birds "in the spirit" and claimed that his Rule in the thirteenth century came completely from the Holy Spirit, just as the Pentecost originally came directly to the Apostles. St. Francis said that he did not add a word of his own. His order broke into "regulars" and "spirituals"—who were more rigorist. His, like many of the orders, is reformist and foreshadowed the later Reformation.

The apophatic, or negative way—the *via negativa*—championed early by some of the desert fathers—culminates in the medieval "Cloud of Unknowing" and then in St. John of the Cross. This tradition, which eschews affirmative statement and cataphoric pronouncement, renounces the light and burrows into the dark. The Spirit here is ineffable, unpronounceable, indescribable, nondiscursive, and penetrable only through the dark night of the soul and direct experience. Thomas Aquinas, the great star of the thirteenth century and patriarch of all medieval theology, wrote the supreme *Summa Theologica*—lynchpin of the Church's grammar of God at 2226 pages. The verdict of St. Thomas, as he is called, is that God is spirit; therefore, of course, the Holy Ghost is also spirit. The *Summa Theologica* is a technical work, and we cannot go into it at length. But to give an idea of the discussions, we can say that Aquinas speaks more of the soul than the spirit. For him, however, the soul is partly what was more anciently thought of as spirit. Thus the soul for Aquinas is the cause and principle of the living body. This form of the body is the principle by which we understand; it is also the principle of human intellect. The body is to the soul as a slave to the master; but, whereas soul and body are one, human beings have a lower vegetative soul, a sentient soul, and an intellectual soul. For instance, Aquinas asks: Can the intellectual soul understand without the sensitive, or sensory, soul?

For Plato, intellect had been akin to spirit, but for Aquinas, after Aristotle, it is part of the soul. For instance, for Plato, intellect needs no sensory medium to operate and is therefore not bound by necessity. As the senses are to things sensible, so is our intellect to things intelligible. Moreover, the intelligible can be immaterial. For Aquinas, however, only in God could His intellect be His essence; in others it is a mere power. The word for essence, however, used to be *substancia*. In Augustine, the mind is spirit or essence. In Aquinas, it is somewhat lowered in power, but for him will and intellect still remain in the soul after destruction of the body.

Intelligence, sometimes associated with angels, is the act of the intellect in understanding. Boethius, earlier, had said intelligence transcends acts of reason. So we can say that, according to Aquinas, for earlier thinkers intelligence represented the spiritual part of intellect and reason. Angels, representing spiritual intelligence, do not need senses to understand or discursive reason to apprehend. (Anyone who wishes to further pursue these Scholastic apprehensions of soul would do well to read chapters six and seven of the *Summa* on "Man and the First Man," questions 75 through 102.)

In chapter two, "God the Divine Persons," Aquinas deals with the Holy Ghost. Question thirty-six concerns the person of the Holy Ghost and questions thirty-seven and thirty-eight deal with the name of the Holy Ghost. Aquinas also calls the Holy Ghost "Love" and also the "Gift of God." The name *Spiritus,* says Aquinas, "in congenial things seems to signify impulse and motion; for we call the breath and wind by the term *spirit.*" A property of love, he says, is "to move and impel the will of the lover toward the object loved."

Athanasius (c.296–373), an early theoretician of the Trinity, had said, "The Holy Ghost is from the Father and the Son; not made nor created, nor begotten, but proceeding." In professing the procession of the Holy Ghost from the Son, Aquinas adds, "The Son proceeds by way of the intellect as Word, and the Holy Ghost by the way of will as Love." "Love must proceed from a word," he says. And Augustine added: "The Holy Ghost is He whereby the begotten is loved by the one begetting and loves his begetter." The divine person of the Holy Ghost is called the Gift from Eternity—given in time. "By the gift, which is the Holy Ghost, many particular gifts are portioned out to the members of Christ."

The twelfth-century move to explain God and Christianity through reason has a bearing on all this. The West, at the time, split between Bernard, who was a conservative of the old monastic type and emphasized traditional faith, and Peter Abelard of Paris, his enemy who spearheaded the move toward reason. From the point of view here, the controversy is of concern to the Holy Spirit, because under attack from reason, Bernard ossified traditional faith into more emphasis on practices of form and doctrine, while Abelard jettisoned the warm feelings of mysticism. True, Abelard argued that reason would expand Christendom ecumenically, because it would explain to all open minds and justify intellectually—to Jews, for instance—the rationale, say, for the second person of the Trinity, the Son, by showing him to be the same as the "Word" of the Jews. In some ways, however, it was a ruse, too, to overwhelm opponents by reason. In any case, both Bernard and Abelard shut down the West to any further influx of influences from the more privatized Holy Spirit revered by the East—Bernard by insisting on orthodoxy and preaching the Crusades, Abelard by insisting on discourse, rationale, and reason.

The final word here for the medievals goes to Dante, the poet, who enshrined the Holy Ghost in Paradise, where Beatrice leads him in the courtly love tradition. The poets emphasize the tension between amatory and religious ideals in matters of the spirit: poetry versus reason. At issue was passion—kill it or enthrone it? The position of the poets was, "In certain states the Holy Spirit reveals two individuals to each other."

The poets are anti-Manichean, in that they believe that matter is capable of salvation. In this they are rather on the side of the Church, but not in all things. Love as a theophany, including sex, is a path as such. Dante's view was to get on with it—don't abstract. Dante, unlike other courtly lovers who achieve their love, still longs for Beatrice. But she does not respond actively on this earthly plane; she dies. When in Paradise, then, she longs for Dante—to save him. The poets, in matters of Spirit, stress theophany of individual vision. The beloved is somewhere between the Church and State. Mystical union was a technical term for a state of consciousness reached after purgation and illumination. Later, Theresa of Avila writes movingly of this unitive experience. It concerns us here, in Dante, because some people think that purgation neutralizes the body, illumination neutralizes the soul—and that in the unitive state, the being reaches the level of spirit. I think it best, for those interested in this approach, to consult Theresa of Avila herself. A good beginning is to view Bernini's statue in Rome depicting her in a state of ecstasy. It is an image of the Holy Spirit as love and ecstasy.

## Chapter 19

# The Reformation

The Reformation, like the medieval ages, is another great chapter in human history, but the Holy Ghost, as in the struggles of kings and popes, takes a back bench to reform and the strict letter of the Bible. Again, we can take only a cursory view of the matter, pointing out a few scenes where the Holy Ghost comes to prominence, and leaving the nitty-gritty of conflict and clerical history aside. Instead of free spirits, a lot of the religious experience in the Reformation has to do with earthly as well as divine politics. There is a violent repudiation of the past and bitter condemnations and anathemas, shadows of heresy, and a hyperactive awareness of sin and an obsession with hell. The Puritans emerge instead of free spirits.

The heresy of Free Spirit emerges briefly in the fourteenth century as a precursor of the Reformation but soon dies. In the course of things, the Spirit is not so much freed as it is forcefully reformed. Not all of this, in my mind, has to do with the heritage of the Holy Ghost or even the life of the Holy Spirit. It often has to do more with conscience, morals, politics, and reform. A lot of the Protestant reform is related to the struggles over the Biblical authority versus oral tradition, the role of priests, and the absolute sovereignty of God and a dependence on him and on the law—not an appeal to the Holy Spirit. But in the end, Luther also makes his feisty appeals to the Holy Ghost.

In Martin Luther's (1483–1546) *Short Catechism,* the German Leader of the Reformation and father of Lutheranism, the monk who, on the Eve of All Saints Day, flagrantly nailed 95 theses, or objections to Catholic practices, to the door of the Wittenberg Castle church. He addresses what is left of the Holy Ghost in a plaintiff fashion. Abuse of the Church practice in selling Indulgences—forgiveness of sin and reduction of days to be spent in purgatory after death—had aroused much public disgust, just as did the recent scandals of Church payoffs to silence the outcry against priests molesting young boys. Luther would be surprised today that, whereas the Church used to be in the business of selling indulgences, today it is in the business of buying pardons for itself.

In 1505, Luther had been studying law at the age of twenty-two, when he was suddenly converted, abandoned his studies, and entered an Augustinian monastery in Erfurt. He applied himself to Scripture intensely and was ordained as a Catholic priest in 1507. Luther was intimately influenced by the teacher John von Staupitz, and his years as novice were troubled by grave doubts and agonizing; he developed nervous insomnia and dyspepsia, which weakened him for the rest of his life. Von Staupitz and his Bible study convinced Luther that Faith and not forms—the rites, liturgy, and practices of the Church—led to the grace of God.

In 1510 Luther was sent to Rome on a business trip; in the Eternal City he was shocked by the moral depravity and spiritual laxity he saw in high ecclesiastical office and in society. Back in Germany, he got his theological doctorate and became a professor. In 1515, still Catholic, he became the district vicar. The selling of indulgences in Saxony by Johann Tetzel, with money streaming to Rome to support the indulgent life of the priests, proved too much for him, and on the Eve of All Saints in 1517 he objected publicly, challenging the world to debate by nailing his dispute with the Church on the door of the Wittenberg Castle church. It marks the break of the Reformation from the Catholic Church and the start of the split in Christendom known as Protestantism.

Luther's propositions caused a wide popular flurry of attention and were brought to the attention of the pope, who ordered the Augustinians to quiet Luther down—he had too much spirit. Luther thought of himself as working for reform within the Church, but Tetzel hired Johann Eck, a gifted pamphleteer, to campaign against Luther and portray him as a heretic.

The Papal legate met with Luther in Augsburg in 1518, but he refused to recant. The next year in a public disputation Eck maneuvered Luther into admitting variances with the doctrine of the Church. Luther hardened his challenge to the Church to reform. He urged German nationalistic control over the German Church, attacked usury and commercialism, and praised the peasant agrarian society. Next Luther published the "Babylonian Captivity of the Church," attacking the papacy and arguing that Rome had Christianity in thrall. In this tract he denied the authority of the priesthood to mediate between the individual and God and rejected the sacraments, except as aids to faith.

His next tract, titled "The Freedom of a Christian Man," presented a new ideal of piety. He claimed that people were free in conscience by virtue of faith and responsible for conducting themselves properly as Christians. In this tract, he proclaimed the famous guideline of "justification by faith alone." It was not an appeal to the Holy Ghost, but to God and the Bible. Rome answered with the Papal Bull *Exsurge Domine,* condemning Luther and threatening excommunication. With popular support in Germany, Luther answered by holding a public burning of the Bull—and of canon law. In 1521, at the age of thirty-eight, he was formally thrown out of the Church. His opposition, The Diet of Worms, called him to account, and when he appeared, the diet was disordered. Although he had been given a safe conduct, an edict of the diet called for the seizure of Luther. His friends hustled him for safe keeping to Wartburg, the castle of the Elector Frederick III of Saxony. There he translated the New Testament and began work on the whole Bible. He left his safe house to return to Wittenberg and fight, but made a damaging break with the humanists and Erasmus, whose *Freedom of Will* argued that individuals could save themselves through their own spiritual efforts. Even so, Luther married a former nun and had six children.

The "Short Catechism" explains the Ten Commandments, the Apostles' Creed, the Our Father, and baptism. Here is where the significance of Luther's important break with humanism and Erasmus—in some ways more important historically than the break between Catholicism and Protestantism—shows. Luther also explains the phrase, "And I believe in the Holy Ghost."

This "prayer" of Luther to the Holy Ghost is fraught with significance and import. It shows the inner human soul of the late Renaissance struggling between rejection of the Catholic tradition of forms and rejection of the humanist and secular future of modernity stemming from Erasmus. Luther writes:

> I believe that I cannot, with my own reason, nor with my own strength, believe in Jesus Christ, my Lord or come to him, Except by the power of the Holy Ghost that calls me through the Bible, And except that I am illuminated by his gifts and am blessed and held in the real faith, As the Holy Spirit calls all Christendom on Earth, gathering, illuminating, sanctifying and keeping humanity in Jesus Christ, in the sole real faith; The Holy Spirit in this Christendom everyday saves all sinners, myself, and all believers And in the Last Day will reawake me and all the dead and will give me and all believers Eternal life in Christ. This is the truth.

It is a terrific statement of witness to an almost blinded Holy Ghost in the new age of conflict and personal schism. The Lutheran hymnbook ("The Evangelical Lutheran Hymnbook") adds:

> We all confess the Holy Ghost
> Who gives us sweet grace and comfort
> And who lives with the Father and the Son
> In Eternal Glory;
> And who holds the Church, his creation,
> In spiritual unity.
> In the Holy Spirit daily pardon and salvation
> Arrive through the merits of Jesus.

It is notable that Luther, rejecting the forms of the Church and stressing faith, resorts more to the agency of a bullish Holy Spirit as an active ingredient of devotion, and that Jesus, on earth through his incarnation and his deeds, earned the merit of the Holy Ghost. The Holy Spirit, in these prayers, becomes the active presence in daily life of God the Father, the Creator, and God the Son, the Redeemer, in a reformist and Protestant mode. However, there seemed to be nothing in Luther's ninety-five theses, which he nailed to the Castle church door in Wittenberg during Halloween month, that dealt with the Holy Ghost. Yes, he said repentance involves the whole life of a person (thesis one); yes, he said grace was an important treasure (thesis sixty-two); yes, in 1520, after his writings had been burned in Rome, in the treatise *"De Captivaitate Babylonia Ecclesiae Praeludium,"* he denied four of the sacraments (he kept Baptism, the Eucharist, and Penance), criticized the Mass, attacked the mystery of Transubstantiation, railed against Papal supremacy, asserted the superiority of Scripture, and claimed some rights for the conscience of the individual. Indirectly, maybe, but otherwise there was nothing about the Holy Ghost. Then he married, and the rest became history.

One distinction he made, however, may concern the Holy Ghost. In a 1523 treatise titled *"Von Wettlichen Obrigkeit"* (Of Earthly Government), he distinguishes temporal from spiritual government. Here, because of terrible unrest in Germany, he claimed part of what he was himself responsible for—that it was a sin to rebel against lawful authority. His own transgression against spiritual authority—he equated "spiritual" with the Church—he ignored, or excused with an appeal to conscience. It seems Luther never concerned himself with any theology itself of the Holy Ghost—or even the responsibility of conscience to the Holy Ghost. Rights of conscience were personal, human, and Church matters. He denied the powers of conscience when it came to matters of state. Luther escaped with his life—and his nun, Katherina von Bora.

Jesus instead, though he preached that Caesar received his due, had taught that conscience is the realm of the Holy Ghost, wherever, whenever. And he died for it. Luther's Holy Ghost is more slavish, somehow, demanding obedience, militancy, and obdurateness based on Faith.

For these reasons, we do not deal with Luther as we dealt with Montanus, the second-century heretic who talked directly about the Holy Ghost. The Holy Ghost, still at large, may or may not have been active at Wittenberg or Worms, where an official diet let Luther go, and a rump diet passed the famous edict that hampered the rest of his life and contributed to his famous indigestion. Montanus, in contrast, was clearly playing with fire in a less accommodating way and did not have the advantage of the German nationalist movement behind him.

From Paul's Epistle to the Romans, Luther emphasized mostly, moreover, that "they shall live by faith," not by the Holy Spirit. The thesis sometimes floated that reform sermons were "outpourings of tongues" sounds odd, since they were in high linear discourse and bound more than they loosened. Yet Luther wrote: "Wherever a Christian is, there is truly the Holy Spirit who does nothing except pray always."

One commentator, noting the firebrand conversions of the age—Luther, Loyola, Xavier, Calvin—called them "cavalry commanders of the Spirit." And Luther, though paying homage to the Spirit, says, "The intellect is the Devil's work." I wonder if the cavalry, artillery, and anti-intellectualism is what Jesus would have seen as the touch of the Holy Ghost. True, the Reformists were adamant that the celebrant needed to be "in the Spirit" if rite or sacrament was to be effective. This was a reaction to the abuse and negligence of Catholic priests. In 1522, Huldreick Zwingli (Letter I:10) asserted that ordination was not enough; he told others not to try mediating for the faithful until they had been themselves filled with the Holy Spirit. Not even a bishop, unless he had the conscious awareness, should minister, while, according to Zwingli, even a lay monk who'd had such an experience could minister.

To recapture the purity of Spirit—in their minds, a form of rigorism—these leaders banished from the spirit the Saints, intermediaries, sometimes music, art and display and most exterior forms. They preached that the sermon word is dependent on the inner word, and that it takes the spirit's activity to open the heart of the believer—not tolerance and charity, however, but to their trademark militancy and political correction.

John Calvin, based in Geneva, also spearheaded the Protestant movement with the monumental writing *Institutes of Christian Religion.* Another austere reformer, Calvin wrote (iii 1.3), "The realization of

God's will in the individual is possible only through the secret working of the Holy Spirit, who unites the soul with Christ in a spiritual marriage." These men were fanatical in linking the Spirit to rigorous religious observances and Biblical belief; but they also hammered out a new awakening of individual human conscience. Still this conscience was hidebound by rigorous doctrine, observance, and Protestant purist fundaments—just as much as it was noble in challenging the depravedness of the priesthood.

Some reformist traditions—most strongly in the Anabaptists—distinguish the true Church "gathered in the spirit" from the "carnal church"—in other words, the Catholics. Arguments about the spirit touched the long-standing controversy over infant baptism, which was denounced by the Schteilheim Confession as "the highest and chief abomination of the pope." Evangelists argued that "inward baptism" by the Holy Spirit must precede "outward baptism" with water. In effect, opponents were claiming that the infant baptism is invalid because the "inward yes" of the spirit is not present.

Philip Melanchthon (née Schwarzerd, 1497–1560) was Luther's chief theorist and author of the *Augsburg Confession* (1530). He tried to mediate between Erasmus the humanist and Luther the reformer by going into the problem of the Holy Spirit's role in conversions. What touches the heart of converts, while other people remain hard-hearted? Is it the natural light of reason, or is humankind, as the Pelagians claimed, inherently good despite the fall—or, as the Manicheans claimed, inherently bad not only from the fall, but also from creation.

Melanchthon, avoiding both heresies, claimed that conversion comes through "the word, the Holy Spirit, and human will." Luther, instead, maintained that humankind had lost all image and glory of God and, with it, the faculty "to choose in spiritual matters"—despite the new preoccupation with conscience. Grace was all—no human will was active as part of the spirit. The Holy Spirit touched a convert, period; the Scripture, the Word, was the Holy Spirit's instrument. According to Luther, "The Holy Spirit does not lie, err, or doubt."

Zwingli returned to a doctrine of the Holy Spirit to elucidate the Lord's Supper. He differentiated the "indwelling Spirit" from "the body that is eaten physically." Calvin in *Institutes of Christian Religion* also distinguished the Word of God and the sacraments from "the light of the Holy Spirit that opens the entrance to our hearts." The sacraments themselves, in some views, are operative by "the work of the Holy Spirit." There were shades in some of this of Eastern Orthodoxy's original views, but the mood was very different.

Eating the body of Christ according to the Heidelberg Cathechism, was possible only insofar as the Holy Spirit lived both in Christ and in us. The operation of the Holy Spirit, as in the real presence, is "secret and incomprehensible," but, according to the Second Helvetic Confession, the "spiritual eating" did not mean—as in the real presence—that food is changed into actual (or essential) blood and flesh. Rather, the body and blood are communicated "spiritually" through the Holy Spirit. This at least was the application of the doctrine of the Holy Spirit by the Reformed faith, which was using spirit as a force against the Catholic Church.

The conflict between Word, Scripture, and the appeal to Spirit was central to the Reformation. Protestants went back to the Bible, but Catholics, in reaction, then resorted to appeals suddenly in the oral tradition to the Spirit. John Calvin pointed out that to appeal to Spirit without the Word was just as unacceptable as appealing to the Word without the Spirit. The whole debate smacks at times of instrumentalizing the Spirit for the purposes of debate. And, in reference to the constant appeals to Spirit, the question keeps arising: But what kind of spirit?

It is interesting that the argument of Biblical reading is easier to understand when we say that Spirit is like loving *meaning*—as in "the spirit, not the letter" of the law. Spirit is like meaning is to the word—as thought is to language. This at least has a positive inflection. Calvin calls Spirit "the inner teacher," but also tries to line up with Luther by emphasizing the Word as "revelation of the Spirit"—and the Bible, sometimes, ends up being as absolute as was Church tradition.

A hundred years later, the poor Holy Ghost—after all this stunning conflict, cavalry charges, debate, and fanaticism on all sides—seems to wake up briefly by candlelight in the seventeenth century in the voice of George Fox (1624–1691), who opens a chapter of "inner light of God in everyman." He speaks of the "inner light" of the Quakers, not of the Holy Ghost—perhaps because the Holy Ghost was already so wounded from the religious wars. "The inner light is never separated from God nor Christ," Fox says, "but wherever it is, God and Christ are wrapped therein." Fox turns his back on the cavalry charges in the Holy Spirit's name and offers peace.

According to the Catholics, the later Unitarianism is one of the leading suspects in the death, or murder, of the Holy Ghost. The same country, Transylvania, that produced Dracula and vampires, produced Unitarianism in the sixteenth century. As a heresy, the seeds of this movement go back to at least the second century, but in 1785 it surfaces again in Boston as a church in a big way. Ever since, it has been strongly associated with Harvard University. Ralph Waldo Emerson was a leading Unitarian for a time—an American spiritual leader who, by the way, has been excommunicated from the Encyclopedia of World Religions (*Merriam-Webster,* 1999), along with the entire nineteenth-century transcendentalism movement. Emerson (1803–1882) ended up zigzagging. He prepared at Harvard for the ministry and was pastor at the Old North Church in Boston in 1829, but retired in 1832 and rejected the real presence in the Eucharist and refused to serve the bread and wine. He turned slowly to a view of the Holy Ghost as the Brahmin "oversoul" of the universe.

The brief on Unitarianism is simple: they denied the divinity of Christ, and then rejected the Trinity—thus casting out the Holy Ghost. In its place came reason and the unity of God. The history of this is more technical and complicated, but much of it does not interest the forensic religious detective. Americans seem to have been first and foremost in modern Unitarianism, but Joseph Priestley, a dissenting British minister, took up the baton there, stressing Jesus' humanity and God's omnipotence and—with his scientific bent—enthroning the rational faculty of humankind in place of the Holy Ghost. Not that he confessed to any crime or seems to have breathed a word about the Holy Ghost. But it was done. Some congregationalists feared that an unwelcome sort of Holy Ghost had reappeared in the eighteenth-century revivalist movement in their ranks (The Great Awakening in the 1730s and 1740s; the Evangelical Revival, 1750 to 1875); and American Unitarianism (the Arminian Congregationalists) was born and institutionalized. It was on the cutting edge. Some thinkers even talked of "free Christians" for fear that the name "Unitarianism," liberal rationally as it was, was too confrontational. Nobody wanted actually to be charged with the murder of the Holy Ghost. And Emerson said that the less one talked about the Holy Ghost the better. Into that cutting-edge movement, however, Emerson was born, and then went his own way.

There was a caveat here, though. The Arminian Congregationalists who formed the Unitarian backbone in the 1785s could look not only forward to a rational future, but also back to a Dutch lineage from the heretic Jacobus Arminius (1560–1609). Arminius, although conservative, had early on tried to moderate the rigid sort of Calvinism that the Pilgrims brought to Plymouth Rock. Doctrinally speaking, he didn't want to be just a slave of God and of predestination; he wanted his free will. He never got it. A fellow Dutch Reformist, Franciscus Gomarus—apparently friend and enemy—trapped him in disputes that do not concern us here, but they absorbed the last years of his life in unwanted controversy and hastened his death in 1609. After he died, an important Dutch statement, called the "Remostrance," was issued sort of in his memory. It mentioned the Holy Ghost, but Point Five argued that, unaided by the Holy Spirit, no person is able to respond to God's Will.

## Chapter 20

# Lady Philosophy

Lady Philosophy, the handmaiden of theology, brings the spirit to us in another way. In the person of Sophia, the great tradition of wisdom, she is present in esoteric tradition from the times of the Egyptian Goddess Isis and Trismegistus, right through to the Gnostics and beyond. As dialectics and philosophy as we know it, from the Greeks, knowledge of the spirit comes to us through Socrates, himself possessed of a *daimon,* or spirit genius, and then Pythagoras, Plato, Aristotle and after the turn of the millennium, after Christ's time, through Plotinus and the neo-Platonic tradition.

Aristotle's God—after concepts replaced the spirits of plants, trees, and animals—was conceptual: the First Cause. Different from the anthropomorphic Gods of Olympus, this God was theistic, not a personal God. The God of the Greek philosophers differed, too, from the Hebrew God of our Fathers, who was more connected with being, prophecy, and the psychology of faith tradition. In the later Jewish Kabbalah, for instance, spirit is willing to suffer temptation and exile in order to achieve true spirituality and self-consciousness. But, in the Jewish tradition, spirit is always dependent on the world and human beings for fulfillment. Not so with Greek philosophy, which spawned the doctrinal development of Christianity in the Patristic Fathers and later Aquinas. We have already seen Jesus' dispute with Pilate over the nature of truth and the effect of Greek dialectic on the development of the doctrine of the Trinity.

The Hebrew tradition, through Jesus and the Apostles, and then John the Evangelist and Paul, collides with Greek culture, and the Patristic and Alexandrian Fathers, Clement and Origen, conflate Greek *nous* and reason and dialectic with the prophetic tradition.

The philosophical tradition, as we saw in our chapter "The Medievals," reaches a new pitch with Abelard, Scotus Eriugena, Albertus Magnus, Duns Scotus, and St. Thomas Aquinas—the Angelic Doctor of the Church, a Sicilian. This tradition hammers out paradoxes of the Holy Spirit in a rapprochement between faith and reason.

We can only sample the philosophical tradition as regards its links to Spirit. Plato, of course, inaugurated the doctrine of the immortality of the soul before Christianity, and Pythagoras offered the threefold doctrine of body, soul, and spirit, just to show that the Holy Ghost, in the form of spirit with a small "s," has not been the exclusive property of religion. In effect, philosophy depersonalizes the Spirit. It also takes the Holy out of Spirit and renders the Holy Ghost a non-person—either denying the Spirit, or presenting it as an Absolute Principle. But some philosophy also makes an impassioned case, on these grounds, for spirit with a small "s." In this book, we are not doing philosophy, but we need to touch base with the thinkers who deal with spirit, and one of the first, of course, was Plato, for whom the ideas of things, the archetypal forms—sometimes called *species*—were spiritual realities. We still use the expression Platonic love, for instance, to describe a pure love that is not of the flesh.

Philosophy often abstracts the spirit even more than theology, which dematerializes the Spirit, but at least it recognizes the person of the Holy Ghost. Philosophy, instead, tends to abstract the being of the spirit and turn it into an Absolute Principle. Early on, Plotinus had elevated the concept of Spirit to the "Alone talking to the Alone," reminiscent of the "still small voice."

Augustine, who gave us a heavy case of original sin, tried to use Plotinus to comprehend a spiritual world above us. Plotinus experienced "the One." Augustine himself complained of not having the direct mystic experience of the One, but he set up this table of equivalents (*Confessions* XIII:11):

| | |
|---|---|
| The One Being | The Father |
| Idea, World Knowing | The Son |
| Psyche, Life, or Love | The Holy Spirit |

He said that Being corresponds to creation from God; the knowing, through the Son, corresponds to the self-representation of being; while the Holy Spirit corresponds to willing—or love—in which the being and the knowing embrace each other.

The last followers of Plato and Plotinus were exiled from the West to Persia, where they founded the Academy of Gondi Shapur. Justinian closed the philosophers' schools in the Greek world of Athens in AD 529.

Thomism, in the thirteenth century, from St. Thomas Aquinas, as we saw, culminates the medieval ages and holds that the human soul is immortal and a unique substantial form; knowledge is based on sensory perception, however, but also the mind possesses the reflective capacity to proceed into fuller perfection in faith.

By the time of rising humanism, we meet a middle figure like Desiderius Erasmus (1469–1536), a humanist philosopher and, in some ways, an antagonist of Luther who wrote *The Education of a Christian Prince* for Charles V, laced with anticlercalism, and eschewing doctrine as the substance of schism. He wanted to grant the chalice to laymen and permit priests to marry. In 1524, writing on free will, he backed human choice in salvation, and in his later years saw Christianity as a religion of spirit based on human reason and tolerance. He was against religious exaltation—even as in Luther—and saw the Sermon on the Mount as central to the life of the Spirit. His contemporary, Machiavelli, also wrote to educate a Prince, and although there is a lot of common sense and the beginnings of political science in Machiavelli, there is no longer any pretense of an appeal to the Holy Ghost, but only to human nature.

But consider, then, an obscure figure like Judah Abravanel (1460–1530). He had been the treasurer to the King of Portugal during the time when Queen Isabella, who aided Columbus, was expelling Jews from Spain in 1492. Abravanel had fled to Spain in 1483, then to Italy. His book, *The Dialogues of Love*, promoted love as the "cosmic principle" of being and its spirit as the mirror of reality. The Dialogues stressed the spiritual character of physical beauty, and out of this developed the tradition of aesthetic idealism. True happiness was said to be the "union of the human intellect to divine intelligence" (a Judaic reference to the Holy Ghost). This union was connected to aesthetic enjoyment, and Abravanel's work became a landmark in the development of the Western science of aesthetics: beauty as related to Divine Intelligence.

These were perhaps the exceptions to the abstracting line of development that led to the Enlightenment—as was, for example, the French physicist and religious philosopher Blaise Pascal (1623–1662) who stressed a personal rational sort of mysticism in which spirit was still a personal experience. "Thou wouldst not see me, if thou hadst not found me," is how Pascal quotes the Spirit.

Everyone is familiar with the dualism between mind and body generated by René Descartes (1596–1650), but it was the German Emmanuel Kant (1724–1804) who systemized the split by saying that pure reason and knowledge must be based on sensory data, whereas matters of the spirit cannot be known except by faith. This virtually ended metaphysics, which had begun with the Greeks. It also led to the later positivism in the nineteenth and twentieth centuries, which denies any place for spirit and, in the end, reduces the mind to the factor of the physiological brain—a hypothesis, a scientific physicality—a notion embraced by many modern thinkers and scientists.

Gottfried Leibniz (1646–1716), during the age of rationalism, became one of the seminal thinkers who led to the Enlightenment—and, paradoxically, to the apparent death of the Holy Ghost. Earlier philosophers such as Leibniz, Spinoza, and then Bishop Berkeley, still held a place for metaphysics. For Leibniz, spirit was akin to reason; for Spinoza, everything was one substance, God—and by "natural substance" (*natura naturans*) he implied spirit. Bishop Berkeley sometimes inferred that the world did not exist as such, but was all a sort of abstract, ideal spirit.

Samuel Butler (1835–1902), after Darwin's *Origin of Species* in the nineteenth century, said that Charles Darwin had "banished mind from the universe." The naturalist Alfred Russell Wallace (1823–1913) had hit on the idea of "natural selection" before Darwin. He acknowledged Darwin but rejected the idea that natural selection could produce higher mental and spiritual faculties. He believed in the necessity of some nonphysical agency to produce mind. Darwin's version of evolution did not allow for this.

A later compromise thinker in the mind-body dualism was the French philosopher Henri Bergson (1859–1941), who posited life as the creative impulse (*l'elan vital*) of all evolution; for him, life was the spirit. We gain the feeling of life by immediate consciousness, or instinct. The intellect, instead, develops mathematics, for example, and best apprehends matter, or the static, whereas life, *elan,* is dynamic. Evolution fuses intellect and instinct to give us intuition, which, rather than faith, is the faculty by which we gain immediate knowledge. *Elan vital,* in this system, replaces the Holy Ghost.

These are just samples that show what philosophy has done about spirit. George Santayana (1863–1952) at Harvard wrote a philosophy of spirit, but he was a critical realist at heart, for whom even mind is matter in motion. Spirit comes into being when mind becomes conscious of itself. And out of the mind's likes and dislikes, values arise, such as goodness and beauty, but these are essences, not existences. In this system, an essential value such as truth is a divinity, but still only an ideal, not an existence.

Edmund Husserl (1859–1938), the father of phenomenology, sidesteps any duality of mind and matter—or spirit—and reduces experience to the act of being conscious, the object of consciousness, and the data by which the object is known. Spirit is just another byplay of phenomenology.

Yale's Paul Weiss (1901–2002), a presiding spirit there through much of the twentieth century, exalted human freedom as creative and social, but God, or Spirit, was but the explanatory concept for teleology, cosmological relations, and ontological states.

Bertrand Russell (1872–1970), a British rationalist representing logic and positivism, wrote a tract called *A Free Man's Worship.* Spirit or mind for him is totally brain-dependent—that is, physical—and reality is a system of perspectives in no way dependent on a knowing mind. As far as the human being is concerned, a pessimistic picture was presented even though the human being was freed theoretically from the vicissitudes of spirit by the rigors of logic and positivism.

Some philosophers accepted the ground of an Infinite Being, but even the celebrated religious theorist Rudolf Otto (1869–1937), influenced by the advances in rationalized theology of the nineteenth and twentieth centuries, wrote his famed *Idea of the Holy,* reducing spirit to a subjective category that creates the numinous out of moral, rational and non-rational needs. The Holy Ghost, in his view, was just such a non-rational creation.

Lest it be forgotten, which is a prevailing danger, there was once such a thing as "the spirit of the enlightenment," too, and in modern dress a modest example of this spirit, according to the *Los Angeles Times,* can be found in the Italian semioticist Umberto Eco's small booklet, *Five Moral Pieces.* Eco's watchword is tolerance, disciplined by prudence and charity, but even the ethical dimension of such a view has jettisoned any indwelling Holy Ghost.

Perhaps the most important modern negator of spirit (as in metaphysics) was Ludwig Wittgenstein (1869–1951), who reduced philosophy itself to the study of more or less meaningless statements. He eliminated metaphysics—speculation on the soul and spirit, God, and much else—because, supposedly, it is not based on experience and observation.

We have taken only a brief, scattered sampling of philosophers, but in dealing with the Spirit we need to do this to spell out what various thinkers—those who are not believers from church or theologians of the Holy Ghost—have thought about spirit, insofar as Spirit with a large "S" differs from spirit with a small "s." Overall, the great exception to this stream of rationalism and reductionism that led from the Enlightenment to the denial, negation, and alienation of modernity, postmodernism, and contemporary thought—so overwhelmingly dominated by today's scientific physicalism—was German Idealism.

For Johann Wolfgang von Goethe (1749–1832), truth is made when the mind participates in the external world. He tried to overcome the abstraction and categorical imperative of Kant's spirit, but the granddaddy of all idealistic philosophers was G. W. F. Hegel (1770–1831)—George Wilhelm Friedrich Hegel. Just before him, the more poetic Johann Gottlieb Fichte (1762–1814) posed the finiteness of humankind against the Absolute Mind immanent in the universe. Fichte said that the transcendental ego projects into the absolute world perceived by the idea. For Hegel, spirit becomes all; history itself is the unfolding of spirit. His *kenosis,* or manifestation of spirit, is the spirit emptying itself to become incarnate and immanent in the world. Spirit is the agent for the transphysical element in evolution. Hegel, a professorial type with an uneventful life, was a professor at various German universities, including Jena, Heidelberg, and Berlin. His landmark book was the *Phenomenology of Spirit*—or mind—which appeared in 1807.

We should remember that *Geist,* the old word, also means mind and the mental activities in German, as in the fine arts, *Geisteswissenschaft*—literally, science of the spirit—remains closer to this dimension in German than in the Romance languages or in English. Spirit appears in three states or stages for Hegel: subjective, objective, and absolute—examples of the world soul becoming, through the dialectic of thesis, antithesis, and synthesis. Subjective spirit is when nature becomes conscious; in objective spirit, mind establishes law, morality, and the state; in absolute spirit, the spirit shows up in great personalities, and art, and realizes its ends. History is the realization of the Idea; spirit reaches its apex in art (the infinite visible); religion symbolizes it with greater reality; and philosophy brings it to thought. Although socialism and Marxism latched on to Hegel, the philosopher himself spoke of Christ as the union of God and human, spirit, and matter.

Following Goethe's act, Rudolf Steiner (1861–1925) began as a philosopher who made thinking the lynchpin of spiritual activity in a corresponding theory of knowledge. His followers pursue the "wisdom of the human" (anthroposophy) and normally attribute clairvoyance to his writings, insights, and sayings. Steiner, an Austrian seer, was brought up Catholic but rejected the tradition. He developed research on the Holy Ghost as much as anyone did, particularly in his later work on festivals and Pentecost. His adherents often do not distinguish between "the mystical spirit" (the Hegelian Spirit of German Idealism) and the traditional Holy Spirit, although, according to his own claim, Steiner's work is considered in some texts to be "written through him." Although raised a Catholic, apparently he never actually claimed to be inspired as such by the Holy Ghost, the third person of the Trinity. Moreover, he pursued a German Idealism fused with Eastern and esoteric wisdom, seeking to avoid the abstractions of Idealism. He did claim to be clairvoyant and to write out of inspiration from the spiritual world, and he urged everybody to try, on scientific grounds, to do this for themselves. He considered his spiritual research to be scientific, and he considered it to be the wisdom of humankind—not necessarily the wisdom of the Holy Ghost. Some followers think the Holy Ghost spoke through him, but because of his teachings on, for example, preexistence and reincarnation, the Holy Office would—and has—viewed him as a heretic. He also founded a religious movement, the Christian Community, based on a 1920s reform of the liturgy and Mass. For Steiner, however, thinking is a spiritually free act that involves "a gesture of inner effort."

Rudolf Steiner's life was an overwhelming endeavor to revivify the spirit. He dropped the word Holy, turning his back on Catholicism. He unified strands of Christian esotericism, Gnosticism, oriental Theosophy, alchemy, Rosicrucianism, Geotheanism, and scientific method into a syncretic phenomenology based on perception and thinking. But he spoke long and often on the *parousia,* the descent of the spirit at Whitsuntide; it was central to his researches on spiritual life and Christology.

In America, Ralph Waldo Emerson (1803–1882) picked up the transcendental stream from the Germans. William James (1842–1910) saw two persons in Emerson: one, the sharp-eyed Yankee, who viewed the imperfection of America without despair; and two, the Platonic Emerson who saw the Oversoul as greater than time, space, and nature. James told Americans that there was no inconsistency between Emerson's shrewd side and his ideal side. Consistency, for Emerson, was the hobgoblin of little minds.

Was the Oversoul actually the Holy Ghost? Emerson spoke of the soul as mind—and spirit. He said that Spinoza, Kant, and Coleridge all spoke about spirit from firsthand insider knowledge, while philosophers like Locke or Hume spoke about it second-hand—spectators who had heard of it from others. This latter kind of philosopher, like later positivists and behaviorists, were course translators of sensory life who knew nothing of the relationship of the soul to the divine spirit. James said Emerson "lived by perception"—a sort of phenomenologist of the Oversoul. But for Emerson no facts were too sacred, no facts were unworthy, because he saw them as symbolizing the history of the living soul. Therefore he did not distinguish as sacred or soulful only that which was touched by religion, but held worthy what came from myth, history, law, custom, proverbs, and the creative spirit of artists and poets, heroes, or the person in the street. Everyone was a portal to the universal mind—the Oversoul, seemingly the bearer, in other words, of what had been the Holy Ghost.

## Chapter 21

# The Holy Ghost Conceives

In one of the greatest mysteries of all time, the Holy Ghost stands far from philosophy at another pole—this is the Conception: the Virgin Birth. It is an irony of language that *conception* means both the birth of a thought, as in philosophy, and the birth of babies. The Virgin Birth is the doctrine that Jesus had no natural father, but was born from the Virgin Mary, who had been filled, or impregnated, if you will, by the Holy Ghost. Unlike the Immaculate Conception of Mary, the Virgin Birth—although a traditional teaching appearing early in the Apostles Creed as an article of belief—has never been raised to dogmatic status by a papal decree ex-Cathedra or Bull or infallible pronouncement. Its sources are in the Bible story of Jesus' birth in Mathew and Luke.

The Immaculate Conception— widely mistaken for the Virgin Birth—is really the dogma that Mary herself was conceived and born free from the taint of original sin. This view is also an early teaching and was already held in the second century. St. Justin Martyr (100–165)—a pagan born in Palestine who studied philosophy and who then converted at the mystery center of Ephesus—combined philosophy and faith and makes an "apology," or explanation, for the Immaculate Conception. St. Irenaeus, who established the identities of the Old and New Testament deity as the same God, also supported the concept of Mary's Immaculate Conception. It was rooted in the Gnostic tradition that Mary, among the disciples, was a very special person.

St. Bonaventure (1217–1274)—a Franciscan who reconciled alms and the beggar orders with Christian tradition and led the Franciscan School of Paris in 1254—opposed the Immaculate Conception, as did the medieval scholastic doctor of the Church, St. Thomas Aquinas. But the Council of Basel of 1439 backed the doctrine as in accordance with the Faith. In 1709, Pope Clement XI made the Feast of the Immaculate Conception a holy day of obligation, and in 1854 Pius the IX issued a Papal Bull making it official Church dogma—*Ineffabilis Deus* (Dec. 8).

Early on, concern arose in the eleventh century that a debate over Mary's virginity and her own conception would taint Christ's unique redemptive mission, but John Duns Scotus argued that Christ's own grace had retroactively covered Mary in advance—that it was not her own doing—preventing original sin from reaching her. Original sin, promoted by Augustine, was the doctrine that Adam's original disobedience in eating of the tree of knowledge of good and evil—not necessarily a sexual sin as many believe—was transmitted for all time to his descendents. The source for this idea is not found in Genesis but through St. Paul and Augustine.

By the grace of the Immaculate Conception, her own conception, by God's act and not by her own merit, Mary was free of the consequences of original sin, including slavery to the devil, tendencies to concupiscence or lust, and darkness of intellect. Because of this freedom from the hereditary line, she became a vessel for the Holy Ghost and the Virgin Birth—the birth of Jesus announced by Gabriel, the spirit of Revelation, and conceived by the power of the Holy Ghost.

Incidentally, under the Blessed Mother's title of the Immaculate Conception, Rome and the U.S. hierarchy dedicated the United States to Mary's patronage. In 1847, the American Bishops petitioned Pope Pius IX to make Mary Immaculate the patroness of the United States. In 1920, in Washington, DC, her shrine was begun at the corner of Fourth Street and Michigan Avenue. Dedicated in 1955, it is the largest Catholic Church in the United States.

Mary's virginity—meaning the Virgin Birth—was prophesied in the Bible by Isaiah (7:14). Celibacy, chastity, and virginity were all precious treasures in ancient times and in the Church, and even in Pagan times virginity was thought to have something to do with spiritual powers. The Vestals, priestesses in Rome, were virgins, and the doctrine of perpetual virginity, both the physical and spiritual, surrounded Mary during her life and after. Mary's own Immaculate Conception prefigured the Virgin Birth and made her a suitable vessel for the Holy Ghost. The Virgin Birth is a story of external generation, similar to parthenogenesis, or reproduction from virgin females by ova that do not require the male element in order to develop. Pagan Gods like Zeus were married. Greek Gods married and mated. But Yahweh, Abraham's father, never married, nor did God, the Father of Christians. No woman generated Adam or Eve—God breathed the dust to generate Adam and pulled Eve from Adam's rib. In Greece, Athena sprang from the brow of Zeus.

The teaching of Mary's perpetual virginity (as differentiated from the Immaculate Conception and the Virgin Birth) means that she bore Jesus free from the pain of child birth and remained virginal all her life—even though Matthew 1:25 says that Joseph "knew her not till she had brought forth her firstborn son." The Council of Chalcedon approved the teaching in 451. The Virgin Birth means that Jesus himself had no natural father and was conceived in Mary through the power of the Holy Ghost. The infancy narrations appear in the Gospels of Luke and Mathew and were universally accepted early on. The Eastern Orthodox and even Islam recognize the teaching, as well as Anglicans and many Protestants.

In Mathew (1:18–25) after reciting the book of generation drawing Jesus' lineage back to Abraham and to Kings David and Solomon, says, "Before they came together, she was found with child of the Holy Ghost." Joseph thinks to put her away, but the angel Gabriel appears to him in a dream and tells him to take her as his wife, "for that which is conceived in her is of the Holy Ghost." In the book of Isaiah, the prophet had said a virgin shall be with child. In Luke, again, the Angel Gabriel tells the old priest Zacharias, who is burning incense in the temple, that Elizabeth too, with her child John, "shall be filled with the Holy Ghost even from his mother's womb." When she receives her annunciation, Mary says, "How shall this be, seeing I know not a man?" To which Gabriel answers, "The Holy Ghost shall come upon thee, and the power of the Highest shall overshadow thee."

Mary visits Elizabeth, and when she salutes her, "The babe John leaped in her womb," and Elizabeth was filled with the Holy Ghost. "Blessed is she that believed," says the story. "Mary says, "My soul doth magnify the Lord, and my spirit hath rejoiced in God." Then Mary gives a remarkable speech that foreshadows Jesus' own Sermon on the Mount: "He that is mighty hath done to me great things and Holy is his name." She says the Lord regarded the low estate of his handmaid, showed mercy, strength, scattered the proud, put down the mighty, exalted them of low degree, filled the hungry with good things, and sent the rich away empty.

Zacharias is also filled with the Holy Ghost, and his muted mouth opens again after John's birth and he gives a remarkable prophecy—the "horn of salvation" speech.

This remarkable chain of events is told beautifully and lovingly in the Bible and is a meditation, at the least, on conception, pregnancy, intuition, generation—even on today's issues of contraception and abortion—as well as the interplay between the divine and human. Every mother and father can be inspired and sobered by the tale.

A teaching, or doctrine (*kerygma*), is different from a tradition or dogma; *dogma* (a term much misunderstood in the modern world) usually refers to an esoteric teaching cloaked in mystery, obligation, and infallibility, an officially held matter of faith.

The Annunciation, the claim goes, is the sense that Joseph in his own right as a man could conceive a child informed only by tribal spirit and family blood; but the angel announces to Mary a child penetrated by the spirit of universal humanity. This, informed commentators say, is the meaning behind the conception by the Holy Ghost. This, then, was conception by a Spirit overcoming differences of body, race, tribe, and blood: a Holy Spirit. Mary's own Immaculate Conception frees her from the gravitational field of original sin, thus preparing a vessel that in all senses, especially spiritual, can be fully infused by the Holy Ghost. Virginity is also esoteric in meaning here, not just physical.

This background prepares Jesus for the incarnation of a personality free from the blood stream of the rabbinical Hebrew or any other people—free from all tribal and patriarchal ties and dominion. In the esoteric sense, then, Mary's Immaculate Conception and Jesus' Virgin Birth mean that, in him was born the vessel of the Christ, to follow at the baptism, the first truly new, free, and modern human ego—in divine purity.

This evolutionary event was, according to Gospel, the work of the Holy Ghost.

# Chapter 22

# War and Music

Holy Spirit is not usually invoked in war, but God, or Allah. The concept invoked is the justness of our cause against the wrongness of the enemy — not the immateriality of Spirit. The Spirit of enthusiasm, yes — Jihad and Patriotism — but not the Holy Ghost. Prayer and invocation strengthen the troops through exhortation and a sense of mission: "God is on our side." But the Holy Spirit is considered too immaterial to help with weapons, bombs, and heavy equipment. "Praise the Lord," the all-powerful, instead, "and pass the ammunition." In fact, if anything, the Holy Spirit is considered slightly subversive around headquarters, because it doesn't give or take orders; it thinks and feels too much and is too closely associated with freedom. I never heard anything about the Holy Ghost at boot camp.

Joan of Arc (1406–1431) was probably a great military exception. Joan of Arc, like Mary, was a virgin, and we have mentioned the special spiritual gifts that sometimes adhere to chastity, especially virginity. At Chinon, Joan was supposedly questioned by Churchmen before her trial for witchery at Poitiers. Jean de Valois, Duc d'Alençon, related to the Dauphin himself, is said to have testified that Joan answered that she had "heard voices and a source of advice that told her what she had to do." At Poitiers, according to Friar Sequin (the future dean of the faculty at Poitiers who also testified at the Nullification trial in 1455), while watching over the animals, Joan had received her vocation from "a voice that revealed itself to her." This was the call to lead the French over the British and to see the Dauphin anointed king. The French have always had both a special fondness and a special scorn for virgins, and Friar Sequin is purported to have asked Joan what language her voice spoke—perhaps French? Joan is reported to have answered, "Better than yours." At Poitiers, she supposedly said she had understood it was an angel's voice. Of course, if she had said it was the voice of the Holy Ghost, she would have been burned immediately.

The Christian Emperor Constantine (288–337) saw the Cross in the field leading him on—not the Holy Spirit. The Byzantines and Romans fought over the nature of the Father and the nature of the Son—the filioque dispute—but it was really about East versus West in a wider sense, not just the Holy Ghost. The Crusades were fought in the name of the true God and Christ, not always the Holy Spirit. Rome never fought in the spirit of a ghost or for Greek truth; it fought for the law, judicial code, and bureaucratic turf. Its banner was glory and power. Charlemagne fought for the Holy Roman Empire, substituting Paris for Rome.

The Holy Roman Empire of the Hapsburgs and the Hohenstaufens put Vienna and Berlin on the map, not the Holy Ghost. The Church got involved on the temporal side, but it usually wasn't about spirit; it was about nation, investiture, property, and turf. The Thirty Years' War and religious wars during the 1600s were also political; they were fought between Protestant and Catholic power groups, although they did involve religious matters, control of the Bible, revelation, ordainment of priests, freedom of conscience, and the emergence of the individual. Spirit was instrumentalized as a weapon by both parties.

Napoleon's banner was secular enlightenment, the Napoleonic code, the confiscation of monasteries and Church resources, and the French concept of *la gloire*. He was not campaigning for the Holy Ghost. And Hitler was in it for *Lebensraum* and Aryan supremacy—a racial and nationalistic agenda, not a spiritual concept. The Russians waged a world campaign for atheism against the Holy Ghost, a classless society, economic determinism, and the workers' state. Pan-Slavism was part of it, but not the Holy Ghost. Meanwhile, the British launched an empire in the name of commerce, democracy, reason, fair play, Anglicanism, and the rights of kings to serial divorce—not for any other spiritual agenda, unless the struggle against Rome is seen as a grand power play for possession of the Spirit. The Japanese were in it for the Sun Emperor. The Jews, the Puritans, and "the spirituals" on the whole, however, tended for a time not to fight.

Yet the concepts related to the Holy Ghost—truth, freedom, conscience, personal dignity, virtue, inspiration—all lurked at the back, the side, and in the trenches of war. This is because the spirit, or the Holy Spirit, haunts the concept of civilization itself. The Geneva Convention, the Red Cross, the rules of war—laughable as they sometimes may seem to potentates and to those of a violent nature—are inspired by humankind's sense of values other than pure brute military might, conquest, and guerilla tactics.

Outrage at terrorism, schools for assassins, Gestapo-run gulags, the SS, Soviet and American intelligence tactics, the Mossad, and torture and inquisitional chambers all arise from a source in humanity that rejects the very struggle for survival that it espouses to children in its schools, universities, and science labs. Civilization teaches materialism and brute power and survival of the fittest, and honors them, but fails to accept them as the final litmus test for what is human. A different spirit—not even that of the common good—inspires civilization's higher values, and maybe this value is related to the Spirit.

At the Council of Trent, with hopes of ending the religious wars, the sitting took place in a Basilica. The schism, the Reformation, the duet between Mary of Scots and Queen Elizabeth, were passing. The Holy Ghost was a refugee. The august Council met, meant to heal five years of breach, and, according to religious historian C. J. Jordan, pronounced, "Here the Holy Spirit spoke for the last time"(*Postremum Spiritus Sanctus oracula effudit*). Libertarians secretly hold the view that, in 1588, the Holy Ghost entered naval operations on the side of the English at the Battle of the Armada between Spain and England. Sir Drake, the knight of the seas, was the beneficiary. It was maybe the first and last time that the Holy Ghost actually entered into battle—secretly on the great Elizabeth's side. As Elizabeth said, "The pope was against me in my mother's womb."

It was a long way from doctrine to actual naval conflict, of course, but in the Channel, some say, the small ships won against the flotilla of Tradition. The great ships of the Catholic Spanish State went down, and the next three hundred years, until World War I, were almost settled.

It is arguable, however, that Queen Elizabeth, like England itself at that time, had "a spiritual awareness of herself." Whereas the Holy Ghost impregnated the Virgin Mary in her time, some, including Henry VIII, felt that the Holy Spirit was somehow responsible in his remarkable case for five miscarriages from his canonical wife Catherine of Aragon. Henry did two things: he blamed Rome for the sterility of the Holy Ghost, and he questioned the nullity of marriage, another treacherous realm of the spirit. Henry himself, a spirituous man, went to Anne Boleyn personally and in no ghostly manner, and the result is history: Queen Elizabeth (1533–1603). How she ruled is well known. What she herself believed is apparently unknown.

In Elizabethan times, the Holy Ghost did not always go to Church either; it went to the theater. It had a presence, too, in the common language. Way before the age of psychobabble and medications, there were expressions like "high spirits" and "mean spirited." Being in "low spirits" meant not so much vulgar or coarse, but simply depressed; and "spirited," as in a spirited horse or person, meant the opposite. It did not mean that one was possessed by a demon or evil spirit, but rather that one was genial, enterprising, and energetic. In those times, this kind of person was appreciated, not medicated. High spirits were not exorcized; only demons and bad spirits were banished. Priests long ago gave up exorcism for confession, penitence, and other rites. But in Shakespeare's time, it seems, the Holy Ghost spent a lot of time at the theater—specifically, at the Globe Theatre. It is interesting that, after the Puritans came to America, for 200 years—between 1620 and 1820—there were no theaters; in Boston, theater was considered bad for the Spirit.

Others said that the Spirit lurks outside the Church. Consider Montaigne (1533–1592) and the spirit of skepticism. Half Jew, born the same year as Queen Elizabeth, and from Bordeaux (where Montesquieu would later practice), Michel de Montaigne was the mayor. An aloof spirit, he withdrew from politics to a rural rather than to a religious retreat. The word *aloof* may come from *hlephan,* an Anglo-Saxon root meaning to laugh. Consider for a moment: Does the Holy Ghost like to laugh?

In any case, *aloof* means distant. Montaigne would later write the famous *Essays* (1580) and, although his name sounds like Montanus (our early heretic), Montaigne may have been closer to Emerson, who emulated the essay style for Americans almost three centuries later. Whereas Emerson used the essay to ascend to the spirit, Montaigne fathered the creed of skepticism. On his deathbed, however, he took communion.

By the way, for those who are interested in my own credentials as a journalist writing on the Holy Ghost, my father, on his deathbed, professed nothing and shrugged his shoulders. My mother (they were divorced) persisted to the end as a lifelong believer "in the Spirit," and said that the story I was telling should be titled, "From the Holy Ghost to the Holy Spirit."

Since the Holy Ghost may, of course, be in more than one place at any one time—unlike mere armies and soldiers—it may also be that it stopped in Spain on its passage North, from Rome to England, to write (in our humble opinion) the poetry of St. John of the Cross—instead of, perhaps, another Papal Bull. St. John of the Cross (1542–1591) was Juan de Yepes. Instead of a doctrine, de Yepes penned this: "If a man wishes to be sure of the road he travels on, he must close his eyes and walk in the dark." The proper place for ghosts, after all, is in the dark. And Yepes had a passion for loss. Here, the imagery for the Holy Ghost is like the eroticism of love unrequited—it is never consummated and the lover despises himself, yet the marriage to nothing is a great mystical union. Theresa of Avila, who touched Yepes in the Spirit, felt the same way. Not much more can be said or proven about history in all these meanderings of the Spirit. The reader must visit the ghosts of such great figures to sense the ghost of a Ghost. I suppose the admonitory counsel that can be added to those who vanish in the dark with Theresa and St. John of the Cross is this: Don't hate or despise yourself too much. They were solitaries of the spirit. The dark is alone.

Speaking of Spain, the Jesuit Constitutions are aimed at taming the "haughty spirit." This needed to be complemented by the *Spiritual Exercises* (1548), a handbook for training the spirit and intellect. Spiritual renewal was the goal. Surprisingly, in his unpublished essay "Christendom in Europe," Novalis (1772–1803), the great German Romantic poet and a leading forerunner of the "free spirit," paradoxically greeted Jesuitism with these words: "A newly arisen order ... on which the dying spirit of the hierarchy seems to have disbursed its last remaining gifts." These gifts, or course, were none other, in Novalis' mind than those of the Holy Ghost. Novalis attributed to the Jesuits "newfound strength ... wonderful charity ... steadiness of purpose." He lauded their goal of reviving the papal imperium to its former majesty and supremacy. This tragic and youthful poet of the blue flower, so revered by spiritualists and esotericists, said there had never been a body of men like the Jesuits before to "design for world dominion with greater certainty of success, nor has the realization of such a great idea ever been thought out with such great sagacity."

Novalis, the champion of poetry and free spirit beyond all others, revered by some as the reincarnation of great personalities, and the spiritual poet in person, said of the Jesuits: "The society will furnish an eternal example to all others that feel within themselves the yearning to extend their sway and to endure forever."

In contrast, Thomas Jefferson, in a letter to John Adams in 1816 had said, "Like you, I disapprove of the restoration of the Jesuits, which seems to portend a backward step from light into darkness."

Although Ignatius of Loyola (1491–1556) had two conversion visions—one at the river Cardines in Marrera, and the other at La Storta—neither involved the Holy Ghost. In the first, God taught him personally; in the second, Jesus and the pope appeared. Loyola, in any case, was a mystic of action, not contemplation. The *Spiritual Exercises,* incidentally, prescribe four weeks of intense experience: the first week, sin and torments of Hell; the second week, whether to follow Satan or Jesus; third week, the imitation and visualization of Jesus Christ's life; and the fourth week, forethoughts of Resurrection and eternal reward. Jesus, not the Holy Ghost, is the model. As for spirit—taming "the haughty spirit" is the goal, and concomitantly, docility to the Holy Spirit. Instead of the Holy Ghost, the model for this is the Holy Father, the Pope. A Jesuit serves not the Holy Ghost but the Holy Father, under strict obedience to service in the world. In this mission, "discernment of spirits" is crucial; this faculty itself, however, may be a gift of the Holy Ghost.

Iñigo, as he was called (until changing his name at the Sorbonne in 1834), grew up on dancing, fencing, and riding. He was brought up early on charges of statutory rape, and a court at Pamplona described him as "treacherous, brutal, and vindictive." His older brother sailed with Columbus on the second voyage in 1493. Iñigo became a courtier and then moved on to knightly deeds in the military as an ensign. A shot from the French shattered his hip and a knee. He received extreme unction, but lived, although knighthood was no longer available to him. He limped thereafter. Idled, he read two books: *The Life of Christ* and a legend called *Flower of Sanctity*. Recovered, he boasted, "I can dance again."

Nevertheless, his reading—and noting that some passages uplifted him, while others left him void and desolate—led to his gift of "distinction of spirits." In Jesuitism, this came to mean that one presents oneself to the world not as oneself but in imitation of Jesus Christ, in service. Before the Black Madonna of Montserrat, he vowed to do just that. Giving away his doublet, tunic, and belt to a beggar, and leaving his sword and scabbard with his crutches in front of the Madonna, he became homeless. Then he "killed" his soul. The rest of the story is well known and leads to the institutes of order and to papal approval in 1540.

But in 1553, however, the Archbishop of Toledo, in critiquing the *Spiritual Exercises,* has this to say:

> As everyone knows, this Ignatius, or Iñigo, of Loyola was summoned before the Holy Office as a notorious heretic. As one of the Dejados, or Alumbrados, he preached a doctrine of complete detachment from the world by things ... guided by

> (as an Illuminist) his "inner light" rather than the teachings of the Church ... thus, it is well worth noting that this same Iñigo has fashioned these exercises of his more in accordance with the promptings of his heart and the inspiration of the Holy Spirit than from books.

The Dejados and Alumbrados, persecuted in Spain by the Inquisition, upheld only what the Holy Spirit said to them in their innermost hearts.

In Paris, Iñigo changed his name, turned his back on his own extreme ordeal of homelessness, asceticism, ecstasy, and otherworldliness to found an order devoted strictly to the world and service in the name of obedience. As to the Discernment of Spirits, in the *Spiritual Exercises,* the Good Spirit awakens conscience to a sense of remorse. The "good spirit" apparently replaces the Holy Ghost. Like the Holy Ghost, the Good Spirit gives courage, strength, consolation, tears, inspiration, and peace. Tears are sometimes the spirit of consolation. Desolation comes from the evil spirit, and one should, according to Loyola, not make changes in routine when desolate, because it is then the evil spirit counseling the change. Patience and sometimes prayer is the antidote to the evil spirit. The evil spirit deceives, then provokes and promotes disquiet and disturbance. Loyola discerns between a gentle, light, and sweet sense in the spirit and a sharp, noisy, disturbing one.

In any event, the year of the Armada, 1588, was a date to remember. After that, the secular powers begin to forget metaphysics. The Holy Ghost had, as it were, done its work. Left behind were signs of its mark: people and powers. God became, so to speak, an absentee landlord, and the British Empire took over. The Holy Ghost, it seems, retired.

The rest is intermittent variations on a theme, except perhaps for Blaise Pascal (1623–1662), the French philosopher. A mathematician himself, he knew the doctrines of chance and of infinity, and he was a mystic. Life was a wager. Pascal opted for belief and fought the echo of the skeptic Montaigne. But the Holy Ghost itself was a receding shadow. "I am because I believe." It was not enough. Frederick the

Great ascended the throne in Prussia, and rather than the soft comforter of any Holy Ghost, the great wave of the Enlightenment took over—human reason. The Church's better self, the Holy Ghost, was largely forgotten elsewhere.

Voltaire (1694–1778), for example, claimed that since history had recorded more than one thousand Messiahs, it was proof that there had been no Messiah. The delicacy of the matter of Spirit was lost on him, despite his sharpness. But the infamy of persecution and intolerance was not. The Holy Ghost was itself already *hors de combat*—out of the struggle. Voltaire and human reason was in. On his death, his body was rolled to the Parisian Pantheon and an inscription readied: "He made us ready to be free." That used to be the Holy Ghost's task. Perhaps the Holy Ghost retired for exactly that purpose—but carnage was the result.

Enter Moscow. Grand Prince Ivan III marries Zoë—a niece of the last Emperor of the East, brought up in Rome. She inspires the Prince. The Holy Ghost, about this time, seems to have undergone a sex change—at least outwardly. Those adepts who observed the esoteric secrets had always suspected the Ghost there was female—the sacred Sophia. But now it was public knowledge.

The Prince put two eagle heads on his coat of arms—one for Byzantium, one for Rome. It was 1472. More than five hundred years later the outcome was clear: the Soviets lost. The eagles—Siamese twins—were split, and after the fall of the wall (1989) Russia was left again with just one Eagle: the eagle of the East. But she had become a buzzard. The other Eagle reigned supreme in Washington, DC. Somewhere, the Holy Ghost may have been sitting in a divine cave watching it all.

The tide, anyway, had turned the other way: John Wesley in England and Alphonse de Liquori in Italy, for example, turned their faces from the Spirit to humanity and the heart. Wesley, the hard-bitten mouth of the North, and Liquori, the common hearted devotionalist of the South, turned their backs on the Enlightenment, the more to cultivate community. We touched on Wesley, founder of Methodism, but not his support of William Wilberforce. This man, somber and austere as Wesley, took England in 1789 to the Bar to outlaw slavery. Something of interest to the Holy Ghost. On his deathbed, Wesley wrote to Wilberforce: "Go on, in the name of God and the power of his might." He did not attribute this to the Ghost. And America did not hear. But Parliament passed the Abolitionist Act of 1807, sixty years before Lincoln died by an assassin's bullet.

In Italy, instead, the folk found a voice for their spirit in Liquori. Laying the path for a revitalization of Roman doctrine, the Vatican, stirred out of its high and low traditions, approved Liquori's worship of the hearts of Jesus and Mary. It also commemorated Liquori with doctrines of Infallibility and the Immaculate Conception. These little-understood dogmas were welcomed by the folk, and Liquori became a Saint, as would Padre Pio, of the same caste, later. Such figures may be the new peoples of the Holy Ghost.

In France, the Goddess of Reason replaced the Holy Ghost, and the Revolution was the result. The head, not the heart, was placed on the altar—and cut off. The French Revolution was a peak experience of the Interregnum of Reason, but, in the backwaters of tradition, a final late tribute to the Ghost was building. In 1897, on the cusp of the change from the clockwork universe to the twentieth-century battlefield for scientific physicalism and the New Age, Pope Leo XIII issued the great Papal Bull—almost universally ignored—*Illud Munus:* "On the Holy Ghost." Some saw it as an epitaph.

The Holy Ghost may have been listening to Hans Christian Anderson's fairytales in Denmark and trying to fathom the riddles of Søren Kierkegaard (1813–1855), concocted on the dunes of Jutland. He equated the Spirit with "the unconditional" and marked the futilities of Christianity and the futility of those opposed. In Germany, Nietzsche (1844–1900) pronounced the death of God in attempt to knock some spirit back into bourgeois Christianity. Perhaps the Holy Ghost had whispered the words, the slogan, "Liberty, Equality, Fraternity" two centuries before we got to a United Europe; but it had been in vain. More bloodshed and a death rattle, and the armies of oblivion in the twentieth century proved the killing fields. Scientism took sway, and we got materialism, consumerism, the car, plane, television, the big bombs, and space shots. The huge world of the former Holy Ghost, in an outwardly cosmic sense, began to shrink as missiles probed further and further into space.

It may be that, in the meanwhile since the days of Marx and the Salvation Army, that the Holy Ghost simply absented itself from High Culture to deal with vexing problems of the poor, labor, poverty, distribution of wealth, health, food, and mass education—and eventually housing, supply-side economics, and issues like abortion, AIDS, and popular culture. But there is no record of it, except for thought itself. The other infamous modern counter-image to the life of the Holy Ghost, in my mind, was Nazism in Germany. Some people thought Hitler, like a ventriloquist in falsetto, was actually speaking in tongues. Instead of a Messiah, however, Germany got the strange message that salvation lay in killing the Jew. The Holy Ghost, as it turned in its grave, was probably sorry it had ever gone north or dealt with Nordics. At Lambeth, England, it is true, a great Anglican Council had met and said, "It seemed good to the Holy Ghost and to us that we confess that we—the Church—have sinned." Pope John Paul II did as much, in a small way, in the 1990s. The afterword seemed too late for the dead.

The German martyr priest Dietrich Bonhoeffer (1906–1945) died opposing Hitler. He took a strong stance against mere soul life—after all, he had matured during the 1930s. The German soul, compelled by the march of "Du musst" ("you must"), with all the banners, beer, and *bonhomie,* was busy. Since the soul—that wonderful sausage of Middle Europe, squeezed between Pan-Slavic love and Western fears—had become a mechanized meal fanned by patriotic fanaticism, Bonhoeffer, perhaps understandably, thought of the soul as "self-centered" and "emotional." This led to his adopting a special interpretation of St. Paul's distinction between Psyche—soul—and Pneuma—spirit. Psyche, then manifesting herself in extreme forms, seemed to him, along with human meat (*fleisch* in German, *sarx* in Greek) was equated with the legacy of fallen nature: emotional, self-centered, and self-gratifying. Germans themselves often use the word *soul* to scorn and ridicule other people's inferior efficiency of feeling, or even the mere intellectual soul which they attributed to the French. But, for Bonhoeffer, the antidote was "spiritual" — which meant some effort at community, based on faith in Jesus Christ.

In 1825, spitting blood, Beethoven wrote a hymn of the invalid: "Doctor close the door to death / Music will also help in my hour of need." Although Beethoven does not go on record about the Holy Ghost, he seems to think of Spirit as music. Beethoven wrote "Ode to Joy" into the famous Ninth Symphony, and it has become the anthem of the new Europe — it could just as well have been written as the hymn of the Holy Ghost. It began as a revelry song in the spirit of the German *Trinklieder*, adopted Friedrich Schiller's words from a song, and then evolved into Beethoven's own words:

Joy, bright spark of divinity,
Daughter of Elysium,
Fire-inspired we tread
Thy sanctuary.
Thy magic power reunites
All that custom has divided,
All men become brothers
Under the sway of thy gentle wings.

This comes very close to addressing the Holy Spirit — for Beethoven a daughter, a gentle dove daughter of Elysium the highest, but a spirit drunk with fire. In the United States, the "Star-Spangled Banner" instead is a battle hymn. Although touched by images of light and stars, it has no words about divinity or the Spirit.

Beethoven's motto was "joy through suffering." Joy was his Holy Ghost — not the vapors of traditional Church. Beethoven saw spirit in the new democratic and republican trends of Europe and welcome national fervor. Socialism adopted Beethoven as a musical messiah unfurling the banner of brothers against "the lie of God" of the Catholic Church, a phrase of later socialist pamphleteer Georges Pioch. Beethoven didn't use the phrase, but he was deeply tinged with anticlericalism.

Beethoven can be thought of as a highly cultivated musical Pentecostal. He loved fervor and enthusiasm. But joy, Beethoven's Holy

Ghost, would not exactly be welcomed by all fundamentalists. For him, the spirit of music raised politics to an ethical level of religious metaphor in which joy becomes a vitalist celebration of "holy orgy" and even "demoniacal passion," according to Romain Rolland, the first major biographer of Beethoven. Rolland saw the melody of "Ode to Joy" as "a veritable God" and said that, at the end of the Ninth Symphony, "Joy descends from heaven wrapped in supernatural calm." Beethoven's was a war against sorrow, and Roland remarks, "Warlike joy is followed by religious ecstasy; then a holy orgy, a delirium of love. All of mankind, trembling, raises its arms to the skies, utters powerful cries and embraces." This sounds again like a Pentecost.

Bach dedicated only one work, a chorale, directly to the "Holy Ghost on Heaven's Throne," but, otherwise, musical literature on the Holy Spirit is scarce. There are some hymns a few centuries ago and, more recently in 1972, an obscure performance in London by a certain Kathleen Clegg of a work for words, music, and drama on the theme of the Holy Spirit. The Sistine Chapel and choir, and high Latin Mass, of course, sing the *Sanctus* (Holy).

Bach's chorale was for soprano, alto, tenor, and bass voices and is seldom sung. Bach's ideal was to get away from conventionally dead church music to a regulated church music for the glory of God. In his Bible, Bach annotated a passage from I Chronicles 25: "Moreover David and the captains of the host separated to the service of the sons ... who should prophesy with harps, with psalteries, and with cymbals." Prophecy is one of the realms of the Holy Ghost. Bach's note says, "This chapter is the true foundation of all church music pleasuring God." Another of Bach's marginalia states: "Marvelous proof that ... music was also especially ordered by the spirit of God through David." Spirit of God, as distinct from the Father God himself, is another name for the Holy Ghost. In church, for Bach, music faced the theologian with equal rights; it was worth as much as a sermon in delivering the Spirit. In his city of Leipzig, rights and functions were strictly meted out and jealously guarded. Church music had been statically regulated for ages. Bach didn't underline David's spirit of music just for the fun of it, though. Pietists and others frowned on music. The organist had to battle for every note.

Bach was fighting for a functionary role for the spirit of music in a strictly regulated and harsh world.

Both Bach and Beethoven were firmly convinced that, whatever else, the Spirit was listening.

## Chapter 23

# Testimony

Before moving on, let's visit a few painters, artists, and poets in helter-skelter fashion and see how the Holy Ghost did over the years in some of the arts. Because it is not always, or even so often, that the Spirit carries a gun, or a spear—unless we go back to the Romans and their ardor and bravery. But the Holy Ghost may wield a paintbrush or a baton.

Consider Leonardo da Vinci (b.1453), accused by chronicler Vasari of heresy and of obeying no religion. Leonardo had probably been the great turning point of the Renaissance, but he worshiped the human eyeball: "This is where human discourse turns toward contemplation of the divine." God was in the miraculous beauty of light. Priests were just rich clowns. The spirit was already at a remove: the *primo motore* or prime mover. In a profile that should say something to the later nineteenth-century rejecters of vitalism, Leonardo worshipped life. He found it in nature. Painting was the higher day of the visible world. A practical sort and a universal tinkerer, Leonard had not much room for theology, doctrine, or theories of quest. He looked. And he looked. Perception, not conception, was his trade.

When he painted *The Last Supper,* he copied—according to Goethe—the actual trestle table and utensils of the monks at the refectory of Santa Maria delle Grazie. The table depicted is not a "spiritual" table—not the Platonic model—but the virtual table of a virtual upper room of a real space of an actual dining room: the Upper Room. Theatrical perspective enhances the depth of vision, telescoping the table of the gospels into real time. The spatial perspective is a new feature of the Renaissance Spirit—a forerunner of the Enlightenment Spirit. Euclidian rules and ruler and compass projected Spirit into perception; mastery moved into the present and the spatial. The center of attention is not the mystery of the real presence of spirit, the Holy Ghost in the Eucharist, or the bread and wine, but the betrayal. The betrayer would be the one who dipped his hand in the dish—the Grail dish—with Jesus.

Painting was "silent poetry," for Leonardo. Celebrated in picture was not abstraction of doctrine, not a conception of dogma, but perceptible gesture and physiognomy detailed by Leonardo in, as it were, a theatrical director's notes. Before Leonardo, Judas was usually singled out by depriving him of a halo. Leonardo took the halo off everyone and identified Judas by his action. To Leonardo, the ermine symbolized purity—but virtue was persecuted and always suffered. Leonardo painted the picture in 1495—Columbus had discovered America three years before. It was apparently around this time that Leonardo first made the attempt physically—not just spiritually—to fly. His writings, despite moving from right to left like the invisible writing on the wall in the Bible, otherwise say nothing about the Holy Ghost. He dissected corpses, creation itself, life perceived, to get at the divine secrets of spirit.

Yet, not a hundred years later, back in Spain, St. Teresa of Avila (1515–1582), *Mater Spiritalium* (Mother Spirit) is still living. The Holy Ghost, it seems, moves by paradoxes. In Rome, there is a statue of St. Teresa of Avila, who was canonized in 1622, with the inscription *"Mater Spiritalium."* In her famous work, the *Interior Castle,* she had written, "I would rather show the soul is not the power of thinking ... seeing that the good of the soul does not consist in thinking much, but in its loving much." Her statue shows her in ecstasy, being penetrated by the Holy Ghost's arrow delivered by a cupid.

Her disciple, St. John of the Cross, wrote the Spiritual Canticle, *Obras Espirituales.* He equated interior detachment with "spiritual poverty," which consisted in "denying yourself of all you may possess." Abjuring "trifling joys and satisfactions of outward things" he urged advancing to spiritual joy which is to be found in spiritual detachment by means of "interior recollection." Images were "motives to invisible things" for him—painting included—but were relevant only insofar as they participated in "the living spirit" of that which they represented. John of the Cross reviled those who painted things "clumsily" and urged the authorities to prevent such persons from painting and sculpting "because of their gross unskillfulness." Their images, he said, quenched devotion. The night for him was the way to God—not amateurism.

In his life of St. John of the Cross, Father Bruno, John's barber, describes having seen *una paloma blanca*—a white dove—on leaving John's cell, and the barber understood that an angel had assumed this shape—or the Holy Ghost. Bernard of Jesus, a follower, also saw this dove—*muy Hermosa,* very beautiful—on the beam over the door of John's cell, a harbinger of peace and chaste affection. Father Bruno says the dove "made no sound, neither did it eat anything or go with any other doves." Thus it is strange that, in *Ascent of Mount Cannel,* John of the Cross writes, "True spirituality seeks for bitterness rather than sweetness in God, inclines to suffering more than to consolation, and to be in want of everything for God rather than to possess; to dryness and afflictions rather than to sweet communications." To seek oneself in God, he says, is the very opposite of love. To seek self in God is to seek only comfort and refreshment. Spirituality instead—if you can believe this—is to seek what is disagreeable. Yet, paradoxically, to carry the cross is to find "great refreshment and sweetness."

John of the Cross goes on to urge spiritual persons to abjure meditation, devotions, and sweetnesses in favor of denying themselves in earnest, inwardly and outwardly, to suffer, and to "annihilate themselves utterly." This, then, according to John, is the imitation of Christ—as distinct from devotion to the Holy Ghost. The result of this, strangely, was poetry of the Holy Ghost:

> My Beloved is the mountains,
> The solitary wooded valleys,
> The strange islands,
> The roaring torrents,
> The whisper of amarous gales;

The tranquil night
At the approach of dawn,
The silent music,
The murmuring solitude
The supper which revives, and unbounding love.

For both Teresa and John, the Holy Ghost—yet living—was some strange and terrible and sweet love. St. Teresa's ecstasy is sometimes pictured as a visitation of the Spirit. As such, it is called, in spiritual terminology the *transverberation* of the heart. Saint John of the Cross, whom Teresa mentored, speaks of this grace in *The Living Flames of Love:* "When the soul is enkindled by the love of God ... it will be conscious of an assault upon it made by a seraph (the highest spirit of the hierarchies) with an arrow or a dart completely enkindled by the fire of love, which will pierce the soul ... and will cauterize it in the most sublime manner ... the soul sees that it has become a vast fire of love ... few souls attain to this state as high as this, but some have done so, especially those whose virtues and spirituality was to be the succession of their children. For God bestows spiritual wealth and strength upon heads of houses, together with the first fruit of the Spirit."

Marjory Kempe and Lady Julian of Norwich earlier had had such experiences: Kempe said that the tears, sobs, outbursts, and dismay that gripped her were attributed to the Holy Spirit. She, however, tried to get Lady Julian to sanctify her outbursts as motions of the Holy Ghost, but Lady Julian remonstrated: "The Holy Ghost moveth n'ere a thing against charity." Nevertheless she blessed Marjory and sent her on her way "to rebuke others, to be a general nuisance, and to go on foolishly concerning herself with her Lord."

The worm turns, however, and by the eighteenth century, approaching the Enlightenment, the Great English genius of language and letters, Samuel Johnson (1709–1784), eschews emotions and ecstasy but still says, "I am so glad to have every evidence of the spiritual world, that I am willing to believe it." As to the "inner light" of Quakers, Dissenters, or some Methodists, Johnson said that it was "a principle utterly incompatible with social or civil security" and that "if a man pretends to a principle of action of which I know nothing, nay, not so much as that he has it ... how can I tell what that person may be prompted to do?"

By the time of an eighteenth-century man as human as Samuel Johnson — a bundle of infirmities lit by eminent reason, whose credo was more or less "the doom of man" — there is no trace of wrestling with the Holy Ghost in this giant of letters. Spirituality, if there is any, is in the heritage of Augustine, the sinner, for whom religion is largely just a subjective proof. Society, urbanity, civility, wit, scholarship, and intolerance of fools makes up "the Spirit" and is so highly cultivated in Johnson that he does not question religion itself, but tries to reconcile himself with church forms, community, and custom. He seeks God, but only because he is a civilized man, and the Church bears the tradition of civilization. He worries not about doctrine and the reality of spirit, but tries to embrace prayer, personal devotion, despite a rabid almost gloomy acceptance of the corruptness and "treachery of the human heart." Even the consolations of prayer, so much more satisfying to him than sermons and doctrine, can be specious because the interior man is so prone to insincerity, he believes, and fooling himself.

Spirituality, in sum, for Johnson, had to do with external ordinances, stated calls to worship, and the salutary influence of example. For Johnson it was not a question of "being in the spirit," but reconciling himself with Church and its established ways. To be of no church is a dangerous religion, according to him, though he could hardly contain his impatience at the inanities of much that he saw. Still, he deeply yearned for an experience of God. Perhaps the futility of British attenuated tastes and gestures of disdain in London's intellectual circles — "elegance refined into impatience" — prevented him from any other approach. Yet he saw through all this too, and said in the Vanity of Human Wishes, "Nor do I think the doom of man reversed for thee." A man whose very essence was the spirit of lively conversation, the Wit, could find no congeniality for spirituality, the Holy Spirit, or the Holy Ghost. He didn't deign to controvert, he was too smart for that. He seems in the end just not to have bothered. Wit and a sort of form was the all of Spirit for him.

On the other hand, John Bunyan, celebrated author of *Pilgrim's Progress,* one of the first novels, said only the Spirit can lift our soul in prayer, "Otherwise it rise not."

Jumping to an Emily Dickinson poem, "A Word Made Flesh ... is seldom," the Maid from Amherst also uses the word *spirit*—a word that has become abstract for her. Dickinson tried to reanimate the discourse of spirit by contact with primary sense. In her poem, the word *spirit* is revived through juxtaposition with the words *breathe* and *expire. Spirit* had already ceased to have living significance as a word and become "a sanctified cliché." Dickinson tried to associate it again with the sense of "breath, wind, air," as in "flow, move, or rush."

A Word that breathes distinctly
Has not the power to die
Cohesive with the Spirit

Another poet, Gerard Manley Hopkins, British, memorably invoked the Holy Ghost "with brooding wings."

We don't think of the poet Walt Whitman as praying to the Holy Ghost, but Whitman saw human action as tied to cosmic life—cosmic solidarity. "I leave all free, I charge you to leave all free." This was, early on, the credo of the Holy Ghost. His poetry is a testament to the unbridled freedom of the human spirit—and underscores the relation of Spirit to the agenda of freedom. His "poet of the cosmos" advanced toward "first principles" through "interpositions, coverings, turmoils, and stratagems." In Whitman, this spirit, arguably of the Holy Ghost as freedom, becomes American.

Goethe, the genius of Germany, on the other hand, had enshrined the Eternal Feminine in the place of the Holy Ghost as a guide to salvation and spirituality, which he associated with culture, while his friend the German dramatist Friedrich Schiller dedicated himself to the "Spirit of Play." Language was essentially itself the supreme work of art ultimately for Schiller—language is identical with "the ideal totality of spirit," or in German, Geist. *Heilige Geist,* cognate with English *gast* (breath), the basis of ghost: the Holy Spirit.

In passing it is worth giving a moment to visiting hymns over the centuries dedicated to the Holy Ghost, for the Psalmist invited the faithful "to sing to the Lord a new song." As the twentieth-century American Henry Sloane Coffin much later pointed out, "If young people grow up to despise what was given them in the house of God, either in words or in tunes, their respect is seriously enfeebled." There is no traditional hymn to the Holy Ghost to match "Onward Christian Soldiers," but surprisingly the *Pilgrim Hymnal*, a Protestant songbook compiled in Boston in 1931 from traditional sources, does include ten hymns to the Holy Spirit. These are worth examining, because nuggets of creed often get condensed into hymns—and also the songs capture the particular qualities and gifts of the object of devotion. Thus the Holy Ghost is equated with the truth, the spirit, love, and peace. These are, in fact, the preternatural character of the Holy Ghost, according to what theology there is. Take the Latin text of the ninth century (translated by John Cosin, 1594–1672):

Come, Holy Ghost, our souls inspire
And lighten with celestial fire;
Thou the anointing Spirit art
Who dost the sevenfold gifts impart.

The theme is inspiration—not God, Jesus, or salvation. The Holy Spirit is endowed with light and celestial fire. Reference is made to the Holy Ghost as anointer—a reference to the baptism in Jordan, when the dove descended and Jesus was selected as Messiah. The seven gifts are recalled. The Holy Spirit comes from "above" and is equated with comfort, life, and love.

Another hymn is, "Spirit of God, Descend Upon my Heart," by George Croly (1780–1860). Here the immanence of the Holy Ghost is stressed: it comes into humankind, into the heart:

I ask no dream, no prophet ecstasies
No sudden rending of the veil of clay
No angel visitant, no opening skies
But take the dimness of my soul away.

In the musty and sometimes stuffy pews of churches we tend to overlook the real vibrancy of this poetry.

The American poet John Greenleaf Whittier, an abolitionist and liberal, addressed the Holy Ghost this way:

Immortal love, forever full
Forever flowering free
Forever shared, forever full
A never ebbing sea!

Edwin Hatch (1835–1889) also catches the character of the Holy Ghost as a breath:

Breathe on me, Breath of God
Fill my life anew
That I may love what thou dost love
And do what thou wouldst do.

"Come Gracious Spirit, Heavenly Dove," by Simon Brown (1680–1732), stresses the descent from above: "Be our guide / O'er every thought and step preside," and "Plant holy fear in every heart / That we from thee may ne'er depart." Fear, remember, was one of the gifts of the Holy Spirit—viewed not as the anxiety and disorder of psychology, but as a natural virtue of the heart. Fear warns, guides, and awakens the heart to danger and reality. It is an organ of perception—a way to measure value and threat.

Samuel Longfellow (1819–1892), the brother of American poet Henry Wadsworth Longfellow, was a pastor at the first Unitarian Church in Brooklyn, New York; he wrote this:

Holy Spirit, Truth Divine
Dawn upon this soul of mine;
Word of God and inward light,
Wake my Spirit, clear my sight.

Holy Spirit, Love Divine,
Glow within this heart of mine;
Kindle every high desire
Perish self in thy pure fire.

Holy Spirit, Power divine,
Fill and nerve this will of mine;
By thee may I strongly live,
Bravely bear, and nobly strive.

Holy Spirit, Right divine,
King within my conscience reign;
Be my law, and I shall be
Firmly bound, forever free.

When we reach the twentieth century, it seems the Holy Ghost, in its traditional form, has pretty much receded from the everyday consciousness of the culture. We shall discuss this further in the closing chapter, but let us cite, for example, three personal witnesses from our time: Thomas Merton, Hans Küng, and Karol Wojtyla (Pope John Paul II).

Thomas Merton, the American Trappist monk, thought, "The most mysterious reality in the mystery of God is—the Hagia Sophia (Holy Wisdom)." He calls Hagia Sophia "God himself," but as a mother. In God it is "the feminine aspect or the feminine principle in the divinity that is the Hagia Sophia.... Hagia Sophia is the dark nameless *Ousia* (being) of the Father, the Son, and the Holy Ghost," or "the darkness that is infinite light." The three divine persons each manifest her, Sophia the wisdom of God, who reaches "from end to end mightily," as in the Tao, "the nameless pivot of all being and nature."

Merton says, "The beauty of all creation is a reflection of Sophia living and hidden in creation," and, "the darkness of wisdom becomes to us inexpressible light." He sees Sophia as "Lady Poverty," with whom St. Francis was married, and says of the desert father, "It was with her that they conversed all the time in their silence." Thus the Holy Spirit, for him, is the Spirit of Love.

Merton charges the Church in its work of salvation of souls with thinking almost exclusively of sacristies and chanceries, of power over souls—of control. The Church editorializes in the abstract about social justice, collaboration, and peace; but in the concrete, everybody who tries to do anything really serious "is blocked, silenced, and forbidden to act." He says "Behind all the Pentecostal wind one can hear, if he listens a little carefully, the hideous merriment of demons.... Each new move, each new spasm that goes through the Body of the Church makes us momentarily hope and imagine that we have not stifled the Holy Spirit: But then we discover, once again, or are in danger of discovering, that we really have lost it."

Merton claimed, "after centuries of Holy Roman empires," the sin of the Church is "in the concept of the absolute need for external control over souls in order to save them." He calls it a "hidden sin." He charged that the Church's compassion for human beings is tinged with "secret contempt" and that "we are pretty slow to attach any real importance to the fact that man may also be the temple of the Holy Spirit" or that, as Pope John XXIII had said, "we have to listen to the voice of history because it is the voice of God." Merton added, "The Holy Spirit is the Giver who, in giving all other gifts, is Himself given by the Father and the Son." The Holy Spirit needs "peace of heart" to do its work.

I met the theologian Hans Küng in the 1960s in Rome at the Ecumenical Council, Vatican II, when his book *Christ Sein* (*On Being a Christian*) came out. Küng was somewhat stocky, middle height, Germanic, with an earnestness in his frock, but also a look of authority. He had a blond complexion, a choleric touch, and a tousled look. He was in his early thirties, but already a name. No other young theologian at the Council carried his weight already. He was on the side of "the Liberals," and the American press quoted him as much as the European media. He was later short-listed by the Holy Office, though he held on to his professorship at the University of Tübingen, where he held the chair of dogmatic and ecumenical studies. He was also visiting professor at Chicago University, and the University of Michigan at Ann Arbor.

Later, I corresponded with Küng briefly about my novel, *God and a Girl,* and he took the Christian charity to respond. He belies assertions that a professor, an academic, a churchman cannot be a Christian. His book on Judaism was a signal ecumenical effort, and he supervised an action group interested in international peace and ecumenism. He is one of the great leading theologians of the late twentieth century.

On the Holy Ghost, Küng wrote: "The spirit of freedom then as the spirit of the future directs men forward; not to the hereafter of empty promises, but to the here and now of probation in the midst of ordinary secular life until the consummation of which the Spirit is the pledge."

I supposed I differ with Küng on the separateness of spirit and flesh, and in the degree to which the Holy Spirit is not a human faculty, a psychic attribute, or a constituent of thinking. Küng polarizes the "spirit" and "the flesh"; he is right insofar as spirit is an essence and a divine attribute. But I prefer to see spirit as in the Jewish tradition—integrating even with the flesh, or at least body, and the fleshly human accessing, despite worldly life, the spirit—in whatever way it will integrate—with the human. Maybe one can find epiphanies of the flesh, or body (as distinct from lower impulses), that are, on closer inspection, reflections of the spirit.

Küng also tends to emphasize more the dotrinal purity of "spirit" as something that human faculties do not achieve or agent, except by bestowal from above, by Grace, from the Holy Ghost. This is in line with traditional Catholic doctrine. Although, as a poet I profoundly respect that the Holy Spirit acts by visitation, bestowal, gifting, and "supernatural" inspiration, I am more Pelagian, seeing efforts of psyche, of thinking, of the heart's attitude as channeling spirit, even the Holy Spirit.

Pelagius (354–418), incidentally, was a non-ordained divine in fourth-century Rome. He preached freedom of will untainted by original sin, and that by one's own efforts a person could reunite with spiritual salvation. He opposed Augustine and was condemned at two African councils, and finally excommunicated by Pope Innocent I and his successor Pope Zosimus.

A footnote to the Holy Ghost's heritage came in the 1966 poem, "Easter Vigil," by Karol Wojtyla (Pope John II), a millennial celebration of the Polish nation. The third invocation here and his very last poem is to "Man who became the body of history." But secretly, the young bishop of Krakow was writing poetry under the name of Andrzej Jawien. Also, before becoming a priest, he had clandestinely performed in the Rhapsodic Theater, where the players performed "the word," not on stage but in a secret chamber accompanied by a piano. Jawien, his pseudonym, meant "coming to light." His secret poems were published in Polish periodicals, no one knowing that they were by the Bishop, once the youngest in the country.

I am convinced that Wojtyla, who would become Pope John Paul II in 1978, was secretly addressing a woman in his poem to the Holy Ghost, if not Hagia Sophia. Listen:

> I call you and I seek you, in whom man's history finds a body.
> I go towards you and do not say, "come," but simply "be."

Be where there is no record, yet where man was, was with his soul, his heart, desire, suffering and well consumed by feeling, burnt by most holy shame.

Be an eternal seismograph of the invisible but real.

> Oh, Man [read "woman"], in whom our lowest depths meet our heights
> For whom what is within is not dark burden but the heart.
> Man ["woman"] in whom each man can find his deep design,
> And the roots of his deeds: the mirror of life and death, staring at the human flux.
>
> Through the shallows of history I always reach you walking towards each heart, walking towards each thought
> (history—the overcrowding of thoughts, death of hearts).
> I seek your body for all history,
> I seek your depth.

A great love poem—worthy of Dante and Beatrice. But there is more. The woman was akin to the Holy Ghost. The young Bishop may even have yearned for her body. She was gone. The body was history. What greater line to the Holy Ghost could there be than this: "Be an eternal seismograph of the invisible but real?"

# Chapter 24

# Americanism

George Washington and Ben Franklin never seem to have gone on record concerning the Holy Ghost. In his farewell address in 1795, Washington urged Americans to imitate Christ's "charity, humility, and pacific temper of mind." It is one of the few presidential mentions of Christ in American history, but he did not invoke the Holy Ghost. Neither did Lincoln at Gettysburg, though the chaplain referred to "the spirit that gathers us together." This spirit often gets invoked in church services and sometimes at solemn occasions, but it has never been clear what spirit this is that is—the spirit of the occasion, the public or civic spirit, congenial and convivial spirit of fellowship, or the real Holy Spirit. Ben Franklin's prescription for America was, instead, to imitate Jesus and Socrates, but he is not on the record either concerning the Holy Ghost.

The only other President I remember mentioning Christ's name in public, other than Jimmy Carter, is George W. Bush in the 2000 campaign. He didn't mention the Holy Ghost or Spirit. Before the cameras and in debate, he was asked who the most important personage of history was, and after a pause he said, "Christ." I admired the answer personally, but a more politic person would have answered, "The Holy Ghost." The Holy Ghost has fewer public and private enemies than Christ does, partly because it has no face, usually stays out of politics, and is dismissed by many as not real anyway.

John Adams, whatever his views of the Ghost—which his biographer David McCullough doesn't record—once quipped as President that "whosever no longer believes in God should take opium." His view was that no truths are self-evident and that truth does not come from the Holy Ghost; it comes from the power structure. He believed not in Spirit, but in government.

For Thomas Jefferson, it was "under the law of nature" that all people are born free. Everyone comes into the world with "a right to his own person." One uses that right "at the power of his own will"—not at the will of a slaveholder; nor, for that matter, at the will of God—or the Holy Ghost—though Jefferson did not deny this. He called each individual's right "a personal liberty" and said it was given by "the Author of Nature." For pursuing this kind of speech, in 1770 Jefferson got gaveled off by the General Court in Virginia when he lost his case to a slave owner. It was the first time Jefferson had spoken the words in public: "All men are born free." In a general sense, the words were considered heretical.

Jefferson considered theologians the corrupters of religion. He suggested reading the Bible as one would the Roman historians Livy or Tacitus. In representing divorce cases, he invoked Mosaic Law, which permitted a husband to discard a wife almost at will. His 1773 note on divorce said, "No partnership can oblige continuance in contradiction to the end and design." This "end and design" was, for him, the "pursuit of happiness," the whole purpose of marriage. A union of hatred was cruel. He didn't attribute this spirit of happiness to the Holy Ghost; he took it from John Locke, the English rational philosopher.

Jefferson considered philosophical systems to be "prisms of the mind." Morals came from pragmatic philosophy, but he followed the advice of the French Encyclopedist Diderot, who said, "Everything must be examined, everything must be shaken up, without exception and without circumspection." He refused to be a godfather, because he "had never sense enough to comprehend the articles of Faith of the Church." He was a deist who believed in natural religion and morality. His patron saints were Bacon, Newton, and Locke. Yet he served as a member of the vestry and remained a nominal Anglican. As an old man he wrote a letter to Adams: "I can never join Calvin in addressing his God.... If ever man worshipped a false God, he did ... a demon of malignant spirit."

A reading of the Spirit of Laws by the French skeptic Montesquieu influenced Jefferson's thought more between 1774 and 1776 than even Locke. The Federalists attacked Jefferson as an enemy of Christianity, which was supposed to be at home on Wall Street with Hamilton or at the Treasury. Yet Jefferson read the Gospels. He underlined simple beliefs of Jesus Christ, but skipped what he thought were later interpolations as "usurpations." Out of it he got a "sublime" code of morals, which he printed in the forty-six-page pamphlet "The Philosophy of Jesus." Not much on the Trinity, however. Meanwhile, gossip and rumor accused him of sexual misconduct.

The Jefferson–Sally Hemings affair came out around the time that Jefferson had told Monroe that James Thomson Callender (the tabloid man who got the Sally Hemings story) "knows nothing of me which I am not willing to declare to the world." What he was willing to declare to the world was the 'Declaration of Independence.' Instead Callender wrote in the *Recorder* out of Richmond: "The African Venus is said to officiate at Monticello." Chief Justice John Marshall, a close ally of Alexander Hamilton, visited the offices of the *Recorder* on the first day the story of Sally broke. And so on....

Was the Holy Ghost invoked in any of this? Did the Holy Ghost generate the phrase, "Pursuit of Happiness"—or did Sally Hemings? I don't know. I'm just a journalist. I don't have sources that high. The record says that, when he was old and sitting in church, Jefferson heard the psalm that his mother Jane used to sing. I know enough journalism to be able to say that he cried—and it was probably the Holy Ghost brooding over Jane's spirit that moved him. More I cannot say. Never reveal your sources.

Jefferson had written an epitaph for Jane that, as a poet, I guarantee was inspired:

> Jane Jefferson
> Shy Jane, best of girls!
> Flower snatched away in bloom!
> May the earth weigh lightly on you!
> Farewell for a long, long time.

Jefferson was appointed in 1776 to the nineteen-member American Revolutionary Committee on Religion. Jefferson said that the committee and the fight over religious freedom was the severest battle of his life, and we know from the Bible and Jesus that the Holy Spirit believes in religious freedom—or at least acts that way. Jefferson then promoted separation of Church and State with a statement that religious freedom was a natural right. Now the horse was pulling the cart.

Religion was also a personal matter for Jefferson. "It does Religion no injury for my neighbor to say there are twenty gods, or no god. It neither picks my pocket nor breaks my leg," he wrote later, in 1784. The state should neither propose nor oppose. Jefferson led the legislative attack on "tyrannical spiritual laws"—things in Anglicanism for instance, that still stipulated death for heresy against doctrines of the Church of England, and imprisonment for denial of the Trinity or Scriptures.

The majority of men in the 1776 assembly were churchmen—and there was fear that Baptists and Methodists might stir up a slave revolt. Jefferson, writing of his life later, said, "Almost daily there were desperate contests" in the Revolutionary Religion Committee. Was the Holy Ghost struggling for another breath here, too, after fading out in Europe? There is not much other record—not much mention. There was a lot, though, about the salaries of rectors, tax levies. In his 1993 biography of Jefferson, Willard Sterne Randall said, "Jefferson's defense of the Bible-beating hillfolk against the rational Anglicans horrified some of his friends. They warned against immorality and enthusiastic bigotry, while Jefferson said, 'Reason and free inquiry are the only effectual agents against error.'"

He read the Hebrew texts, too, and the Koran. Jefferson had won. Madison wrote him in Paris: "In this country extinguished forever is the ambitious hope of making laws for the human mind." He meant church and state, for instance, and never for a moment thought that one day science—positivism, behaviorism, psychology, sociology, Darwinism, anthropology, and scientific physicalism would rule the roost and be busy trying to rewrite the natural laws—at least for humankind—telling people what is and what is not the correct way to think and act.

Jefferson thought it honorable to declare that human reason may be trusted with the formation of opinions. He did not foresee that reason, reinforced by a scientific establishment and technology, could also become an establishment and a labyrinth. But meanwhile, in 1777, he gave more than double what anyone else in St. Anne's Anglican Parish gave to the coffer. If religion is a personal matter for Jefferson, then maybe the Holy Ghost was as well. For him, it may have been, as in mystic lore and tradition, the Great Comforter.

On the whole, Freemasons (Jefferson was not a Freemason, but Washington was) are deists. They believe in a distant, impersonal God who is a builder of the Universe. Their traditional secret society is said to go back to Solomon's Temple. Atheists are not allowed membership. Napoleon, Goethe, and George Washington were members. The Vatican banned Freemasons for political reasons after the French Revolution and Garibaldi's *Risorgimento* in Italy. Although Freemasonry employs rites and secret symbolism, it carries no special brief on the Holy Ghost. Ben Franklin was also a freemason. He believed, as a Presbyterian, that the "Divine Essence" gives values. He believed in common sense, the Duty as Prime Mover, but then found Deism no longer useful. He believed in a guardian angel if not the Holy Ghost, prepared his own prayer book, and had an ethical belief that good actions were commendable because they might be useful.

Incidentally, Abraham Lincoln's famous phrase, "Of the people, by the people, for the people," has an antecedent in Augustine's work on the Trinity, in which he speaks of salvation: "Of Him, By Him, in Him" (De Trin., LVI, Ic10). The threefold theology here was power, wisdom, and love.

In setting the American agenda, Jonathan Edwards (1703–1758) looms huge, no matter how unsympathetic. He would end up his life as head of Princeton College, appointed by Richard Stockton (an ancestor of mine), and future signer of the Declaration of Independence. Edwards, a proponent of fervency in religion, believed that favored nations lead evolution, and that history reflects this—but that the secret work of the Holy Ghost in saving souls was more important. Thus he emphasized the pivotal role of prophetic scenarios triggered by periodic awakenings to the Holy Spirit. He witnessed such an awakening in the New England revival of 1734–1735 at Northampton, Massachusetts.

Largely suspect, the whole episode caused waves of concern throughout America. Edwards, perhaps the dupe of a huge joke in Northampton, saw the episode as witness to the legitimacy of "enthusiasm" in religion, and the American Pentecostal movement owes its theological origins to the Bostonian. It entailed not only mass conversions, but also suicides and Magdalene-like repentances. From it, Edwards justified his millennial predictions of an Age of Spirit, long before any talk of the New Age. Yale College, though on the much more conservative side of divinity questions, even named a college after this American Divine.

Later, in the nineteenth century, for Ralph Waldo Emerson, bondage of the spirit lay in error, laziness, fear, poor instruction, blind obedience, habitual conditions, vices, and temptations. Freedom from spiritual bondage came through awareness of mind, then knowledge of the human condition, and then, based on these, action in the world based on knowledge. Many spirits, according to him, were in deep prisons. He said that, in America, often-spiritual expressions were condemned as fantasy or ignorance. He refers, in the controversial Divinity School Address of 1838 to "the indwelling Supreme Spirit."

For Emerson, "living in the spirit" did not necessarily mean living religiously in any traditional sense. Indeed, he viewed religion as a materialistic embodiment of faith, partly because it viewed God's world as "other." Emerson considered the "subtle" world of spirit not dualistic but indwelling. Subtle laws of the spirit were Gnostic and to be learned moment by moment, esoterically, by living in revelations of the mind. "Of that ineffable presence, which we call Spirit, he that thinks most, will say least." Yet, he devoted six pages in *Nature* (1836) to the Spirit. He called it "that ineffable essence." Having harangued against religion for not dealing with spirit, he says, "Of that ineffable essence which we call Spirit, he that thinks most, will say least."

Nevertheless, he adds that Spirit is present to the human soul as "the totality of aspects, including wisdom, love, beauty, and power, the last of which he reviles against elsewhere.

The life force evident in nature and humanity is where spirit can be witnessed by the human mind in matter—though in *Self Reliance,* it has no name or face and is to be scoffed at in the Church when materialized. Again, the negative: we have shrunken to a drop of our former omniscience when humankind was once "permeated and dissolved by spirit." In order to revive, we are to listen to Emerson.

Intuition, which he also called instinct, was the way back or forward to a sense of spirit. One rule is held throughout nature—that of universal spirit, which applies also to thought. The spiritual act of a person is the subject (the I), observing the object (nature) from the viewpoint of thought (detached observer). In his essay, "Spiritual Laws," he speaks of "looking at ourselves in the light of thought" which reveals, outside the finite of suffering, beauty in the infinite like a "smiling repose." He saw mere magnetism, omens, spiritism, mesmerism, and such as very low levels of spirituality. "Why run after a ghost or a dream?" he asked. He denied the real presence in the Eucharist and, as a Unitarian, seems not to have bothered about the actual third person of the Trinity, the Holy Ghost, in whose place he put the universal spirit.

Americanism takes many forms, from the boat in Boston Harbor—the *Spirit of Boston*—to the Massachusetts license plate, "The Spirit of America," or the Portuguese Holy Ghost Society in Stonington, Connecticut, which celebrates the sixteenth-century feeding of the famine victims by Queen Isabella, and in August, celebrates an outdoor fête with "Holy Ghost" hot dogs. Sometimes it seems that Americans scarcely know the difference between the Holy Ghost and the Wizard of Oz. In Mexico, too, there is the Isla Espiritu Santo (Island of the Holy Spirit) off Baja, California. Back in the States, there is a Holy Spirit Association for the Unification of World Christianity, for example. And the Mormon revelation that founded a whole religious sect, with ten million believers, comes from John Smith and the tablets he received from an angel of revelation, not necessarily the Holy Ghost.

In 1879, Mary Baker Eddy, founder of Christian Science, believed herself divinely inspired. Christian Science promoted the ascendancy of the mind over matter. The mind, in Eddy's view, was the principle of spirit. The glossary of her famous book, *Science and Health*, describes spirit as "Divine substance; mind; divine Principle." Spirit is opposed to "spirits," which are mortal beliefs, evil minds, errors, and hallucinations. For her, the Holy Ghost is the "Divine Science—the development of eternal life, Truth, and love." She equated the "I," or ego, with the Divine Principle and Spirit. This ego, being mental, could bring health to the material. As to the difference between soul and spirit, "Identity is the reflection of spirit," she wrote. "Soul is the substance of life ... soul can never reflect anything inferior to Spirit." That is, through the soul—unlike Spirit—things are individualized, which is not the case in matter. God is a reflection of Spirit; humankind is the reflection of soul. Christian Science is thought spiritual in the sense that it doesn't believe in germs, molecules, or sickness; illness is an illusion, the *soma*, or body, is sort of a fiction, and the mind has power over these things.

The actual term *Americanism* arose in the nineteenth century over a controversy between the Vatican and Isaac Hecker, the American who founded the Paulist Fathers. Hecker argues—on the basis of the Holy Spirit in the early Church—that America and Catholicism were inherently compatible. The equal right of citizenship is a secular expression, for him, of the "indwelling of the spirit," which Jesus taught was available to all. In Judaism originally, according to Hecker, when the Book more or less replaced the Temple, Jews worked the texts, gathered, conversed, and debated. Jesus joined with some of these, and an assumption—essentially a democratic assumption—was used that all could bring or achieve wisdom, insight, maturity, and holiness to pursue truth. Hecker picked up this view to say that the Holy Spirit is language for this view. His view was that such a Holy Spirit is not a narrowly defined "objective truth," but something "living in all," yet for all "shrouded in mystery." He argued that American equality of citizen rights was a secular expression of this religious acceptance of "the indwelling of the Spirit."

At the end of the nineteenth century, Pope Leo XIII—who also propounded "tolerance" as the Christian way (rather than actual religious liberty)—nevertheless denounced the Paulist conception as the heresy of "Americanism," on grounds that the Church defended objective truth from the inroads of personal license or "certain liberties" that would undermine the exercise and vigilance of the Church powers. Leo was against a view that would allow "each one of the faithful to act more freely in pursuance of his own natural bent and capacity."

Commentators who deal with this controversy in American circles reject truth as any kind of objectivity—or for that matter, the domain of the Holy Ghost—saying, as we hear so often, that human beings see truth only in partial ways and "in a mirror dimly." Of course, this is precisely why the Church tries—when it is not swayed by mere politics—to defend the Truth. According to the Church—and others—this is precisely what Jesus, Paul, and John offered in the first place: the true Spirit. According to the American commentators who reject an objective view of truth in favor of relativism, the Holy Spirit is not the Truth but a "mutuality." Mutuality means bringing one's own experience and thoughts to a place where the community discusses and converses, offers and accepts criticism, and honors the positions of others—even leading to self-respect in this creative mutuality. All sense of renouncing one's own opinions in favor of a greater or higher truth is gone in Americanism. The Spirit does not blow where it will; it blows everywhere. There is no need to replace the "me" with the "I" or cultivate special or divine knowledge or to respect Revelation. Equal time at the mike is the theology. Even the "pursuit of happiness" is merely the pursuance of one's own natural bent and capacity—not education or stoic virtue or any other ideal, philosophy, or truth.

According to the Vatican, freedom becomes confused with license and truth itself—and the political extension becomes religious liberty, a civil right, worthy in its own right, but used by various forces of political correction to blindside any other discussion, theological or otherwise, of truth itself—or, for that matter, of beauty. Standards, in other words, go by the board and go to hell.

Some of the commentators, then, have the wit to see that Americanism means any view of the Holy Ghost or of any absolute truth—even as revealed by Jesus, John, or Paul—as not being of the highest value. Pluralism, as in mutuality, replaces truth, the Holy Spirit, and the argument shifts, at best, to love. "Not knowing but loving," becomes the slogan. But the Vatican thinks you end up with drugs and Woodstock this way. The New Age ends up with statements like, "The ultimate meaning of existence, as love, is a classic affirmation of what one might call the pluralistic principle." But according to some, this, without standards, is a big mess. I have heard it said in American circles, "God is the first pluralist," and that religious pluralism begins with this acknowledgement of the universal impossibility of direct or truthful knowledge of God. This is, come to think of it, a far cry from monotheism and one God. Nor, would it seem, is there much left to discuss in "creative mutuality" or in the Church community for, when everybody is right, and nobody wrong, nothing means anything and everything is unknowable. The common good exists, maybe, but that seems to be in the social and legal province, and since there is no truth anyway, as Pilate implied, we are warned by these commentators to find love—yet love becomes "cheap talk of love," and a journalist suspects that the Holy Ghost may have found all this to be an American puzzle.

But Leo XIII at the end of the nineteenth century condemned this view as the "Americanism" heresy. Hecker came under fire. Meanwhile, serious—and I mean *serious*—American theologians also went to work, and my apologies for the abstruseness here. Paul Tillich (1886–1965) became arguably the leading Protestant theologian of the mid-twentieth century at the Union Theological Seminary in New York, having served as chaplain with the Kaiser's army in 1924, but getting out of Germany when the Nazis came to power in 1933. In *Dynamics of Faith*, Tillich asserts that emotion involves a personality in an act of life or "spirit," while intellect "involves it in truth," and the will "involves it in commitment." Together, these constitute faith. Faith is the achievement—"definite in direction and concrete in content," whatever that might refer to—of religion. Religion at its core. Tillich quotes the great Friedrich Ernst Daniel

Schleiermacher (1768–1834) (father of modern Protestant theology), who described religion, at its core, as "the feeling of unconditional dependence"—though this would be considered pathology in modern day psychology.

As a journalist, I can certainly understand a feeling of dependence, but Tillich also equates a sense of dependence with a sense of ultimate concern. This he meant as an antidote to faith as the belief in things without evidence. It was an existentialist view. He makes a distinction between "vital ecstasy" and "spiritual ecstasy"—but says, oddly, that both involve the body: one by fulfillment, the other by rejection. Body, soul, and "spirit" are not three parts but "dimensions" of a oneness. In this kind of theology, the Holy Ghost doesn't have much of a personality. Tillich was very wary of any kind of idolatry, and nowhere in his book *Dynamics of Faith* does he credit or mention the Holy Ghost for anything. How, then, to judge "truth?" Scientifically? Historically? Philosophically? No. By reference to Christ, Jesus, St. Paul, or St. John? No. Truth is measured subjectively by "ultimate concern" and objectively "if its content is really ultimate." Ultimate concern gets its test in symbols, faith, and responses to "the holy"—with *holy* defined as the divine, and the divine is defined as "the content of ultimate concern." A merry-go-round, viz., but no ghost. After all, he was a Protestant. Ultimacy, furthermore, is itself the judge of ultimate concern, but it is simple: yes or no. Still no Holy Ghost. From Berlin to Tübingen, Halle to the trenches, in Marburg, Dresden, and Frankfurt, and then New York, Harvard, and Chicago—he taught in them all—students were cracking on this.

Reinhold Niebuhr (1892–1971)—who helped Tillich get started in this country, and whose name belies his thoroughly American pedigree from Wright City, Missouri—studied at Eden Theological Seminary, but even with his evangelical background, he jumped to Yale Divinity School. He became a pastor in Detroit, where he got an eyeful of capitalism, and turned socialist. He deals no more with the Holy Ghost than did Tillich, becoming much more interested in the persistence of evil in human nature and, particularly, in social institutions. He was also at Union Theological Seminary, where he got Tillich in.

At Harvard, Tillich barely missed George Ruiz de Santayana (1863–1952), a Spanish specialist in a sort of physicalized spirit. Santayana, who had served with William James, managed to write a whole book on spirit without ever mentioning the Holy Ghost. He got involved with animal faith and seems to have reduced spirit to his theory of immediately apprehended essences. As a journalist, it seems to me from his book that he had a mercurial approach, with a touch of the bullfighter. His book was *The Realm of Spirit* (1940), which he prefaced by saying, "The title of this book may tempt some unwary reader with the hope of tidings from the spirit world. Such is not my subject." A materialist, he said spirit sprang from "natural ground." However, he added, "A study of the realm of spirit is therefore an exercise in self-knowledge, and effort on the part of spirit to clarify and discipline itself."

But for a clearer message let us turn to Louis Cassels, a hardened newsman. Although we never talked of spirit at the Ecumenical Council in Rome, UPI's chief religion correspondent, who was there at the first session (the Council went on four years), later, in 1971, wrote his book on the reality of God, in which he gave a few paragraphs to the spirit. This hardened newsman raised the question of "how God acts within us." A tough question. Pointing to "a mystifying but unmistakably real presence of power," he wrote that people have given a wide variety of names to this power: Spirit of God; Spirit of Christ; Spirit of Truth; Holy Spirit; Holy Ghost. Also Holy Comforter; Indwelling God; and Inner Light.

Lou wrote that the reality, not the name, matters. I don't want to argue with him posthumously, but I would qualify this: Names, as spiritual realities, are important. "I shall refer to this Presence simply as the Spirit," he said. He warned against conceiving the Spirit in an anthropological image or limiting it spatially or temporally. "Spirit cannot be imprisoned in institutions or manipulated by rites," he wrote—himself a deacon. He argued that the Church had sometimes behaved as if she had a monopoly control of Spirit. "The power of the Spirit as a motivating force for good is manifested sometimes more dramatically in movements and events that are not specifically religious than within the institutional life of the

Church." Nevertheless, he added, "The Spirit has a special relationship to the Church.

His column was carried in more than five hundred newspapers in the 1960s and 1970s, and he complained that the Church had fallen into a great irony by stressing relevance to modern humanity's secular interest at the expense of its agenda of mediating another supernatural world.

The "power of the Spirit" was again at issue. This again was the direct manifestation of spirit that had happened originally at Pentecost. Cassels pointed out that American Pentecostalists, once known as Holy Rollers, had remained attached to "the power of the Spirit."

Cassels converted from his Southern Baptist tradition to his wife's Episcopalianism, but said of the Pentecostals: "So in spite of my own inability, as a longtime, card-carrying Episcopalian, to enter fully into the joyous informality and spontaneity of Pentecostal worship, I greatly admire this movement." He personally regretted their one-sided emphasis on speaking in tongues, or ecstatic utterance, hoping that they would remember that this was only one gift of the Spirit, and that—as St. Paul had pointed out—speaking in tongues was more likely to confuse or put off inquirers than to edify them.

Nevertheless, Cassels admitted that the Christian Church was created by "the power of the Spirit," saying, "Who knows? It may yet be revived, renewed, and saved from its own folly by that same power."

Jimmy Carter, former American President, a born-again Christian, and, with his wife Rosalynn, head of the Carter Center in Atlanta, speaks of various ways of reaching out to others. One path is contemplation; others are avoidance of sin, or virtuous living and seeking "to be filled with the Holy Spirit." Carter said that his sister Ruth had experiences of this last kind, an intense and powerfully emotional spiritual life. Carter himself chose service to the needy as his expression of Christian life, and is wary of those who delegate responsibility to God or the Holy Spirit. He shook more hands as a politician than as a Christian, he admits, but says, "Although my activities as a Christian witness have been relatively modest, they have given me both experiences of the power of the Holy Spirit that have shaped my life as a Christian and memories I'll never forget."

For the first man into space, astronaut John Glenn, the spirit of Zen was too deep; Zen is for the Japanese. Instead, Glenn, at the battle of Midway in 1944, was "just part of the plane, not separate—as if you are the brain and it is the body." "Bombing runs into antiaircraft fire were a test of skill, severe reparation, and focus, that I relished." Nothing gave him more pleasure.

Under President Kennedy, the Russian Cosmonaut Gherman Titov (1935–2000) and Glenn visited the White House together, after which they attended a Space Symposium in Washington. Afterward, at a press conference, Titov told the Western press: "I went into space and didn't see God, so that must mean God does not exist."

"Did you see God in space, Colonel Glenn?" the questioner asked.

"The God I believe in isn't so small that I thought I would run into Him just a little above the atmosphere."

Glenn never, however, prayed to the Holy Ghost. He never prayed to be saved—even from death. "I prayed for guidance not deliverance," he later wrote. His prayers were not "in the spirit," merely to God. A convinced churchman, his memoirs never mention the Holy Ghost or Holy Spirit. His favorite hymn, however, was, "Be still, My Soul," by Jean Sibelius.

Taking a contemporary American literary sage like John Updike, who writes of "more matter," the spirit is for him tantamount to "a supernatural exponent: a momentary cup of positivity in the flow of electrons, the integral 'I' that no longer exists now in contemporary fiction, let alone forever." Though he confounds spirituality pretty much with religion, he sees artistic and spiritual excellence as both invisible to contemporary eyes and equates art with religion in not being measurable by worldly terms. Interestingly, he equates fiction with acts of faith and says that the writer's asset is often not wisdom or skill but "an irrational, often joyous sense of importance attaching to what little he knows," so much so that it is almost a religious sensation.

President George Bush, the younger, recently appealed to "higher authority" in public life and in 2000 said that the most important historical figure of all time is Christ—but there is never any mention of the Holy Ghost or spirituality. Jesus, the faith, and the Church are the bottom line—the born-again Jesus factor, which, according to *Sojourners Magazine,* is a self-styled twelve-step program that helped him stop drinking and focus on a political career. Divine mission is seen not as a universal Holy Spirit, but rather as "American exceptionalism" and the "language of righteous empire."

After the passage of the faith-based social initiatives in recent legislation, I queried my cousin, an Anglican minister, on them. When they came in, or were proposed, I thought they might interest the old Holy Ghost. Though never quite destitute, I have been on the streets and elsewhere, and I thought this support might be a good thing. I did not know if it would of any interest to the Holy Ghost, although sometimes on the street even the pigeons look like doves, and any help seems supernatural. On the other hand, faith is not always the same as spirit. Nothing in Washington indicated that this program would be "spirit-based." Anyway, my cousin, himself of the faith, was dubious about the support and the program. "I think it's dangerous," he said, out of concern for the separation of church and state, which the Holy Ghost, ever since the time of Montesquieu, seems to support.

American spirituality is often fundamentalist and confrontational. The dispute over body and soul, mind and matter, goes on in low culture, too, as well as high, but very often the American secular attitude in both quarters is dismissive, disrespectful, and licentious. And humorous. As an American bumper sticker recently read: "Your body may be a temple. Mine is an amusement park."

Yet in the National Cathedral in Washington, a cathedral that preserves but also departs from tradition —at the center of this great American Church—a giant cross stands on the floor before the altar. In the bottom foot of the cross is embedded the dove, symbol of the Holy Ghost. That cross, with this symbol in the foot—not the head—signifies the descent of the dove, which is unique in the world. At the recent state funeral for Ronald Reagan, the dead President's coffin rested squarely on the sign of the Holy Ghost.

## Chapter 25

# The Vatican

At St. Peter's, splashed over the apse of the giant basilica, is a gigantic Bernini golden sunburst with a large white dove descending over an empty, resplendent golden throne—the symbolic throne of St. Peter's chair of the doctrine, dogma, teaching, and infallible Truth in matters of Faith and Morals.

"Infallibility," a dogma promulgated in 1870 when the Vatican was under siege in Italy, is much misunderstood. First, it covers not truth in all matters—just matters of faith and morals. Second, it means that only in such matters will the Church be without error. Third, therefore it does not mean that the Church is always right or comprehensive in all ways in such a statement, but only that a position pronounced *ex cathedra,* from the throne, will never in itself be incorrect. The embodiment of this is the throne and descending dove, symbol of the Holy Ghost, inspiring the teaching power of the Church. The Vatican, moreover, is named after the *mons,* or *collis* (a hill), in Rome that was called in Latin the *Vaticanus.* Apparently, the name stemmed from the same word as *Vates,* an old usage for poet or bard—one who is divinely inspired, a prophet poet. In ancient Rome, the *mons Vaticanus* was the site of the *vaticinators,* or soothsayers, augurs, and omen readers.

The name may also have to do with the ancient pot gods, from the word *vat,* the same as in the word *fat,* vats having been used to store fats and oil as well as ferment liquors—spirits. Pot gods were worshipped in the ancient East. The proto-German was *fatan* from Indo-European for vat or pot: *pod.* The Vates were also a class of old Gaul druids. *Vatincinare* in Latin meant to prophecy and foretell events. In India, *Vata* was the wind, and in Latin mythology Yatici made babies utter their first cry.

The concept of Holy Spirit is also important in the history of Church Councils, as we have seen, which in fact derive their authority from the Holy Spirit. Originally, the tradition itself is also the source of the doctrine of infallibility—that a Council was infallible. Christ is supposed to have promised the Church, through the disciples, assistance of the Holy Spirit in matters beyond the reach of human investigation—an esoteric tradition. Thus a Council could be wrong about matters of fact, but not about matters of faith and morals. Since different parties vie for dominance at Councils, this is a version of St. Cyprian's assertion that, even if some parties to a Council have departed from the faith, "the infallible rule is that the majority always persists in the faith and in the truth of the law."

The famed covenant of God with Moses did not, according to St. Paul, guarantee that the spirit of regeneration" would be with the Jews until the bitter end, and this was why Jesus had to renew the covenant as predicted by Jeremiah. This new spirit of the covenant had greater "amplitude" and was applicable to all the nations, not just the Jews. Vatican I, the 1870 council dealing with Faith and Reason, issued a decree on the *Dogmatic Constitution of the Catholic Faith,* which asserts that the tradition from the Apostles makes progress in the Church with the help of the Holy Spirit. In other words, the Spirit keeps acting on and through the Tradition.

Therefore, Vatican II, dealing with *Divine Revelation,* said that there is "a growth in insight into the realities and words that are being passed on." In other words, there is evolution of doctrine. This happens three ways: 1) through the contemplation and study of believers who ponder these things in their heart; 2) from the intimate sense of spiritual realities that they experience; 3) from preaching output coming from "the charism of truth." Thus God continues to converse, and the Holy Spirit leads believers to the full truth. The Holy Spirit also transmits by tradition informed by the Spirit of Truth. A further decree at Vatican II, *On the Renewal of Religious Life,* claimed that one of the charisms of the Holy Spirit was the gift of the religious life itself—religious orders. *A Dogmatic Constitution on the Church* further asserted that the Council itself was gathered together in the Holy Spirit. Pentecost, it claimed, sent the spirit so that "he might continually sanctify the Church. The spirit dwells in the Church and in the hearts of the faithful as in a temple." Missionary activity was declared to be the Holy Spirit "exercising inwardly his saving influence."

I have heard it said that the higher the church and the more powerful the institution, the less likely it is to recognize much of the spirit—or the Holy Spirit. The saying goes that the more organized the religion, the less room it leaves for the spirit. This is not entirely fair, although it applies to some aspects and historical periods of both Anglican and Catholic history. The Gnostics, the Pelagians, the Arians, the Monophysites, the Cathars, the Templars, the Albigensians, as well as Quakers and some Puritans and Pentecostals, would all probably testify to this, though other issues of truth, doctrine, and politics were also at stake.

More widely than is thought, at least outside the Church, Catholicism—though it has not developed much theology of the spirit as far as it has other aspects of its life—has heavily recognized the role of the institutionalized Holy Spirit in the Church, in practical life, and as a source of its religious life. This is true of their position on scripture, on baptism, on the role in the Eucharist, in the life of the Blessed Virgin Mary, and in the practical life of the Church and the faithful. True, in St. Peter's in Rome, the throne of Peter—the Pope's throne—is the center of attention in the apse of the basilica. This represents doctrine and dogma: the Holy See. But the throne is also overwhelmed and flooded by the baroque rays of the Holy Ghost coming from the emblematic dove above it. Moreover, Vatican II, in accord with true Catholic tradition, reasserted that the Holy Spirit has also been operative *outside* the Church in other times and other traditions.

At the Ecumenical Council—sometimes referred to as the second Pentecost—the Primate of Australia, Cardinal Gilroy, then Archbishop of Sydney, gave me an interview. He eyed me carefully, then he carefully said, "The trouble with you journalists is that you don't want just the facts; you want the story." He sort of smiled. But in my mind the Holy Ghost is less of a fact, more of a story.

Today, of course, Gilroy is dead, but I would like to ask him: "Your Excellence, does the Holy Ghost deal in facts?" I think he might smile again. One Methodist observer at the Council that I interviewed did not understand Latin, the language of the Council. He had a paperback in his pocket that he took out during the secret sessions in St. Peter's Basilica. "If you don't mind my asking, what are you reading," I said. He fished the volume out. It was a lurid detective story, featuring a priest in a Roman story—a whodunit. There was also a shadow cleric at the Vatican II Council. He reported from inside the Vatican and divulged some of the secrets of the dark corridors. His pronouncements carried some weight, because it was sometimes associated with famous hidden prophecies about the papacy. Some people at the time confused him with Xavier Rynn, the pseudonym of a source that wrote the Council up from the inside for the *New Yorker* magazine.

Malachi Martin—a former Jesuit and a professor close to the Jewish Augustine Cardinal Bea (1881–1968)—wrote the decree on the Jews and on Christian Unity. Martin judged the Church at the time (the 1960s) to be finished, spent, and without moorings, a religion "replaced, ousted, and drained, in a word, moribund." Catholicism, through the Council, and through the Polish Pope John Paul, made a terrific comeback, enjoying unprecedented power and publicity at the beginning of the twenty-first century; but now, this shadow insider let it be known, ironically, dubiously, and to the astonishment of those who heard him, that toward his death in 1963, the original Pope John XXIII had "succeeded." That is, in the bitter words of Martin, "Everyone was dressed up, at his bidding, but lamentably they had nowhere to go. John awaited the outpouring. There was none. He hoped for a new birth of the spirit. Nothing was born." "The era of compassion" was over, this former priest said. My own view, for what it is worth, is not so dire. The council opened the windows of the Church and, although it then retrenched over the next twenty years, a new impulse nevertheless entered.

Martin lampooned the "Pentecostal dream" of Pope Angelo Roncalli's council for religious renewal as a great buffoon congress of "babbling participants, wild emotions, and unknown languages," with "venerable cardinals screaming, eyes shut, at running patriarchs, careening bishops and jigging monsignors, an orgy of 'spirit' clad in the hubbub, the brouhaha of clerics caught in a Midsummer Night's frenzy."

Witnessing the Council, this insider reported that the Holy Office at the Vatican considered the whole thing to be "*La Commedia*"—the comedy—and that "Sometimes a dumb horror seized those trying to interpret Roncalli's feeble efforts to make himself understood." The council, conceived of by Roncalli as a renewal of the spirit, came from this pope's inspiring belief in "the Spirit as a really existent force, personal, all-powerful, divine, and the truth." But the Council, critics claimed, was turned by his Church enemies—who neither shared Roncalli's vision or the appraisal of reality that the peasant Pope had made—into "a fantastic ecclesiastical amusement park littered with the debris of paper resolutions."

"Cackling piously of God's will," Martin went on in his appraisal of the biggest religious event of the Church's two-thousand-year history, John's religious enemies—despite later putting him up for Sainthood—turned his "forum for renewal" of spirit into a "Ferris wheel of ecumenism, that became fascinated with their own actions and mistook bureaucratization for progress." This vicious critique of the Council and clericalism is not fair, though it is based on objection to the bureaucratization of spiritual life. Pope John's impulse was more honest than that, and he actually hoped for an open window on the spirit to refresh and renew the Church. I think we should honor that and not just caricature the clergy.

But reporting further, this outstanding former cleric and erstwhile professor, high up in the great bastion of the Pontifical Institute Rome, predicted the end of the Roman Catholic and Apostolic Church by the year 2000. *The New York Review of Books* hailed Martin's critique as a "landmark of religious writing," but today the latest Pope has proven the Faith otherwise and reigned as long as any other. And despite Parkinson's disease, he has traveled farther and has been seen by more people than any other man alive. In the United States today, the religion and the Catholicism that was once beleaguered, reviled, and nearly outlawed in 1776, has become one of the most powerful, visible, and feared institutions of the country, curried for favors by politicians and given preeminence by the police and the press, if not by the Holy Ghost.

The Holy Ghost has also been at the Vatican and into banking in a big way at least since 1605. The Bank of the Holy Spirit (Banco di Santo Spirito) was founded by Pope Paul V in 1605. It has managed private deposits and loans to patrician families as well as some public debt, provided capital for churches and hospitals, and dealt commercially. In 1785 it played a prominent role in the introduction of paper currency into Italy, but became a shareholder bank in 1923.

After settling with the Italian State in 1929 (The Lateran Treaty), the Vatican was handsomely paid off. It then appointed Bernardino Nogara to handle Church funds. He was the brother of a monsignor close to Pope Pius XI. Nogara, who had financial experience in Turkey, revolutionized Church finances by divesting investment from any religious or doctrinal consideration and by going global. Would that be what the Holy Ghost would do with money? The ancient Church doctrine against usury went by the boards, and the Vatican moved into armaments productions, munitions, and chemicals—even contraceptives—and gold, some of which was still on deposit as late as 1985 in Fort Knox for the Vatican. Practice was not exactly where the mouth was for the Vatican. In the 1930s, it was Nogara who bought back for the Vatican the ancient Banco di Santo Spirito—the Bank of the Holy Ghost—which, under Mussolini, had been taken over by the IRI, an Italian state industrial redevelopment authority. Later, there were mergers over the years, and finally the Bank of the Holy Spirit merged with the Bank of Rome in 1992. As of 2001, the bank's disclosed assets were ninety-five billion dollars. Though the Bank of the Holy Ghost was a Church bank for three centuries, it is not the Vatican bank today, though it is closely allied. The Vatican bank today is an entity called the Institute for Religious Works, founded by Pope Leo XIII in 1887.

Leo XIII is the Pope who promulgated the only papal decree or Bull dedicated solely to the doctrine of the Holy Ghost—May 9, 1897—and the only document of its kind in the history of the Church. The title in Latin was *Divinum Illud Munus*—literally, "Of That Divine Gift." Leo XIII, before the days of the rights of religious liberty at the Vatican, supported tolerance of religious beliefs. When *Divinum Illud Munus* was released, he was close to dying. It is the only major papal pronouncement on the Holy Spirit in two millennia of history. The document is not remarkable or sensational. In fifteen very long paragraphs, it details stored scriptural and traditional wisdom of the Holy Ghost, quoting from Scripture, St. Basil (Of the Holy Ghost), Augustine, St. Cyril, and St. Thomas Aquinas.

It is a conservative document and does not mention, for example, speaking in tongues. Its opening paragraph speaks of the Holy Ghost's work as unfinished, and quotes John about Christ's warning: "If I go not away, the Comforter will not come unto you" (John 16:7). The Bull describes the Holy Ghost as intercessor, consoler, and teacher, "the indwelling and miraculous" and "the life-giving love." It warns against worship of the Holy Ghost—which has never arisen in cult fashion anyway, perhaps because the Holy Ghost has no face. It claims that the Holy Spirit is "the soul" of the Church, but says that the action of the Holy Ghost in individuals is "more difficult to understand," because such action is invisible. Before Christ, the Ghost lived in "the just"—Zachary, John the Baptist, Simeon, and others. After Pentecost, the Spirit becomes more abundant. Among the gifts of the Holy Ghost, Leo refers to "those secret warnings and invitations" that excite minds and hearts. These warnings and admonitions that come "in secret manner" are "aptly compared in Holy Writ to the breathing of coming breezes. Leo compares them to the movement of the heart wholly hidden in the living body. He says we owe homage of love and devotion to the Holy Ghost, but not worship, and he warns against "difficult and subtle controversies" of those whose dangerous folly rashly endeavors to pry into the divine mysteries."

The sin against the Holy Ghost is equated with malice. Leo quotes the second letter to the Thessalonians: "God shall send them strong delusion, that they should believe a lie" (2:11). And he says the "time has come" when sin against the Holy Ghost is getting more prevalent, people are taking falsehood for truth, and are turning more and more to the "Prince of This World" and to lies.

It is all right to pray to and invoke the Holy Spirit, but not worship it — even though the Holy Ghost gives remission of sins as a gift of God. As to the Blessed Virgin, Leo says, "She is partly called his spouse," and, "You know the intimate and wonderful relations between Her and the Holy Spirit."

After citing David's psalm "Thou sendest forth thy spirit, they are created: and thou renewest the face of the earth" (104:30), the Bull closes with an Apostolic blessing. Karol Wojtyla — the man who wrote the play *Our God's Brother* in Poland during the 1940s — became pope in 1978. An actor, playwright, and activist, Wojtyla, born in 1920, stood firmly in the twentieth century and experienced the Nazi occupation in Poland. He had been weaned on the Polish poet Adam Mickiewicz, who saw history as a deep spiritual dimension in which the suffering of the Poles prepared the soul for glory — so said George Weigel, Pope John Paul's biographer, in 2001.

When I returned to Rome with my German Lutheran wife for her first visit, we stood behind a barrier in a place I had seen so much of in the 1960s. The pope-mobile rolled up with the ailing Wojtyla in papal white. A victim of Parkinson's disease, he stepped out with help and shuffled to the canopied dais on the steps of St. Peter's. I had asked to present my book, *Give Us This Day: The Story of Prayer,* to the Pontiff, but the Pope did not need another book on prayer. The Vatican Secretariat wrote back: "The Pontiff holds you in his prayers."

Under the watchful eyes of prelates and Vatican guards and secret police, tears came to my wife's eyes. The Pope waved constantly to the crowd in a friendly manner. I was remembering Pope John XXIII, Pope Paul VI, and all the turbulent days of the 1960s, thirty years before. I had written a novel about those heady days, *God and a Girl,* but New York's mainline, as persons close to Madison Avenue and the Avenue of the Americas had told me, complained it was not pornographic enough about the pope and popery to get published.

My wife gazed serenely and long at the Pope—at Wojtyla. "I never saw anything that inspired me with so much—serenity," she said. At the beginning of the same war that confirmed Wojtyla in the priesthood, she herself had been born in a Nazi tenement development near Mercedes Benz; it was obliterated in the bombings. Her father had worked there, but he went to Russia. He never came back. "I don't trust Slavs," she sometimes said; but Wojtyla was a Slav, and she felt trust. My wife and I saw something in Wojtyla's robes and role. Is this, perhaps, an aura of the Holy Ghost? I shut up. Who is to say she did not see a glint or a glance of the Holy Ghost. Some fleeting remembrance.

Julius Slowacki (1808–1849), a Polish poet, also influenced Wojtyla. He saw Poland as playing a unique role in the destiny of history—and the Spirit according to him who shaped history resided then in Poland. He wrote a poem about a "Slav pope" who would be a brother to all humanity. He wrote an unfinished epic called King Spirit. The poem describes "the wandering of the Spirit as it informs … leaders, kings, and saints throughout the centuries of European civilization," according to what John Paul himself told Weigel in a personal conversation in 1996.

The Polish poet Czeslaw Milosz (1911–2004), who I heard read at Harvard in the 1990s, says that Slowacki's mysticism raises historical events to a cosmic dimension. The creative proclamation of Sowo the Word would bend history in the directions as the spirit led it, according to interpreters of Slowacki's prophetic poem of 1848.

Wojtyla, as an actor, also learned from Mieczyslaw Kotlarczyk. Already in Wadowicz, Poland, where Wojtyla went to high school, Kotlarczyk was promoting a "theater of the inner word" and introducing the future priest to the dramatic concept of a relationship between proclaiming the word and the dynamics of history. An actor's task was to bring the listener to "intimacy" by effacing the self to the point where the word would touch the listener directly. In his first play, Wojtyla introduces the work by saying a person is "a line inaccessible to history."

In that same 1996 conversation with Weigel, the Pope told him, "They try to understand me from outside. But I can be understood only from inside."

Through the War, Wojtyla came to believe that the modern world was a crisis of ideas. If the idea of a human person was flawed, he believed, cultures would get destructive or be unable to reach their dreams. Weigel asks what this "inside" of a person is, and tells us what Wojtyla believed, but he does not say this "inside," this idea, is the Holy Spirit—or the individual spirit, for that matter. But isn't that what it is? From his training as actor, though, Wojtyla saw the structure of the world as dramatic—and he saw humankind as a moral agent, or actor, who surrenders "the personal I am" to the drama of "the person I ought to be." Wojtyla saw hope, Weigel says, to be truth—and, personally and as a priest, Wojtyla saw hope as Christ-centered.

Thus his first encyclical, in 1979, *Redemptor Hominis* centered on Christ—not the Holy Spirit. There hadn't been a Bull or encyclical on the Holy Spirit since 1897, and that one was the first in Church history. *Redemptor Hominis* stressed the redemption in spirit and in body, though, and linked it to dignity of the human person. He equated the life of Soul to the human rights movement. Without love there is only remoteness. Religious freedom, in the Iron Curtain context, was his mission. He began his drive against the immorality built into modern materialism.

Also in 1979, the Holy Office declared that Hans Küng could not be considered a Catholic theologian. The new Pope was seen as doctrinally conservative, retrenching after the Second Pentecost of the Council. But I doubt this is personally so. He also launched into a four-year public audience on the topic of human sexual love as an icon of the inner life of God. This was, no matter what critics say, a theology of the body, but broaches the difficult realm of the relationship between spirit and sexuality. The pressure here, of course, was the Church's continuing hard-line stance against birth control—itself refused by many Catholics ever since the encyclical *Humane Vitae.*

It seems these audiences were of very high quality, although I was not there. The question arises whether they were delivered—that is, if sex really was treated in the light of the Holy Ghost—whatever that might mean. Certainly they were theological, but theology, though of God, is not always of the Spirit. The newspapers and journalist—who always shred everything the Pope says about birth control into bits—barely registered those deliveries on sexuality and love and the body. They were dear to John Paul. He had even worked on the research papers that he originally brought to Rome during the conclave that elected his predecessor.

Some of this is heady stuff. According to Wojtyla, Mark's rather appealing record of Jesus saying that, in the Kingdom of Heaven, men and women "neither marry, nor are given in marriage" (Mark 12:23) doesn't imply any devaluation of marriage. How so? In the Resurrection there is a "divinization" of even the body, which is the "nuptial meaning" of the human body. This sounds like heavenly sex, as if the Resurrection body, as in St. Teresa's ecstasy, is part of the erotic body. It's what happens in love even before the resurrection, and its something maybe associated with the spirit. The power of eroticism seemed to sometimes be the shining through of the spirit—in other words, whatever else the responsibilities involved. The Pope added this up in a theological dimension, that is, in the light of the Holy Spirit, which can dictate theology or poetry, as in Dante, who found this all centuries ago more through Beatrice than through Jesus.

I thought John Paul was right on, too, when he talked of the man's solitary aloneness in the Garden of Eden before meeting Eve—"original solitude" instead of original sin. He says "original nakedness" is the third part of the mystery, and it becomes the original sin only when the guy, or anyone, treats anything or anyone as a mere object: "a thing to be used."

Whether the Holy Ghost should use a prophylactic, of course, has been one of the hottest issues of recent times. The fourth part of the Pope's deliveries on sex and the body concerned birth control. The Holy Ghost's views on the subject, I hope, are not irrelevant. The Vatican's position has drawn criticism and fire, but I admire the Vatican for speaking out on the subject and to the importance of life. Whatever the taboos, whatever the means of regulation, whatever the choices, Wojtyla seems to say—and it is all on record elsewhere—that love itself "is poured into hearts as a gift of the Holy Spirit."

Conflicts in theology itself are not always about spirit as such, but rather neo-orthodoxy against liberalism—orthodoxy against hyper-orthodoxy; evangelicalism against fundamentalists; process theology (which rejects revelation) against orthodox; and so forth. Conflicts among types of ecclesiasticism also often outweigh disputes about materialism or spirit, or, nowadays, even disputes with science.

In fact, Spirit is sometimes as routinely dismissed by religion as it is by science. The burning issues are abortion, gay priests, a married clergy, celibacy, canon law, money, and property—not spirituality. The Church has gone for the secular agenda in many ways, forgetting its task of mediating the human and divine. The Catholic Church, in the homosexuality issue, has even given up citing natural law, much less any spiritual background of union.

The area in which the Vatican remains hard-line is disciplinary—against married clergy and in the right to life. Often, here, they no longer appeal to spiritual positions, but to civil and disciplinary positions. The Vatican, remember, is not just a spiritual fiefdom, but also a world power.

# Chapter 26

# Mr. Science

Where Lady Philosophy left off, Mr. Science moves in to take up the slack. The Holy Ghost, without theology to defend and cut the path, in some ways fades. But also, without theology to confine and pin the Spirit down, the Holy Ghost in some ways becomes more active in the field of free inquiry. Spirit, freed from what some view as the shackles of organized religion, comes into its own as science. But Spirit becomes more of a ghost, too, because, with the turn of the century in 1500, sense-based knowledge gradually becomes more important. Sensory data based on perception of the physical world comes to the fore everywhere, especially in the new scientific disciplines. The gold Byzantine background, the halos, and the Holy Ghost all fade from the world in the glare of everyday exploration and reality. In the new empirical reality, the ineffable, nonphysical, and immaterial become ever more distant.

With Science, knowledge turns its back on the spirit and the "ghost in the machine" arises—a clockmaker who isn't there, finally a quantum too small to be seen or even counted. Yet scientists, in the decline of the divine, were often concerned with the passage of Spirit and even with the demise of the Holy Ghost. The Holy Ghost, of course, cannot be weighed or measured—although Egyptian science, according to the ancient Book of the Dead, had tried it. Spirit, from the point of view of science, however, cannot be quantified. Even for the Greeks, spirit was non-Euclidean.

In the jargon, the shift from religion to science is the shift of the episteme, which focuses on secondary rather than primary causes, and that shift is from the authority of moral and divine worlds to social and natural worlds.

Medieval theology had downgraded the created, natural world and associated it with the relative worthlessness of matter. Natural theology, true, dealt with creation, but divine theology dealt with the Creator, Revelation, first principles, the heavens, the other world, the Bible, and the world beyond and the unknowable, in other words: the spirit. The telescope knocked this out, and the key conflicts that ushered in the brave new world were Galileo, Copernicus, Newton, Darwin, and Freud. We will not repeat the well-known stories of Galileo's conflict with the Church over the earth's movement, the outcome of astronomy, and Newton's clockwork universe. These were grand and dramatic confrontations over huge matters, including the being of the Holy Ghost. Science and deism won.

A word, however, about Newton's view on the Trinity: Newton was a deist after being a scientist; he was convinced that contemplation of the universe proved God's existence. "This most beautiful system of the sun, planets, and comets could proceed only from the counsel and dimension of an intelligent and powerful Being"—God, Newton said in concluding the *Principia.* But in 1670, he writes on the Trinity and calls it "this strange religion of the West" and "the abomination of desolation." He concludes that it, along with the mystery of the Holy Ghost, is a conspiracy of St. Athanasius (296–373) and his cohorts to convert pagans in the early centuries. Newton abhorred the cultivation of mystery; his reverence was for the new truth of observation of secondary causes, and the Holy Ghost was for him just a mystification.

In the new post-Newtonian world, the scientific categories are space, time, motion, causality, and the pervading ether, now replaced by atomic physics. At best, deism left no room for the Biblical God, a creator God active in history and with lives of persons. Where the turf shifted from a mechanistic to an electromagnetic perspective, the signals became electromagnetic, gravitational, and sometimes luminiferous ether forces, and there were thoughts of matter-free space or nonmaterial force fields where the Holy Ghost once lived. Otherwise, it was all "matter in motion under the influence of forces."

This didn't leave much room even for philosophy of spirit or for mental and psychic factors. Psychology has recently denied even the mind-matter duality and downgraded mentality to physical and corporeal forces; even dreams are just physical epiphenomena.

Sir Oliver Lodge (1851–1940) was the last spokesperson for a "spiritualized ether," and he got some hearing only because he pioneered electromagnetic wave theory. Nevertheless, he got interested in telepathy, telekinesis, communication with the dead, and personal immortality. By the 1930s, the new physics had demolished both this and mechanistic theories. The ethers were gone. Space, time and motion, simultaneity, and even causality were modified, along with energy—the wave particle theory of both matter and radiation emerging. But all of this based reality in particles, and matter—not spirit—emerged in mechanistic science.

The "new alchemy" in chemistry and the discovery of argon led to the acknowledgement of chemical elements with no chemical properties; but matter was still almost as solidly in place as ever. We review all this to see where spirit disappeared—perhaps into some black hole. Electrons were still discrete particles of negative charge and small mass. Note that science, though denying spirit, is speaking of matter in ever finer and finer quantities.

Einstein knocked out absolute notions of space, time, and motion, posited a four-dimensional universe of relativity, and said, "God does not play dice." He also recognized that energy annihilates matter. The search for antimatter—not spirit—began. So the question arises: Did the Holy Ghost escape into the sphere of antimatter?

Rather than opening a window for spirit, rational critics like George Bernard Shaw (1856–1950) greeted the demise of Newtonian mechanics and the annihilation of matter this way: "And now, now, what is left of it? All is caprice: the calculable world has become incalculable." Newton's great respect for the order of the planets had arrived, with Shaw's scoffing, at universal caprice—even though the Sun still runs on time. It all led to the bomb, of course, but not even X-rays, radioactivity, quantum theory, or the photon theory of light made any waves or room for spirit.

Strangely enough, some theologians, not particularly interested in the reality of spirit itself, nevertheless found hope (read "faith") for religion in the new physics; but this was only insofar as it denied determinism and relativized materialism itself.

James Jeans (1877–1946), a British physicist, said that, whereas the old classical physics bolted the door against free will and cast the universe as a mechanistic prison, the new physics viewed the world as "conceivably the suitable dwelling place for a free man"—emphasizing science's relation to the possession of free will and the existence, perhaps, of human spirit. But religion has never been particularly interested in free will anyway (though the Holy Ghost had). Radioactivity opened for some the concept of a dynamic instead of a static universe—relevant to spirit and the Holy Ghost inasmuch as the presence of spirit favors a changing, living, growing universe. Some hailed the discovery of cosmic rays in the 1920s as "the birth cries of atoms." British astronomer Arthur Stanley Eddington (1882–1944) saw relativity as evidence of the mind in nature.

In another corner, Rudolf Steiner, the neglected Austrian philosopher who tried to bring science to spiritual life throughout his career, argues that evolution itself testifies to the work of spirit on matter—not just physical forces of survival and genetic fitness.

Some theologians used Einstein's fourth dimension as evidence for the realm of the Holy Spirit. Canon Arthur F. Smethurst in England proclaimed: "If the Christian view is true, surely we should expect to find evidence of the Holy Spirit in the physical sphere in just such signs of dynamic energy and activity as are indicated by modern physics. If energy is the essential basis of the whole material world, this to the Christian is a clear manifestation of the active, creative spirit of God in the physical realm." With Einstein, the problem of spirit arises philosophically, since people—including the Archbishop of Canterbury—asked what the theory of relativity had to do with religion. Nothing, Einstein answered, but he also said, "God does not play dice." The question was whether the theory favored Idealism or Materialism. If it favored Idealism, the Spirit had a chance.

It was important too because new foundations were being laid for the role of the observer in science, and thus the very formulas of the universe were being mapped out. The era of clocks, of mechanistic physics—material and mindless—was over. When Einstein visited London, the *Times* remarked: "Observational science has, in fact, led back to subjective idealism." Reality, according to the theory, not only needed to be taken in the concrete—just as the Spirit needs to be taken immanently—but in Einstein's new world, to observe became part of what he observes again. So the human spirit, if not the Ghost, at least had a role again. Whether the human spirit is part of the Holy Spirit is not up to Einstein.

Einstein, a traditionalist in matters of faith and morals, never wanted his theory used religiously or for religion. But Philipp Frank, in his biography *Einstein: His Life and Times,* quotes an interesting passage from the British *Hibbert Journal* published in 1939, which sheds some light on the subject:

> If the idea of time as a fourth dimension is valid, then the difference between this mortal life and the "other life" is not a difference in the time nor in the quality of life. It is only a difference in our view of it—our ability to see the whole. While we are limited to three-dimensional understanding, it is mortal life. Where we perceive it in four dimensions, it is eternal life. (p. 239)

Undoubtedly, the Holy Ghost may be four-dimensional—this is also the report from movements raising or altering consciousness, as we see in another chapter.

Einstein attended a Catholic elementary school in the 1880s in Munich and was the only Jew in his class. He got instruction in religion and, on the whole, liked it. He tended to conflate the Catholic teaching with what he knew from a nominally Jewish background, by looking at the various symbols of religion not so much as symbols of truth as things that were more or less beautiful—as artistic tokens. He married a Greek Orthodox woman and complained, when his own children had to take religious education, that with what the schools teach, "eventually the children believe that God is some kind of gaseous vertebrate." Gaseous is about the extent of many American's idea of spirit today.

Einstein believed in pure mathematical construction. Theories, however, he held, were products of free imagination that then needed to be tested by physical observation. He held, however, that experience alone could not be the source of mathematical concepts. "In a certain sense, therefore, I hold it to be true that pure thought is competent to comprehend the real as the ancients dreamed," he maintained in an address at Oxford (ibid., p. 282). This, too, is one reason why, in this book, we look for a connection between thought and the Spirit.

Einstein held pretty much to the view that experience tests theory in a universe where there is "rationality in nature"—and insofar as the "rationality of nature" makes one think of a spirit superior to the human, yet similar, Einstein's view is somewhat compatible to the views of religion.

"The most beautiful emotion we can experience is the mystical," Einstein once said. "It is the sower of all true art and science. He to whom this emotion is a stranger, who can no longer wonder and stand rapt in awe, is as good as dead" (ibid., p. 284). The Holy Ghost, I think, would be glad to hear this, and if it could still speak, would say the same kind of thing—but in a whisper and with the fear of being overheard. Einstein himself, meanwhile, had not much regard otherwise for the formal side of religion.

In 1940, in a short paper on "Science and Religion," Einstein said that the main conflict between science and religion lay in claims for a personal God. His bias was for a "Cosmic religion" based on the "rationality of nature" (ibid., p. 283). The point was challenging for Churches, theology, and believers. Einstein did not want the Church saying how nature worked—but he did not think science could ever say what man's aims in life could or should be. He allowed that Churches had an important role in dealing with this.

From our perspective, Einstein's view is revealing, because he talks clearly and positively of rationality and thinking, but very little of the spirit. And not at all about the Holy Ghost. Like God, the Holy Ghost is a person—and that probably bothered Einstein just as it had Newton. He was dismayed, too, at science ever teaching people their goals. "It is clear that no path leads from knowledge of that which is to that which should be," he said. He added: "No matter how splendid the knowledge of truth as such may be, as a guide it is ... impotent" (ibid., p. 287).

So, despite Einstein's overwhelming human value of awe and emotion, and rationality and thinking—even of mysticism and cosmic religion—he had no brief for the Holy Ghost as a person, certainly, or for the guidance of the Holy Spirit as a bringer of any truth that can lead men to their aims and what they should do in any scientific sense. This dimension of a reality of spirit is lacking. Yet he adds: "If one should ask whence fundamental goals receive their authority, since they are not set up by reason and cannot be founded on it, one can only answer that they do not come into existence as a result of argument and proof, but instead by revelation, and through the actions of strong personalities" (ibid., p. 288). This may seem to have implications for democratic process, but that was not what he was talking about here; besides, Einstein was committed to democratic process. More surprising would be his appeal to "revelation" for values, which naturally found a sympathetic reaction in clerical circles. To the question of how one judges such values, he adds prudently: "One should not attempt to prove them, but rather to recognize their essence as clearly and as purely as possible" (ibid.).

Turning elsewhere in the scientific community, at Yale, the plant morphologist Edmund Were Sinnott (1888–1968) saw the new science as advancing a synthesis of matter and spirit. Werner Heisenberg (1901–1976) expounded his principle of uncertainty in 1927, which was seen by some apologists as the lynchpin for existential and religious spiritual belief. At one point Arthur Eddington (1882–1944) invoked the principles as leading to "supernaturalism." The finding of indeterminacy, accident, and chance in nature was adopted by some as pointing to the Biblical idea of Providence, if not the Spirit. The spirit, however, may yet be found working at the subatomic level.

As to the big bang theory of creation in astronomy, Robert Jastrow in 1978 concluded: "For the scientist who has lived ... by the power of reason, the story ends like a bad dream. He has climbed the mountains of ignorance; he is about to conquer the highest peak; as he pulls himself over the final rock, he is greeted by a band of theologians who have been sitting there for centuries."

When it came to Sigmund Freud and the battle between the new psychology and religion, the Great Professor opted out. A thorough search of the Freud literature and the Carl Gustav Jung literature did not turn up any mention of Holy Spirit or Holy Ghost—quite an oversight for psychology—except for an irrelevant reference in *Psychology of the Unconscious* by Jung, in which he says that the Virgin Birth is represented in a Germanic painter of the Middle Ages "by a tubular pipe coming down from heaven and passing beneath the skirt of Mary. Into this flies the Holy Ghost in the form of a dove for the impregnation of the Mother of God." Jung seems to have had a good laugh.

Jung also said that certain early Christian sectarians attributed a maternal significance to the Holy Ghost as world soul or moon. He says that the libido in its "incestuous bond" is repressed in fear of the avenging Father and that this can be led over "into sublimation through the symbol of baptism (birth from water) and of generation (spiritual birth) through the symbol of the descent of the Holy Ghost."

As for Freud, he avoids the Holy Ghost. An American doctor wrote to Freud in 1927: "I beg you as a brother physician to give thought to God ... if you look into this subject with an open mind, God will reveal the truth to your soul." Freud, purporting to open other peoples' minds, wrote back: "God has not done so much for me. He never allowed me to hear an inner voice; and if, in view of my age, he doesn't make haste, it will not be my fault if I remain to the end of my life what I now am—'an infidel Jew.'"

Freud was a special case. Fascinated by spiritual and occult phenomena, he rejected them all. "There is no appeal to a court above that of reason," he stated. He scorned the idea that "inner experience bears witness to the truth." As far as spiritualists were concerned, he said, "The appearance and utterances of their spirits are merely the products of their own mental activity." Religion, for him, was full of fairytales. The spirit for Freud, then, is an illusion—wish fulfillment. Illusions, not always errors, are nevertheless derived from human wishes and very close to psychiatric delusions. Their reality value is in question, whereas a delusion is in contradiction to reality and reason. Yet he agreed that no one should be forced either to believe or to disbelieve. God himself, much less the Holy Ghost, was "a vague abstraction" tantamount to "an unsubstantial shadow." Freud left to the ages whether spirit has "truth value."

By the time we get to modern psychology and even parapsychology—which studies "spiritual phenomena," like trying to predict card sequences—preconception is the name for prophecy; clairvoyance is the name for revelation; telepathis is the name for some prayer phenomena, psychokinesis is the name for some so-called miracles; and natural principle of communication is the name for divine agency.

There is no microscope or telescope powerful enough to see the Holy Spirit, of course; for scientists, academicians, and materialists, this most often means it does not exist. But these are the same people, scientists themselves, who once said that other planets, protons, neutrinos, electrons, antimatter, black holes, and other phenomena did not exist—until new scientists saw them by electronic means.

Church people, too, of course, denied these things. X-ray crystallography pictured molecules as early as 1917, but spiritism still denies their existence, claiming they are only models and paradigms. X-rays and radium were disbelieved until finally demonstrated. Spiritism denied that photos could be taken on the far side of the moon, until space ships got there with the cameras. The Church went against Galileo and Copernicus. But science itself has been full of rejections of phenomena and theories also—until evidence supported them. Science routinely rejects things that it says it cannot know about—in fact, the whole realm of metaphysics and spirit. Even doctors at one time bled patients for wrong reasons, killing them, and for centuries rejected the existence of germs. They claimed remedial qualities for a host of substances that they now scoff at. And they also rejected genes and the double helix at first.

Immateriality, of course, or the Holy Spirit, are not likely to come into focus this way—no matter how powerful machines get—orgon boxes, scientology, Duke university, and ouija boards aside. A telescope or microscope is not likely to suddenly see an angel. It is scientifically likely that, when we come to the spirit or the Holy Ghost, if we are talking about anything, we are talking about a different domain. A different dimension.

If anything, science could probably recognize immateriality or spirit only with other criteria of evidence or new and different paradigms—for example, in linguistics, when phonology and phonetics "discovered" the phoneme. Unlike a sound, the phoneme does not "exist"; it is a pattern. It has a structural, or formatic, dimension and a psychic dimension, but it is not a reality, like a thing. It organizes perception and can be used to predict structures and even sound, but it is immaterial. If one wanted, one could call the phoneme "spiritual"—though the linguistic scientists of course do not do this.

In the big picture, science still excludes the spirit and has—the sin against the Holy Spirit aside—an account to settle.

# Chapter 27

# The Pentecostals

The rise of Pentecostal Churches in America and elsewhere in the twentieth cenutry is tremendous, and they may have bearing—great bearing—on the heritage of spirit for the twenty-first century and beyond. Harvey Cox, in *Fire from Above* has done a great service by surveying the rise of Pentecostal spirituality and then calling it, "The reshaping of religion in the twenty-first century. This Pentecostal movement has a dubious name in some quarters due to its association with "enthusiasm"—read emotion—a feature of zealots and evangelicals. Pentecostalism as distinct from tradition and from cognitive spirituality. The fact that some Pentecostal sects appeal to the lower class and populistic and poor segments of society influences this prejudice.

For example, in 1893 hopes for a new Pentecost were entertained at the World Parliament of Religions held in Chicago at White City, only to give way to bickering and a devastating fire. The American worldwide Pentecostal movement was born in a livery stable in Azura, California, which gave way to a shopping plaza. Newspapers lampooned the "fanaticism and unseemly contentiousness" that allegedly accompanied Pentecostal revivals. Yet today this movement looms large not only in America, but also in South America and Asia, and Catholicism has revamped its own Pentecostal spirit in response. This movement, rather than ascending to spiritual heights and esotericism, reaches into primal spirituality and primal language beyond creed and ceremony: primal speech, primal piety, and primal hope. These are touched by dreams, glossolalia, and trances. For traditionalism and elitists they are scary. For example, in Rhodesia (now Zimbabwe), John Maranke (1912–1963), founder of the African

Apostolic Church, claimed to be touched by the Holy Spirit in a way that his European mission school education did not prepare for. Given two books of "revealed" instruction, only the Holy Spirit unlocks their meaning. His church was credited for preparing the *chinunenga* for the struggle for independence. Many other Africans also learned to appeal to the Holy Spirit for liberation from European domination.

Mainstream churches dislike Pentecostals, but so do fundamentalists, even calling Pentecostalism "the last vomit of Satan." It is the old battle, in a new form, of spirit versus the letter; fundamentalists side with the letter of the law. Also, Pentecostalism is interracial.

Take the performance of Korean Hyun Kyung Chung at the World Council of Churches meeting at Canberra. Chung showed delegates a rice paper roll of victims of oppression who were now dead and *han* (spirits). The theme prayer of the assembly was, "Come Holy Spirit, Renew thy Whole Creation." She burned the role of names, then told the assembly her beliefs: "I no longer believe in an omnipotent God. I rely on a compassionate God who weeps with us in the midst of the cruel destruction of life. The spirit is like a bodhisattva, an enlightened being, a goddess of compassion and wisdom. Indeed, the Holy Spirit might also be the feminine image of the Christ who goes before and brings others with her." She ended with a dance to protest the overly verbal idiom of Western liturgies.

Sally McFague, an American feminist theologian, openly touts "God the lover" in female imagery. The phrase "full of grace" is lifted from the Hail Mary to exalt the female lover and mother aspect of God.

The early Pentecostal movement still called the Holy Spirit the "Holy Ghost." Experience, not doctrine, is a key word and concept for them. They live between "the already and not yet." The movement readily identifies with the poor and meek and envisions the Kingdom of God—not Caesar's. Healings, tongues, and prophecies abound, rather than rites, canon code, and verbal ceremony. Speaking in tongues also got a bad name in some Pentecostal quarters, and they have dampened their eschatological fire in recent years for a vision of Jesus as helper, healer, and companion.

In the 1980s and 1990s, when mainline churches were losing members, Pentecostals gained about thirty percent. In Stepney, East London, incidentally, there sprouted up the Holy Spirit Apostolic Church.

Jonathan Edwards (1703–1758) cut a swathe in colonial America for the Pentecostals early on, leaving the moorings of authority and tradition for the uncharted waters of "enthusiasm." But still, it is a long way to the modern movement. Charles Emmanuel "Sweet Daddy" Grace (1883–1960), born in Cape Verde, was a cook on a Southern Railway, but left that job to preach. He took the name "Grace" and opened a church in Charlotte, North Carolina, and ordained himself "Bishop." Later he moved to Newark. He invoked God as his source, but not the Holy Ghost. God, he said, had given him authority to grant or withhold salvation. His death led to litigation and a dispute over his succession.

The American community of Evangelicals, forerunners of the Pentecostalists, was built on English and European streams of the Evangelical movement, including that of John Wesley (1703–1791), father of Methodism. These streams had a relation to speaking in tongues, prophesying, and miraculous healing. By the 1820s, this phenomenon had also arisen in Scotland, but the General Assembly of Church of Scotland, dominated by conventional evangelicals, "condemned" such goings on. Edward Irving (1792–1834) and other radical evangelicals, however, "confirmed" that these occurrences were the work of the Holy Spirit. And in England, Cardinal Henry Newman (1801–1890)—the leader of an English Catholic reform movement that was a forerunner of the Ecumenical Council at Vatican II—tried to mount a bulwark against rampaging evangelicalism with a call to tradition.

Ironically, what Samuel Taylor Coleridge (1772–1834) termed "the spirit of commerce" informs some of the conventional Evangelical sects with a spirit of wealth, competition, and values—sincerity, justice, honesty, fairness of trade, and contracts—that they regarded as the work of the Holy Spirit.

Jonathan Edwards, a Yale graduate, was one of the first in America to embrace the Spirit of God in revivalism as the Holy Spirit. In

"A Faithful Narrative" (*The Great Awakening*, 1734) he remarked, "God seemed to have gone out of his usual way" in New England, and sober, orderly, good people, shocked by the sudden deaths of two young people, were getting born again and developing religious fervor. As Karen Armstrong writes in *A History of God*, "It must be said, however, that the Holy Spirit sometimes manifested in some rather hysterical symptoms" (p. 223). People were "broken" by fear of God and sunk into an abyss under a sense of guilt. Elation would follow—tears, laughter, and loud weeping with shouts of praise. This showy emotion was far from the *apatheia*—the detachment—and discipline of mystics through the ages. It was a new birth attendant with violent convulsions, pain, and effort. A new frontier version of the dark night of the soul and Jacob's wrestling with the angel. People poured over Bibles and forgot to eat. Two years later, emotions began to die down, and Edwards said that very sensibly "the Spirit of God is withdrawing from us." But he thought that the phenomenon had been a direct revelation of God. Where God left off, Satan took over—people began to despair and cut their throats. People went mad. Abnormality and distress surfaced.

The outbreak marked an American frontier syndrome of the masses meeting an unfettered and "uncivilized God." It occurred in the poorer colonies and went counter to the sedate Enlightenment of the American Founding Fathers. But it ushered in the popular tradition in America of evangelical revivalism and born-again Christians. It contributed, too, to lower class identification with the Revolution. For Edwards, God the creator would bring about the Kingdom of the New World, and in it His Son was the deity generated by understanding—the blue-printer of the new news. But it was the Spirit—"the deity subsisting in act"—that would accomplish the master plan in time, according to Jonathan Edwards' "Essay on the Trinity."

This was when God, according to the Edwards vision, would contemplate his own perfection in the New World of America. New England would be the "city on a hill" of John Winthrop, ravishing all. Is this Spirit of God the same as the Holy Ghost, or have the revivalists gotten hold of some jolly father figure, a sort of Santa Claus of rock and roll heaven? The traditional Holy Ghost, insofar as he was allowed to exist, was often a contemplative spirit of the thinking heart, or a community soul. Edward's Spirit of God was an act—a manifestation of will.

In Catholic Pentecostalism a twentieth century revival aimed at meeting the rise of Pentecostals, prayer groups, student activities, conferences, and social activities are directed toward the action of the Holy Spirit. Catholics still harbor concerns, however, about the lack of accountability to Episcopal authority. The Pope issued three principles in this regard for judging what is truly of the Spirit: fidelity to authentic doctrine; discernment in striving for the gifts most useful to the community; and the presence of love.

In the Catholic Charismatic Renewal, for instance, in February 1967, twenty students and faculty at Duquesne University cited Acts 1.8: "Ye shall receive power, after that the Holy Ghost is come upon you: and ye shall be witnesses." They claimed that they got the powers of tongues, prophecy, discernment of spirits, and exorcism. The movement spread to Notre Dame, Michigan State, and Michigan. The Bishops of the US (NCC), wary of the threat, nevertheless issued a statement saying, "The natural man does not accept what is taught by the Spirit of God. For him, this is an absurdity. He cannot come to know such teaching, because it must be appraised in a spiritual way. The spiritual man, on the other hand, can appraise everything, though he himself can be appraised of no one" (1 Corinthians 2:14–15), and then it warned the priests and Church "not to extinguish the Spirit."

A leading liberal at Vatican II, Cardinal Suenens (1904–1996) of Belgium, welcomed the charismatic movement as "ecumenical," and the Council itself, in the "Dogmatic Constitution on the Church," said, "It is not only through the sacraments and church ministries that the same Holy Spirit sanctifies and leads the People of God and enriches it with virtues. 'Allotting his gifts to each as he wills' [1 Corinthians 12:11], he distributes special graces among the faithful of every rank. By these gifts he makes them fit and ready to undertake the various tasks or offices advantageous for renewal and up-building of the Church." Note that it says "Church," not society in general; but the Church thinks of itself as the society in general.

Louis Cassels, the UPI columnist and reporter, a Baptist by birth and Anglican by conversion, begrudgingly recognized the power of the Pentecostals and actually looked to them, in *The Reality of God* as a great source of hope and revival for the traditional Church.

America, cut off from the tradition in some ways, is a strange land. For example, in *A New Religious America* (2001), Harvard author Diana L. Eck devotes 416 pages to isms, sects, confessions, diversity, and pluralism, but not one mention of the Holy Ghost or the Holy Spirit. There is no discussion at all of what spirit represents or what spirituality, in whatever guises—the societies, denominations, churches, confessions, or groups—say about spirit. Her thesis, that religious pluralism has replaced racial difference as an issue, is in some ways appealing. Certainly it is potentially more interesting than racial hatred, but if there is no spirit to new religion, is the pluralistic openness she sees forthcoming much different than bingo?

In Elizabeth Lesser's *New American Spirituality* (1999), something different happens. The Holy Ghost and the Holy Spirit get no mention here, either, nor do charismatic Pentecostals get any recognition, but Lesser does something else. She really seems to go for the jugular of spiritual life in more ways than one. Besides, in real life she was a midwife. She even sees the value in poetry as a shaker-up of souls—as an eye-opener to further spiritual seeking. A template. Without even a further nod to womanist theology, knowing here and there someone might be disappointed I can highly recommend this treatment of how to make a spiritual go of American life to most readers who otherwise miss the Holy Ghost or Holy Spirit.

Lastly, of course, is the black spiritual, an abiding source of the Pentecostal movement—if properly understood and not theologically segregated. As Anthony Pinn observes, they originated out of slavery in their American form because slaves could not complain to overseers and owners; so they voiced their concerns to a more eternal presence: God. He notes that drums were outlawed on the plantation, another example of establishment obstruction of enthusiasm and messaging. In his book *The Black Church in the Post-Civil Rights Era* (2002), Pinn shows that the spiritual, although it owed debts to secular experience, was "a complex, multilayered, and syncretic style of song shaped by religious and theological regulations" (p. 50). Something that spirituals had sometimes in common with glossolalia, or speaking in tongues, was double talk. Such double talk, on the surface sounding otherworldly, below the surface meant a call for divine justice. Call and response in performance often involved, and still does, extemporaneous inspiration. Even in church blacks will move out of what is regarded as Sunday etiquette to sway, gesture, break into utterance, and get "in the spirit." Pinn quotes a former slave:

> Some ob de sarbants, mos'ly de ole ones 'ud preach ter us. An' den de black folks 'ud git off, down in de crick bottom, er in a thic'et, an sing an' sout an' pray. Don't know why, but de w'ite foks shot didn't like dem ring shouts de cullud folks had. De folks git shuffle, den hit gits faster, 'an faster as dey gits wa'amed up; an' dey moans an' shouts; an' sinngs, an' claps, an' dance. Some ob em gits 'zauseted an' dey drop out, an' de ring gits closer. Sometime dey sing an' shout all night. (p. 51)

The claim for this is that, when performed properly, spiritual power manifests; people get "happy in de spirit" and souls are saved.

## Chapter 28

# The Ghost in the Machine

A major example of the popular power of a spirit even in the contemporary world is found, no less, in the secular theater. *The Phantom of the Opera* may indeed be looked at as an incarnation of the Ghost—though not so holy. Look for a minute at the lyrics of the outstanding song, "The Music of the Night:"

> Turn your face away
> From the garish light of day,
> Turn your though away
> From the cold unfeeling light
> And listen to the music of the night...
> Close your eyes and let your spirit soar
> And you'll live as you never lived before.

The Phantom (a spiritual figure, after all) sings this from "the land beyond the lake," and the public—a young secular public—goes crazy. Indeed, the Holy Ghost, as a spirit from "the land beyond the lake," may be seen in another light as a bringer of consciousness. I mean not just medical consciousness, or reflex to stimuli, but special kinds of consciousness—the kind of thing that draws people to the *Phantom.* Spirit may be a kind of consciousness that awakens and is aware. Awareness is a state that reaches beyond the body of things and beyond itself.

Medically speaking, consciousness is the organism's neurological response to stimuli. It is distinguished from a comatose state. But there is a broad band of conscious states, including medical, waking consciousness, sleep and dream states, responsive consciousness, self-awareness, higher consciousness, awareness, attentiveness, enlightenment, imagination, inspiration, intuition, concentration, contemplation, intellectuality, psychedelic and altered, visionary, hypnogogic, hallucinatory, schizophrenic or abnormal, paranormal, telepathic, ecstatic, and cosmic. These have some relation to spirit, however it is defined.

The opposite of spirit—small "s" and capital "S"—is in many ways the doctrine of scientific physicalism, prevalent during the last century and the present one. It is the idea that all human activities must be explained according to physical brain processes or in relation to physical stimuli and responses. In his introduction to *Essential Sources of the Scientific Study of Consciousness,* leading cognitive scientist, Bernard J. Baars, admits that in the twentieth century "the universal fact of human consciousness came to resemble a scientific taboo." It was an embarrassment to the scientific community, because there was no physical evidence for spirit soul, or self—or even for mental concepts, recall, memory, much less anything like imagination, inspiration, or intuition.

The latest research has begun to recognize certain elements of consciousness: explicit cognition, immediate memory, novel and informative events, attentional information, focal contents, supraliminal stimulation, recall, grammatical strings, wakefulness and dreams, autonoetic memory, intentional learning, and so forth—all elements that, in another age, might have been signs, or gifts, of the spirit. The Holy Ghost was not just good—that is, "moral"; it was also a cognitive personality. In the jargon, psychologists and neurologists talk of a mental state as having consciousness *if it has a qualitative feel*—an associative quality of feeling.

All great religious leaders, and even philosophers, have spoken of nothing less—of *qualia*: phenomenal qualities as the problem of explaining consciousness. When the Holy Ghost hears such talk, it may well sit up and awaken again in the graveyard, assigned by so much modernity and materialism to things of the spirit.

William James, at the end of the nineteenth century, had already told scientists, "No account of the universe can be final that leaves other forms of consciousness disregarded." But they didn't listen. In

1932, the philosopher Henri Bergson also warned them: "There is more in the mind than a corresponding brain."

In our time, the Spirit, spirit, and Holy Ghost compete with the secular spirit, the "spirit" of materialism (a contradiction), the spirit of science, and the Ghost in the machine. If science is the sole arbiter of truth because of its gradual expulsion of other human consciousness from its object of study, then the Holy Spirit, we might say, is at a certain level a void filled at least with our human consciousness. Or, in a still more advanced speculation, we might say daringly—in one kind of parlance—that despite science our consciousness is the void filled by the Holy Spirit. Early in the history of modern Europe, a "peak experience" of the poet Petrarch (1304–1374) literally helped mold the growing new perceptual consciousness of Europe. The Italian poet climbed Mt. Ventoux and described the experience of the new expanding horizon, as Lindbergh did when he flew the Atlantic. Petrarch feared at the time that he had transgressed against law and that he had, with the new "wide and freely shifting vistas," transgressed against the Holy Ghost and slipped into "another world."

Another poet, William Blake, said, "Where man is not, nature is barren." We can add that where man is not, spirit is barren, or even the reverse: where spirit is not, man is barren.

Some commentators have suggested the obscure realm of intention is the locus of the Holy Ghost—intention being that free prompting by which the will chooses. Awareness of intention is a slippery field, of course; there are virtual, actual, habitual, trained, and ordinary intentions. A sense for consciousness, or spirit, might help sort out these levels.

Usually, existence is viewed either materially or, sometimes, intellectually. Our universities intellectualize the universe, generally concluding that it is all material. But, on the whole, common people act out existence instead by feel. They have a feel for survival, for matter, for the everyday world. It is faith, rather than intellect, that often appeals to this "feel" for the world—for creation, life and death, religion, and afterlife. Thus, where intellect is cognitive, faith is affective. A person of faith (as in, "Keep the faith") holds to the great truths through an affective (read "emotional") experience. Accompanying this feel are mystery and miracles: past myth and reflections of the unconscious. Teaching and doctrine appear as dogmas—almost as conundrums—that, backed by authority, appeal less to the mind than to belief and the heart. The Trinity itself is closer to the Zen *koan,* a paradox meant to empty the mind, than it is to rationality in the modern sense. But the heart used to be, even for the Greeks, an organ for perception—not just a muscle. It, too, can be trained, disciplined, and oriented. Common folk accept the wisdom of the heart without talking about it. It is only modernity and academics and schools that laugh at and scorn this kind of knowledge.

Again, it is the reality not just of truth but also of being. The Holy Spirit, as we have seen, is supposed to participate in both realms. This dualism, the split between truth and being, is almost as great as the celebrated dualism of mind and matter. Science tends to deal in "truth." Here it broke from faith and religion, from the truth of being as well as from the truth of doctrine. Religion, too, deals in truth, but also in being and heart knowledge. If reason and religion would separate their terms of truth into these two categories—heart and mind—there would be less futile controversy over the separation of science and religion, faith and reason, church and state. For instance, in many ways, except for technology, evolution may not have been so much up from the Neanderthal to the modern person in the street, or the new nerd, but truly *down* from great elephants and the wise ape and the cunning monkey to the modern jerk and contemporary punk, from goddess to feminist, from righteous prophets to technocrats and death machines.

Faith keeps a dimension of consciousness for the Holy Spirit, but the domain of religion does not hold a monopoly on spirit itself (though it has tried). Spirit also deals with cognition as well as emotions. And poets deal in "inspiration" as much as religion is supposed to. Knowledge, as we saw, is supposed to be one of the gifts of the Holy Ghost. So regardless of science, we can also ask: What is the Spirit's relation to cognition? To thinking? To knowing? To the branch of study known as epistemology, the study of how things are known? Faith sometimes pigeonholes spirit, and even the Holy Spirit, associating it with certain beliefs: inspiration of the Bible by the Holy Spirit; the Ghost as a person in the Trinity; the Pentecost; the Baptism by the Holy Spirit; and being born again. People who reject these religious beliefs, then, mistakenly reject spirit itself also.

But there is yet another way of looking at Spirit: as a factor, a player, in the mind–body dialogue or, cognitively, as a description of some element in mental consciousness and behavior. What is the role of this ghost, whatever it is, in the life of the mind, in thought, imagination, and inspiration—regardless of religion and creed, churches, and the tenets of faith?

Socrates—and Jesus for that matter—did not see the spirit as a compartment, a dogma, or some temple or church. Indeed, for them, the spirit blows where it will. Some New Agers claimed it might blow the mind of a druggie or themselves, just as well as that of a saint or an archbishop. Or it may visit and inspire a scientist to decipher the molecular structure of carbon. Or inspire Walt Disney to found an empire on a mouse—or was that merely the inspiration of the mouse itself? In response to this kind of "spirit" a critic might ask if it is the same as that of the Holy Ghost; or is the Holy Ghost, like some divine collective consciousness, the sum and total of all these individual "spirits" of humankind? I sometimes like to think that, as a linguist, one has to do with signs and sounds—a province of data—but that, by ascending the structure, one comes to "meaning." Language, Owen Barfield pointed out, preserves for us the inner living history of man's soul—just as spirit, now so often abstract, once meant breath. Barfield also claimed that in earlier times consciousness participated in a primary way in the world and was not, as it is now, a sort of ghost hovering above it.

Emerson, too, spoke of language as "fossil poetry." Ghosts, of course, leave no footprints—except, perhaps, in language as words, expressions, and etymologies. To make an analogy, then, as meaning is to language so may the Spirit be to consciousness, and perhaps to history itself. Language—a haunted house, the mansion of the soul—may in fact now be an attic of leftovers, or a flea market of haunted meanings, the beautiful empty shell of a spirit that once lived there. There may, in fact, be a ghost in our attic.

Again the poet Emily Dickinson captures the reality consciousness when she says:

> The brain is just the weight of God,
> For lift them, pound for pound,
> And they will differ, if they do,
> As syllable from sound.

One poet I encountered viewed the Holy Ghost as a special kind of writer—that it practices *apperceptive ego consciousness,* which is to say it reflects. It reflects itself in history through the sign and symbol: writing. In fact, history comes about only through reflection of the culture on itself. Until then, there is no history, which is made not just by action, but also by writing. This is not only why writing itself is important, but why the history of writing, the alphabet itself, is spiritually important. Writing is, in fact, spiritual, even if science denies that. The alphabet is an archeological sign in history that history has begun. The spirit has reflected. This gift was the gift of wings—Pegasus, the winged horse, as a kind of spirit.

Myths, creation stories, sagas, legends, fairy tales then become not just accounts of superstition, old wives tales, and nonsense fiction, but records or "mind prints" of the rise, or descent, of spiritual consciousness. They are pictures of man's first self-consciousness. They may even be records of the imprint of the Spirit in man's first grasping of his own awareness—the Holy Ghost. They are fossils of the emergences from the unconscious. It is in this sense that we meet the early Judaic name for God: "I Am that I Am." And there was, on the first day, light—awareness.

If the Holy Ghost has to do at all with consciousness, it may be as *a process*—that is, Spirit itself is not a conclusion or a definition but a process of arriving at itself. The poet T. S. Eliot expressed this by saying: "Time present and time past are both present in time future." And the Russian guru P. D. Ouspensky suggested, "To be conscious is not to be in time."

The taste for consciousness has left modern times, but it was pursued earlier by figures like the obscure American original Richard Buche (1837–1902), who wrote extensively of cosmic consciousness long before the New Agers. Buche saw higher consciousness evolving beyond the routine everyday world by awareness of the cosmos and intellectual enlightenment. He staged consciousness on four levels: 1) simple awareness, 2) responsual consciousness, 3) self-consciousness, and 4) higher consciousness. And he gave a typology or phenomenology to recognize higher consciousness, which, he said, recognized goodness in the universe; the universe as alive, not dead; immortality of the human soul; and illumination arriving from within.

In my mind, the history of the Holy Spirit itself—as apart from some other aspects of religion, like piety and church life—may be associated mostly with coming to and inspiring consciousness. It is not often, as are demons, associated with the dulling of consciousness or the dimming of awareness. Despite trances, at least this case can be made. It is not just that the Holy Spirit is Apollonian, associated with light—many mystics have chosen the path of darkness, of negation, the apophatic path—to reach the Spirit. Dante goes to hell before going to heaven. But such mystics also associate the Spirit with higher consciousness, a vision of greater virtue and greater righteousness, more than those who choose downward transcendence—stoning the ego, demonic spirits, black magic, hyper-stimulation of the senses, dervish frenzies, drugs and psychedelics, and satanic cults. Such souls achieve a wide assortment of powers and paranormal experiences—sometimes, great insights, even more than is gained through Sunday School and the catechism—but they are not so consistently associated with clear and raised consciousness as the Holy Spirit.

Sinners sometimes know more than the righteous—do-gooders are often more awkward than sophisticates, technocrats, and experts. But sin—the separation from the divine, indeed, separation from the spirit—often comes at a great price and, often, with a lot of demonic darkness, trauma, despair and alienation or risk and damage. Faust achieves all, but his bargain is with the devil, and it is not the devil that saves him in the end, but Gretchen. The Holy Ghost may witness sin. But the wages of sin are paid in many ways—by lonely individuals but also by history, culture, and nations, as Adam and Eve discovered on their expulsion from Paradise, and as the Germans and Russians found out, along with the rest of the world, in World War II.

Was the Fourth Way and "new consciousness"—as developed in the 1920s (and later in the New Age) in the London journal, *New Age,* forty years ahead of the 1960s explosion of the American New Age and the Age of Aquarians—a manifestation of the Spirit or the Holy Ghost? This movement was led by G. I. Gurdjieff, P. D. Ouspensky, and A. R. Orage, and tended to by such influential figures as T. S. Eliot, Aldous Huxley, Gerald Heard, A. E. Waite, Katherine Mansfield, George Bernard Shaw, G. K. Chesterton, and H. G. Wells. It drew the attention of consciousness to consciousness itself. Its goal was "a new contemplative and imaginative order," arising around the time that behaviorism began to debunk consciousness in any form. A method of training and meditation was "consciousness without thought"—perception without a sensory object. Orage talked of "winged thought," "winged judgment," and "winged sympathy." These do not equate readily with the Catholic list of gifts of the Holy Ghost, but it is tempting for others to see the "universal consciousness" as something akin to the truth of the Holy Spirit.

Sometimes all this depends on parlance and one's degree of orthodoxy—the faithful and church theologians tend to equate the Holy Spirit with given doctrine, the truth defended by the Holy Office, and the fullness of the faith in church congregations. But free spirits and poets and mystics may see a parallel in the touch of the Holy Spirit in cognition, in thinking about thinking, and in the attention to consciousness—a sort of new Pentecost of the mind. After all, the prophet Joel and Jesus talked about the new outpouring of the Spirit, and it didn't mean just the catechism or Canon Law; it meant a new mental experience, as well as a change of heart. For Orage, consciousness is the equivalent of spirit; it arises from a flat, single dimension of sense impression to a folded state: memory itself and self-consciousness. Then it curved further in on itself, consciousness achieving a kind of continuity. If this consciousness is again raised—if a higher self becomes aware of the ego that is aware—consciousness reaches a cosmic level, an ecstasy. This cosmic consciousness, one might say, is a touch of the Holy Spirit, too.

P. D. Ouspensky, a Russian, was on a search for the fourth dimension. We must remember that a fourth dimension had been posited through Einstein's studies in physics—consciousness that he experienced momentarily in 1908 in Turkey's Sea of Marmar, when he watched the waves hitting the boat:

> Suddenly I felt myself go to them. It was only a moment, maybe less than a moment, but I entered the waves and ... at that moment *I became all*. The waves—they were myself. The violet mountains in the distance—they were myself. The wind—it was myself.

This kind of cathection to the world—being carried away—can be dangerous, and nowadays it is often a cause for medication in our clinics.

But Ouspensky describes the moment as one of "extraordinary liberation, joy, and expansion"—again, maybe, tantamount to a touch of the Spirit. But are there differences, too, among cults of consciousness, the mystic embrace, and a visit of the Holy Spirit? Some would say yes. Religious guides, Fathers, and counselors are very careful about such moments; one should not just cathect madly with the universe. One should not just fall in love with oneself. For this reason, in religion, the Holy Ghost is surrounded by careful responsibility; its gifts are carefully qualified. It is associated, too, with proper training, the virtues, sobriety, grace, and holiness. Often New Agers, sometimes mystics, and users of psychedelic drugs dispense with the virtues and holiness and discipline when reaching out to embrace "the spirits." Even evangelicals sometimes jettison sobriety.

Nietzsche and others spoke of a new consciousness and a superhuman mentality that goes beyond convention, routine, and worn-out mores, and beyond good and evil. But, without the virtues, without the holiness, without the sobriety, others adopted these concepts to potentize a new consciousness that, in Nazism certainly, fell to new depths of evil. New Agers, cultists, hippies, mystics, and psychedelic users—as well as secular skeptics—might ponder these truths before turning up their noses at the traditions of religion, monks, nuns, the faithful, Christianity, Judaism, and the churches.

Closer to our own time, the spiritual outsider Colin Wilson has said, "The External world that our eyes reveal to us is just a limited version of the larger inner world." The outsiders, however, should not forget the outside world either.

Holy Spirit is a qualification of Spirit that has technical, doctrinal, moral and other dimensions; it is not just an empty name, nor is it just a religious foible. Whereas elevated consciousness, or enlightenment, is desirable, it is not necessarily equivalent to "the fullness of the Holy Spirit."

Secular science, spiritual science, Eastern tradition and sects like Christian Science as well as the New Age—even Evangelicals—can learn by observing more closely the phenomenology of the Holy Spirit and by sifting the mystical observation of the Holy Ghost and Catholic doctrine. The Holy Spirit, in the Western sense, has things to learn from the East, but also things to offer, like community.

Not everything modern is automatically better than what came before. In matters of the Holy Spirit, the Cappodocian Fathers of the sixth century may be more advanced than twenty-first–century evangelicals, or scientists and their fads of cosmic theories of "chaos" or "complexity." Early Christianity in Jerusalem may have been closer to the Pentecostal breath of the spirit than Rome and the Vatican of the twentieth century. In this sense, the Holy Spirit transcends time. Though it came before, it may be more modern than what came after. Truth does not always march in lockstep or deal in relativity and chronology. This relation to the eternal may itself be one of the gifts of the Holy Spirit. A sense for our destiny beyond the immediate daily bites of everyday news and the latest atrocity, the latest murder, the latest scandals, might be an unseen gift of the sense of a forgotten Ghost.

## Chapter 29

# Amen to the Future

The dove descends; it doesn't ascend. Humankind is its nest. If the name Holy Ghost seems dead, the being of the Spirit may still be alive. There are no traditions, even in the time of Columbus, hinting that the Spirit lived in the New World, America, or that it would be found there. The search here was for the Promised Land and El Dorado, the fountain of youth — not the Holy Ghost, which seems to have had more of an Old World heritage, going back to Jerusalem itself and Biblical times. America seems to offer the born-again factor, if that is the Spirit. Otherwise, the New World was better known for opportunity and the American Dream and Pursuit of Happiness.

Some people say — and I found this lead in an 1866 American Tract publication — that the Holy Ghost lived in the Fortunate Isles. The Fortunate Isles were thought by the Greeks to lie beyond the Rock of Gibraltar in "the Western Ocean." This might have meant the new Indies, America, or the Caribbean, but when I pursued the matter further, the Fortunate Isles turned out to be the Canary Isles, off Africa and now belonging to Spain. Curiosity aroused, I pursued the matter. The trail at first led to Hell. The Western Ocean appeared in dictionaries to be the location of Hades, the God of the Underworld, who quested for a magic helmet that made him unseeable, the invisible. Intriguing, because the Holy Ghost is invisible, too, but Hades was a Greek version of Hell. The heretical thought came that the Holy Ghost was then none other than Pluto in disguise — Pluto being another Roman and more congenial name for Hades. Hades had been fierce; Pluto was somewhat gentler. Both were Invisible, and both came from the West.

If Pluto was some semblance of the Holy Ghost, the Invisible One, though unlikely, then to become the Holy Ghost of the early Christians, he must have been mysteriously converted. Unable to speculate further, I retraced the trail to the Fortunate Isles. Hades, the natives said, had apparently not lived here; the confusion arose from the Greek literature, which said that the dead live in Hades but also said that the dead—the blessed—live in the Fortunate Isles. The dead in Hades, however, are banished dead souls in dank, damp, shady places, flitting about like bats as ghosts.

The Fortunate Isles were home instead to the blessed, a place where souls of the virtuous were placed after death. So then I thought, maybe my informant meant that the Holy Ghost had retired to—not come from—the Fortunate Isles. A quick trip to the Canary Islands convinced me that it was a pleasant place. Perhaps the Blessed could have lived there in Greek times, when Greece itself was still utterly pagan, but what I found on the islands was mostly tourism. That and the queer story that the Fortunate Isles were the home of Mona, a mysterious figure said to be the daughter of (and this again gave me the shudders) Pluto! She was said not to have died there, but to have been born there. It was said that this figure Mona had been fed on drunkenness and impertinence, slowly becoming queen of a powerful empire. Her realms spread far and wide but, sadly, included no church properties and no churchmen, monks, nuns, friars, or bishops as subjects. This angered Mona, so she decided to lavish favors on the churchmen and priests, giving them wine, food, baubles, and women—even boys. Still, the Churchmen would not vow obedience to her, although most everybody else did. Enraged, Mona spread rumors that bishops, monks, and priests were bewildering themselves with theology and dialectics and she slandered them saying they were disorderly, ignorant, and filthy.

I returned to the Fortunate Islands to track the story of Mona and look for the Holy Ghost, but I could find her nowhere. It turned out that the whole account was a fabrication of the Humanist Desiderius Erasmus (1466–1536), and it appeared in a book called *In Praise of Folly* (1516), printed in, of all the sober and reformed places of Europe, the city of Basel, Switzerland. Erasmus, a great moralist and wit, had moved to Basel and written the joke on the Holy Ghost in exile, because, like Martin Luther, who knew him well, he had neither the stomach or desire to play the reformer. Luther said of him: "Erasmus is very capable of exposing error, but he knows not how to teach the truth."

The Fortunate Isles turned out not to be the home of the Spirit, though it seemed nice enough to qualify, so let us reconsider the somber wisdom of Seneca, at the end of Rome's glory, the stoic and moralist. Before the Christians had usurped the spirit, he told the Caesars:

> Nothing can be more commendable and beneficial if you persevere in the pursuit of wisdom. It is what would be ridiculous to wish for when it is in your power to attain it. There is no need to lift up your hands to heaven, or pray to the servant of the temple, to admit you to the ear of the idol that your prayers may be heard the better. God is near thee; he is with thee. Yes, Lucilius, a holy spirit resides within us, the observer of good and evil, and our constant guardian. And as we treat him, he treats us; no good man is without a God.

It was said early on that no one worships a spirit—but if not, doesn't one just worship an idol or a human being? Novalis, the shining German lyric poet, said: "The world of spirits is, in fact, already open: it is always manifest. If we were suddenly to have the necessary elasticity we would find ourselves among them, in the world of spirit." After the age of idols, the Holy Ghost was the first Spirit—not just a spirit of religion, but also a spirit in culture; religion does not have a monopoly on spirit. The "Holy" in Spirit, of course, is religious, but Spirit spills over into culture. The Holy Ghost may be hiding in churches, but also hides in culture—in Hollywood, museums, the Internet.

Since secular culture has won so much of the domain of life, we need to remember more than ever to look for and respect the spirit in our political, our artistic, our scientific, and our cultural and social life. One need not look for spirit only in the pews of churches. One need not turn just to religion or fundamentalism to be reborn. One can find the spirit in nature, in the marketplace—just about everywhere—but one has to have a sense for more than just materialism.

To persons who dismiss a personal God, there is still spirit in the realm of knowing, and it is provocative to represent this area of life as the realm of spirit. The Christian may think of the Holy Spirit as a name, a being, or a presence—even as a personal feeling—but to others, it is enticing to see the unconscious as the realm of the Holy Ghost. For Christians, who view the Holy Spirit as a "higher being," the unconscious is a lower world. Again, the difference between the name and the reality plays a role—many other Churchgoers and Christians think of the Holy Spirit as a mere name, a theological category of the Trinity. As such, they "know" it nominally, if at all, as a supposed immanence—something said to enter life or the life of the Church. For those who deal with the Holy Spirit as a presence, not just a name, it is something to be treated in the here and now.

Even outside the Church, people often use "higher" and "lower" when referring to spiritual and material realities. This usage derives from thinking of God as the "transcendent"—that which is beyond, unreachable, and over us. This spiritual world is "above us." But for others, the Holy Spirit is, as it is meant to be in Catholic thought, immanent—that is, it manifests in the world and is perceptible in creation. It visits people. It leaves "signs." Thus history itself may be the evolution of the human spirit—or, the Holy Ghost. History, then, is the incarnation of Divine Spirit—and, sometimes, demonic spirits—working on earth. For those who are not religious or theistic, such an evolution may be seen as the manifestation of the spirit—without the "Holy." Such people differ, naturally, from those who take a Darwinian materialistic stance or those who stand with Marx, seeing evolution and history as the record of chance matter surviving by natural laws—chemistry, chance, and survival of the fittest and strongest. Darwinism is, according to some, a "lower" view, or a view of the lower world. But in Jewish and Kabbalistic spirituality, as in some alchemy, the rule is: As in the Upper, so in the Lower. The sign for this is the hexagram: an upper triangle for transcendence, with a reversed triangle below for the lower, or immanence. The two intersect and mirror each other. The lower and upper are integrated. What is divine purpose in an upper sphere may appear as chance, atoms, and random molecules in the submicroscopic world. That which is a higher clarity in the transcendent world might be an obscure drive in the lower unconscious.

Again, to some a fourth dimension beyond space, time, and mass may be an area of mystery, the unknown, or it may be the domain of the Spirit—even the Holy Ghost. Just because the Holy Ghost is a religious name does not mean that it should be taboo to psychology and science.

P. D. Ouspensky (1878–1947), a Russian, liked to say that the shadows of a hangman, a sailor, and a saint all look the same. And the matter, the body, of each would also be very similar. But still there are huge differences among the three. This realm of numinous difference, then, is the zone spoken of by spirit. An aspect of this difference was called in Indian philosophy the *Ling Sharira,* or "long body of life," which differs from the spatial and temporal body, just as a snapshot differs from a biography. The Eternal Now lives in a past that is not wiped out and in a future that is already taking place. In other words, this "long time body" may be a dimension of the Holy Ghost. This need not lessen our wonder nor increase the mystery, but it may make mystery more understandable and clear. The American poet T. S. Eliot (1888–1965) spoke of this dimension in his poem "Burnt Norton" as time present, time past, and time future being contained in one another.

Deep prejudice and sometimes ignorance surround a term like *Holy Ghost*—as they do sometimes our thinking about spirit, even with a small "s." Educated, scholarly, empowered Ph.D.s and professors—not just everyday locker-room secularists—often snobbishly poke fun at such mysteries, yet they belong not only to the very roots of religion, but also to psychology, astronomy, and science.

Also, the Spirit is sometimes represented as an absolute, static, eternal truth. It is worth asking, however, whether the Spirit itself evolves toward Doomsday. Free will or divine grace may be arms of evolution just as much as the struggle for survival. The fittest may survive in many cases, but free will may also forge survival. Where the fittest survive, there is little choice, and maybe, if we're talking only about brute strength, little evolution. After all, the meek inherit the earth, no? Where the free survive—and they may not always be the strongest—there may be evolution.

There is not much talk about "the signs" of the Holy Ghost. It is hard for even those who confess the Spirit to always see the presence. In evolution, a sign of the spirit might be where the free survive, though they are not the fittest or the most brutal and materialistic. Such speculation need not diminish science, and it may even add to the parameters of its research and sense of inquiry. The spirit leaves no fossils, unless some prankster wants to think of the dinosaur as a fossil of the Holy Ghost.

After all, the *noosphere*—Teilhard de Chardin's term—may inform civilization along with the computer and the Internet. In fact, the Internet may be the noosphere—a network of noumenal, mind-like qualities enveloping the world. But even the Web, for all its vaunted technology, needs "content providers," and Spirit, not just dinosaurs, provides content. It should not be left out of the equation.

Asking ordinary people about spirit and the Holy Ghost leads to remarkable answers. A waitress, for example, answered that the Holy Ghost is the guide of God and God's guardian angel. A Yale alumnus said, "Spirit is that which raises attention above the everyday routine of the body."

Often the difference between religion and spirituality is little understood. Religion—meaning literally "to tie back to," or to reconnect—is most often associated with organized religion, churches, temples, institutions, and community life. It has hierarchy, property, administration, rites, and liturgy. Spirituality has to do with the life of the spirit. It may be, and often is, religious in character, but it may also be individual, philosophical, or cultural in character. Whereas religion is often worldly, spirituality is often not, although spiritual life, or the old contemplative life, may also be carried on in the midst of active life.

Thus, in the end, the Holy Ghost may be a Spirit that haunts history, dead or alive. The Holy Ghost may be gone, the Holy Spirit, we hope, is not. Somehow time, it sometimes seems, has turned the once-living Spirit into an echo, a ghost in the modern sense. Some commentators might say that the Spirit is the ghost of God, or the ghost of Christ; after all, there, hung on the cross, a body and God "gave up the Ghost." But Spirit became a "person" in its own right. The great Cathedrals were seen as houses of God and no one worships the Ghost. Yet all over, in the Churches, in history, in culture, in the inward person, it may still linger, hover, brood—and still animate.

In another sense Spirit is a ghost, too. It was the immaterial, the unphysical—the essence. *Essence* is no longer a popular word, as in "the essence of a thing." But this distillation, this pure nature of a thing, was for millennia thought to be the secret of life, the principle of the universe, the basis of the soul. Essence was, ironically, the substance at the heart of things. Now we think it to be nothing but matter.

Although *ghost* came to be the word for a dead being, the Holy Ghost, now in some kind of exile, is perhaps closer in real meaning to the animating spirit of life than it is to death. And often in religion, *spiritual* is linked to the renunciation of the world and the flesh. This is not the original meaning of spirit, which meant breath and life. Like many words and expressions that originally referred to activity in the world, spirit has been abstracted; the meat has been removed from the shell, and the core meaning is gone. The term, the definition, and the abstraction remain. Like a lobster, the succulence has been eaten; the mess and cracked shells are left over. Spirit, like a dead lobster, sometimes looks at us from the plate of history with lifeless eyes and empty feelers.

Today religion is sometimes passed off as suppers and bingo, or as tedious disputation and argument, as a definition, as spiritual life. Bingo and supper are social, but are they any more "in the Spirit" than TV is? Perhaps. Often, only the name remains in any case. In olden times, the names of God and the Ghost—Yahweh and the Holy Spirit—were holy. They were so magical and powerful that they were unspeakable: "Hallowed be thy name." A caveman could use a name or a picture to cast a spell. Names were realities—because they were attached to experiences. Now they are attached to bingo. But language was also the thing—*economy* meant householding; *church* meant a gathering, not a building; *handkerchief* meant a hand scarf; *sin* meant separation; *spirit* meant breath. Nor had the language been overused yet; it was still a process of discovery. It didn't submit to sound bites and television dissolves. "Spirit" was a new name for old gods—a new experience of the divine.

The desert fathers went to the sand in the sense of turning off the TV; they got rid of sensory impressions, stimuli, and the haranguing marketplace in order to embrace a new life, not renounce it. For a while, spirituality was opposed to the world. They emptied their lives, like the desert, of clutter, to absorb the candle, the flower, the fruit, the word, and the water. There they reverenced silence so that they could hear and not be deafened by the noise of civilization. They observed the silence of the sand in order to talk with Hagia Sophia, or holy wisdom. The desolation of the desert enhanced their very sense of life. Spirituality was often an attempt to reform society, just as Christianity was an attempt to clean up pagan culture and Rome. Ascetics renounced life to embrace it. Some organized religion and cults have promoted renunciation, scorn of the flesh, *ascetisini,* but in my view it is not that "the spirit is willing, but the flesh is weak"; rather, the flesh is strong, but the spirit life, breath, understanding, and the mind is weak. In the modern world, we need to bring the spirit to the flesh—not to turn our backs on TV, dance, movies, theater, politics, and love. We need to bring breath, life, mind, the wit, and spirit to them.

Religion "links back to," but the spirit looks forward to. Churches sometimes organize the spirit out of religion in order to institutionalize and control. The Church itself stifled the Holy Spirit, which is a commonplace to many mystics, many reformists, and to many dedicated monks or theologians like Merton and Küng. Of course, these kinds of office, rites, and arrangements are not all bad or negative—far from it. Even an Episcopalian minister said, "In the Anglican Church, a lot of the time Spirit seems to be about keeping order."

It is not that the Church and churches do not nourish and defend religion and devotion. But when it comes to spirit, often, the stakes are different. The temple, it seems obvious, is the house of the Spirit.

It was that way in Solomon's time, and it is supposed to be true now. Spirit is supposed to drip from the altar, not blood. But sometimes it seems the church has been turned into God's old-age home, and, like many older persons, He seems to prefer TV most of the time. He even seems to want to run away from home. After all, most of the time a cathedral is really a tomb; the altar is a slab. The Mass enlivens things, true, as hymns are supposed to, but much of the time it is silent. Silence, however, is a good place for the Holy Ghost, and maybe an old lady or two still find the Spirit in their memory or prayer. And memory, too, is immaterial, and maybe the Holy Ghost hangs out in memory—or, if Scripture is correct, somewhere in the future, the time to come. In this space age, the Holy Ghost may also be cosmic as well as personal. It may be the unknowable essence of God made manifest and knowable—but, in a real sense, it may also be just you.

If God can raise the dead, the Ghost might have something to look forward to. After all, Lazurus got up again. Not even science raises the bodily dead yet. Society and science spend a lot of time killing the spirit, abhorring silence, and filling up time. But if we cannot raise bodies, at least we should try to raise spirits. Paradoxically, as I grow older I am attracted more to an immanent Holy Ghost—the presence and fullness in us—than to the transcendent Spirit, the one above and beyond us. It should be the other way around—in youth trying to reach down into immanence, to join this earth, the spirit in this world, and, nearing death, looking to the above and beyond. It doesn't always work out that way.

It is a truism to say that spirits, immaterial as they are, leave no footsteps. Dinosaurs leave tracks. As anthropologists know, humankind—the bodies and bones—leaves traces. Civilizations leave ruins. Temples, sanctuaries, Stonehenge, and megaliths are all still there. But otherwise, except in some literature, inscriptions, and graveyards, there are many fewer traces of spirit or the Holy Ghost in history—unless history itself is seen as the residue. History, to be sure, in legends, myths, and records—and in Scripture—testifies to magic, spirituality, hermeticism, and religion. Laws, commandments, formulas, and prayers leave some record, but the prayers in particular are only a whisper. Nevertheless, temples and church ruins say something.

A broad survey of great figures and personalities throughout time—with the few exceptions of saints and comments here and there—turns up few references to the Holy Ghost. Maybe acts speak louder than words. The record from Eisenhower—the commander-in-chief of Allied forces in the great mission against Nazism, the commander at Normandy, and two-term President of the United States—shows no references to the Holy Spirit or to spirit, even with a small "s," and almost no references even to religion itself. If the Holy Spirit is incarnated in human history—and I think somehow it might be—it leaves fewer records and talk, and perhaps more in deeds: Columbus' journey, Normandy, Beethoven's symphonies.

Hegel thought of history as the dialectic of spirit, but the spiritual witness of both the great and small alike goes mostly without testimony and attribution. What people thought or felt in large part goes without saying, even if like Napoleon they conquered the world. Monks and nuns, who may have lived the life of the spirit, very often lived silently. The prayers of countless billions left nothing in writing. Of course, even written secular history, like the tip of the iceberg, very often fails to record much of what really happened and existed.

One of the very huge ideas and inspirations of humanity—the Holy Ghost—left few imprints except here and there in the Bible, on a few tombstones, in the writings of some divines, by a few philosophers and poets, in a few Church doctrines, in a few prayers, by some saints and mystics, and in a few hymns. War has a much richer and more extensive documentation by far. I found that actual attribution to the Spirit, like the Holy Ghost, was itself "immaterial." Maybe I shouldn't have been surprised. Or maybe the story of the Holy Ghost is less about its death than the fact that it was never fully born—at least, not yet. If the Holy Ghost truly proceeds from the Father creator and the Son redeemer, it seems sometimes that it has not yet surpassed commercials, sports events, and wars. Maybe the Holy Ghost just doesn't boast or talk out loud much. Maybe the sin against the Holy Ghost is to talk or write about it (though I hope not). In my forty years around the news business, I don't think I have seen the Holy Ghost—a major player in a way—mentioned more than once in the *New York Times.* And it certainly doesn't make the evening news. Only the Internet is exceptional in this regard, with more than a million and a half postings. Much of this, however, may relate more to business than it does to news.

Incidentally, we should mention the Holy Ghost Fathers. This society, called the Spiritans, was founded in Paris in 1703 by a wealthy Breton lawyer, Claude Poullart des Places (1679–1709) when he was just twenty-four. He formed it to help the poor and to help students. It had no doctrinal mission or "message," but it has missionized for three hundred years out of service to the Holy Ghost and exists today in sixty-two countries, combating poverty, illiteracy, civil wars, ethnic cleansing, slavery, tribalism, and military corruption. It's message is hope. Though I have not had personal contact with Spiritans, one would think that such an effort would catch the attention of the Holy Ghost.

One of the surprising things I have found is that many people who are interested in spirituality, enlightenment, philosophy, Yoga, life after death, as well as a host of other frontiers of mind and consciousness are not interested in the Holy Ghost whatsoever. To them, the great dove of inspiration and peace seems to belong to a Church of the past and does not connect in their lives or minds with their ideas of spirituality.

A doubt came into my mind: Is this the people's fault, or is it a failing of the Church? After all, the Church has somewhat institutionalized and regulated the idea of the Holy Spirit, yet the theology of it did not develop much, and many people who go to Church go for God and Jesus and the architecture, or even to be seen, but not for the Holy Spirit. As to secular people, you might think the Ghost would titillate their minds, too, but the very thought often seems simply to turn them off. For them the great ghost and Spirit of the past just happens to be a Catholic.

Where has the enthrallment, the rapture, the ecstasy gone? Was Pentecost the end of the beginning? A punk rock concert spooks the young a lot more than the Holy Ghost. Or did Alfred Whitehead, Bertrand Russell, Ludwig Wittgenstein, the logical positivists, Francis Crick and James Watson, Jay Gould, the rationalists, the determinists, and materialists nominally kill the Holy Ghost? Have artificial intelligence and virtual reality won the day? Are Newton and the scoffers right? Are we all better off without a spook?

To the Jews, the spirit originally meant life and vitality. To the Romans, *spiritus* came to mean not just breath, but also ardor, vigor, and a passion for action. In the beginning, the Logos, or Word, was part of it, too; you couldn't have much speech, after, all, without breath. Then at Pentecost, when the disciples were gathered, it wasn't just a funeral. Everybody was talking all those languages. The idols, the superstitions, and the different magic formulas all tumbled into the dust at the approach of the dove. Not a hawk, mind you, but a dove. And the Holy Spirit wasn't a statue, but it wasn't an abstraction either. It was a kind of oneness. They were born again under an umbrella of light—not in the shadow of an idol. And, in fact, it was a spirit. Some observers today wonder whether churches are now the haunted houses—in this case by an empty ghost. Personally, I get another message when the pope travels or when real bodies—live people—visit the Church, and the bread and wine still become flesh and blood. But there are empty churches, too; the Boston Diocese just shut down sixty buildings and put them up for sale. There are also churches of nominal worship, and there are Evangelicals and Pentecostals who sometimes whoop it up.

Then I think, well, the Ghost goes to Rock concerts; the new glossolalia is in all that scat singing, reggae, and hip-hop. And I'm torn. These young people are getting spooked, all right, but are they getting the wrong spirit?

I sometimes wonder if the Ghost has cut out Church altogether and is really hanging out on the Internet and television. The TV tube looks enough like a flickering will-o'-the-wisp, a ghost, and maybe this is the real thing? Across the world now, in homes everywhere, the eerie neon efflorescence of television light flickers like the homes' inward light, and it may indeed be all that is left of the world's inward light. Evolution may have gone from the light of the Holy Ghost to the light of TV. The marvels of technology, themselves a gift, may have merely made the invisible visible, as Martin Luther King's expression put it. TV and Internet may be the modern sacraments of the mind. The global village may be a theological development. If so, there are those who would say it is sometimes much abused.

I do not want to go into a polemic about the virtues or ills of TV, but everybody knows about the commercialization, about problems of attention span, about image and channel surfing, about sound bites, and about the porn. The shock comes when one views TV itself as the Holy Ghost's modern communication channel. With TV, as well as with the Internet, the abuses and marvels become sensational, but they could also become a new, possibly more reverential light and perhaps even help viewers and programmers toward a more startling perspective on the scope and possibilities of TV.

So it makes some sense and sobers us to ask whether the Holy Ghost has gone from religion into the entertainment business. Personally, I often wonder if the real Holy Ghost, working at close to the minimum wage, is not just silent and long-suffering and in the service sector of the economy—that is, not up there with the bankers, priests, professors, and journalists, but with those who are cleaning up the streets, waiting on tables and cooking dinners, taking care of the children, trucking the farm produce, picking the strawberries, and cleaning toilets. If the Holy Ghost were actually in the minimum-wage service sector, it would explain why there is little history of his or her doings. Even so, it is sometimes a question of whether High Culture or low culture is of more interest to the Holy Ghost. Often the high and mighty, the rich and powerful, are the ones who will not let the spirit blow where it listeth. Academicians, Ph.D.s, and the overeducated are often the ones who scoff at the Holy Ghost and the immateriality of spirit, not just the locker-room boys or poor people, and sometimes it is merely the dentist who admits, "We have all shared in killing the Holy Ghost."

Another reason the Holy Ghost may not talk or boast about itself much in history is that it "infuses" itself into humankind. At least, that is the wisdom provided by tradition. It infuses itself into humankind and touches souls, minds, or hearts, with a kind of "fullness." So the real question is: Why do so many people, after turning off the TV or witnessing a political campaign, sometimes feel so empty?

History does record more about wars and less about sources of imagination, inspiration, and intuition. But *something* continually moves people to new ideas, new likes and dislikes, and new actions. And it isn't just Darwinism—otherwise, a lot of us would already be dead. People are motivated in mysterious ways to choose a career, to marry, to travel, even to go, unfortunately, to war. History does not record the inner deed, only the outer. The Holy Ghost, invisibly, may infuse motivation directly into people's will and their actions. There would be no record of this on the books, in the ledgers, or in the X-rays.

This observation is in no way a positive claim or proof, but just a speculation, which may be the way the Holy Ghost would work. Indeed, the Holy Spirit probably does not always pronounce decrees and issue dogmas. Nor is it likely to publish theorems or mathematical or algebraic formulas—calculations for pi and the golden section aside—though such formulas may, indeed, be "spiritual." The Holy Ghost seems to offer no proof. Perhaps it is, like new science, a principle of uncertainty.

Tibetan temples, Aztec monuments, Stonehenge, Chartres, medieval temples, Eleusis, Delphi, and the Pyramids may all have been, indirectly, centers of the Holy Ghost. Besides the dove, the mysterious sphinx may have been our only real icon, an early forerunner, of the Holy Ghost. Surely she is strange enough to be the very image of mystery.

The Holy Ghost may not mind being plainer than the nose on your face either. It might not object to not having a license, a certificate, a diploma, or a Ph.D. The Holy Ghost may not be a lawyer—it may not specialize in obfuscation, fraternities, secret societies, handshakes, and dossiers marked top secret or confidential. It may be an open secret. Many people reject God because he will not show his face. Many people reject God because they dislike Christianity, can't accept Jesus, or don't like the Church. Some people don't care for Moses either. Some reject the Church because they can't accept that God's world is also full of evil, concentration camps, tanks, machine guns, murder, and injustice. Others reject God and the Church because, like Newton, they find the theory of the Trinity foolish and fraudulent. Does any of this disprove the Holy Ghost? Is the theory of the Big Bang and the start of creation any less valid if someone suggests that it was the combustion of spirit—the Holy Ghost blowing up and expanding?

If God is dead, as Nietzsche claimed in the nineteenth century, and as *Time* magazine successfully publicized in the 1960s, maybe the Holy Spirit lives on as a ghost. God began to die under the Jews and Romans; then Jesus was crucified, so we had lost two key players, but perhaps the Holy Ghost, because it was immaterial, escaped and lived on. Being invisible, it may have snuck through, so to speak. Those manly Romans couldn't find and persecute it. But then, because of Newton, Marx, Darwin, Freud, Skinnner, Crick, Dennet, Hobson, and a few others—not to mention much worse men like Hitler, Stalin, Mao and that ilk—people gave up on the immaterial. Despite the wonders revealed by telescopes, microscopes, X-rays, crystallography, cameras, and radars—making the invisible visible—people still gave up on the invisible. The Ghost itself didn't give up; people did.

In 1955, the American congressman Charles R. Burnham managed to get "In God we trust" placed on the currency and coin of the realm. That may not say much about the Holy Ghost, but it says something about money. Given the separation of church and state, and after knocking out the prayers and the Ten Commandments from public life, it is inexplicable that people haven't gone after that money. Burnham, at the time—known derisively as Mr. Clean—said that any nation that loses its faith in God will not survive. Well, that's what happened to the Soviet Union. As to the Holy Ghost, he or she or it might not like being on the money. The Holy Ghost, as we saw, is shy of history in some ways, so, unlike Caesar, the Holy Ghost might not like being on the coin of the land.

An irony of our times is that the spirit dies—just consider Alzheimer's—while the flesh, the body, and matter lives longer and longer. At least, this is the scenario written by scientists, so there should be little hubbub over it. In an age of materialism, it seems entirely appropriate that a Ghost vanishes, while the body lives on. Maybe our global society itself will be some kind of old age home. For several millennia before science, it was the other way around: the body died, the spirit lived on. Science has simply turned the scenario around and upside down. The *corpus delicti* now is spirit—immaterial, an essence, and a ghost. So there is not even evidence of a victim. Not much proof. A mere ghost is not a body. We don't read about this in the media along with the rest of the murders. Yet it is sensational in its way: the perfect crime. Nevertheless, there is a suspect: the ancient and modern sin against the Holy Ghost.

Then again, after this demise of the Holy Ghost, it is sometimes as if the thing would never completely die. So the Holy Ghost, in a way, proves there is life after death. From the Vatican to Grub Street, Madison Avenue, Tin Pan Alley, and even Hollywood Row—in culture both high and low—ghostwriters have begun to work. They are of two kinds: paid, and unpaid. Instead of the Spirit, a ghostwriter could be hired to write a book, a play, or a president's speech. Behind the mask of such ghosts, however, are real men and women. Is there a face, too, behind the Holy Ghost? A true ghostwriter writes and says, "This is written through me." Then the mystery becomes: Who is the ghost—a person, a spirit, a demon, or a lady of the dark? Here a tattered remain of the glory days of the Holy Ghost may still echo on. Again, the Bible, the original ghostwritten book, foreshadowed modern times and so much else.

As actors say when they don't get paid, "The ghost won't walk this time." It is an allusion to *Hamlet,* act one, scene one, when Horatio asks if the ghost of Hamlet's father walks only for pay. Maybe, all these years, the Holy Ghost just hasn't been paid enough. In fact, the treasurer of a theater came to be called "the ghost," which was also why "the ghost walks" meant it was payday. In other words, the ghost never paid enough. Perhaps that was it.

As technology advanced, the term *ghost* became further and further abused until people, as we noted, spoke of "the ghost in the machine" as a reference to lost divinity. In telecasting, the term also has a technical meaning: the secondary image on an old television screen beam. Then materialized light reappeared as holography took off, and this principle was utilized in laser projection to produce holograms on the basis of interference light: the ghost seemed to come back to life. They called it interference theory, and it became the basis of a new physics, which ultimately claims that all reality and ourselves are ghosts of light.

The further and future whereabouts or demise of the Holy Ghost is shrouded in obscurity. The new millennium ushers in not flowers and peace and starlight, but 9/11 and "the spirit" of terrorism. Such a demagogic spirit is then embraced, for example, by Arabs, by some anti-materialistic Westerners, and even by intellectuals. It is celebrated as a spirit of death and games that offer suicide as a thrill and a way of defying life and a system of culture and civilization. Some of these theoreticians of the "spirit of terrorism," bored by conventional war, even prefer terrorism.

As a veteran of the Cold War, which eventually destroyed the Soviet Union (unless it was the sin against the Holy Ghost that did them in), I can see some advantages of cold war over hot war. Europeans — inured to events like the bombing of Dresden, which theoreticians of the spirit of terrorism say had "no symbolic value" — don't always care much about terrorism, because it kills only insignificant numbers of people, mostly Americans, anyway, and some Jews. The point is that, in a demented way, even the terrorists relish spirit — the "spirit of terrorism."

As for Spirit Land, it is an esoteric place — either nowhere and thought of by many Americans as the land of Oz, or beyond the rainbow according to others. Geographers have placed it differently at different times and in different languages. Once it was the lost Atlantis, then the Far Isles, the Paradise Islands, or even the New World — as unrecognizable as it might be today. Arcadia was another name for Spirit Land — a true Garden of Eden, lost in a world where life once existed in a pure state, and where thought and deed were free from punishment by Church and State. Sir Francis Bacon (1561–1626) said that Arcadia could exist only far outside Europe, and he called the place New Atlantis, where freedom would be guaranteed and religious liberty tolerated. Nova Scotia was once named L'Arcadie, and Longfellow wrote "Evangeline," a dreamy poem about its loss.

Sometimes Spirit Land is, mistakenly, called Utopia, and people think that the Holy Ghost lives in Utopia. But there have been many utopias and castles in the air. Others spoke of a New Jerusalem. Yet, as far as I know, no such place (except for the Fortunate Islands) has ever been considered the home of the Holy Ghost. Indeed, the Holy Ghost seems never to have had a home outside the Church and its congregations. Some people, therefore, think that the Holy Ghost is homeless. Others think the Spirit is now buried in cyberspace on the Web, and they may be right.

In the twenty-first century, a new consideration presents itself: Is the noetic web of Internet spiritual? In one way, the Internet—cyberspace—is less material than books, paper, leather, bindings, hardcopy, and libraries. It is light and electricity; it moves and vanishes. It is evanescent. It travels in a flash. It is global. Hardware aside, it is more mental. It is more picture and image, less word and letter—but it is still based on hardware. If the Internet is the incarnation of the noosphere, the Web also poses an interesting threat, in that it sometimes—as a noetic web—threatens to generalize the minds of its users into a universal program, possibly at the expense of individuality. The spirit, instead of blowing where it will, clicks as a program.

But the thesis in this book, if there is any—apart from a fragmented history—is only that the Holy Spirit is a dimension of personal, public, and perhaps supernatural life that, like music and inspiration, should be taken into consideration. It would be part of the equation. Like music, the Spirit belongs to all. Like music, it raises awareness and IQ. Like music, it speaks to affect and the heart. Everyone hears. Like music, the Holy Spirit belongs to the very act of human cognition. It belongs to all peoples and to each individual.

It could well be that the Holy Ghost is in exile, or dead, haunting the past, only to have given way to the Holy Spirit. But it helps us understand what the Holy Spirit is if we understand what the Holy

Ghost *was.* The future of spirit is up to us, not just God. Whether spirit, in the various guises we have met, has a role in the future is also a matter of how we come to think, feel, and will; no spirit, no dove, can come to us unless we are there to receive and nurture the gift. And it may behoove us to look first in simple things and in common places.

Whether history itself is the emanation of the Holy Spirit, only history itself and time can tell. There are those who will object here that the Holy Spirit is only another gene. Or an atom. Or Chemistry. Some will say, more wryly, that history is a demon's stage play. Some will go on saying none of this really matters—that history is a game of chance and a question of pleasure. However, the manifest destinies of the Americas, China, Russia, Europe, and Africa will enact this history. A last judgment will eventually come, whether with a bang or with a whimper. The dead will rise or forever hold their peace.

Here in this book evidence is offered, but no proof. No outcome. Only a short partial record, one voice urging that the ghost in the machine may be, like music, the Holy Ghost.

As one woman said to this journalist as I wrapped up this book, her definition of the Holy Spirit is "the spirit of love yet to be born." This may be the best news there is from the street. Amen.

# Bibliography


Aquinas, Saint Thomas, *Basic Writings of Saint Thomas Aquinas: Man and the Conduct of Life,* ed. Anton C. Pegis, 2 vols., Hackett, Indianapolis, 1997.

Armstrong, Karen, *A History of God: The 4,000-Year Quest of Judaism, Christianity and Islam,* Ballantine Books, New York, 1993.

Bamford, Christopher, An Endless Trace: The Passionate Pursuit of Wisdom in the West, intro, by Philip Zaleski, Codhill Press, New Paltz, NY, 2003.

Baars, Bernard J., ed., and William Banks and James B. Newman, *Essential Sources in the Scientific Study of Consciousness,* MIT Press, Cambridge, MA., 2003.

Barfield, Owen, *History in English Words,* Lindisfarne Books, Great Barrington, MA, 2003.

Barry, Alfred, D. D., *The Book of Common Prayer,* London, 1881.

Barthel, Manfred, *The Jesuits: History and Legend of the Society of Jesus,* trans. by Mark Howson, William Morrow, New York, 1984.

Basil, St., the Great, *On the Holy Spirit,* St. Valdimir's, Crestwood, NY, 1980.

Baudrillard, Jean, *The Spirit of Terrorism,* trans. by Chris Turner, Verso, London, 2003.

Bate, Walter Jackson, *Samuel Johnson,* Counterpoint, Washington, 1998.

Bock, Emil, *The Three Years: The Life of Christ between Baptism and Ascension,* trans. Alfred Heidenreich, Floris Books, Edinburgh, 1995.

Bokenkotter, Thomas S., *Essential Catholicism: Dynamics of Faith and Belief,* Image Books, Garden City, NY, 1986.

Bonhoeffer, Dietrich, *The Cost of Discipleship,* Simon & Shuster, New York, 1995.

———, *Life Together: Prayerbook of the Bible,* trans. Daniel W. Bloesch & James H. Burtness, Fortress Press, Minneapolis, 1996.

Bramly, Serge, *Leonardo: The Artist and the Man,* trans. by Sian Reynolds, Penguin, New York, 1994.

Brennan, Rev. Richard, *Church History for Schools,* Benziger Brothers, Cincinatti, 1881.

Broderick, Robert, ed., *The Catholic Encyclopedia,* Nelson Reference, Nashville, 1990.

Bruno de Jésus-Marie, Fr., ed., *Three mystics: El Greco, St. John of the Cross, St. Teresa of Avila,* Sheed & Ward, New York, 1949.

Buch, Esteban, *Beethoven's Ninth: A Political History,* the University of Chicago Press, Chicago, 2003.

Burkett, Walter, *Ancient Mystery Cults,* Harvard University Press, Cambridge, MA., 1987.

Burrini, Gabriele & Alda Gallerano, eds, *Padre Nostro Che Sei Nei Cieli: Le Piu Grandi*

*Preghiere did Tutti i Tempi e di Tutti i Paesi,* Tascabili Bompiani, Milan, 1998.

Cahill, Thomas, *Desire of the Everlasting Hills: The World Before and After Jesus,* Anchor Books, New York, 2001.

Carrol, James, *Constantine's Sword: The Church and the Jews,* Mariner, New York, 2002.

Carter, Jimmy, *Living Faith,* Three Rivers Press, New York, 2001.

Cassels, Louis, *The Reality of God,* Doubleday, Garden City, New York, 1971.

*Catechism of the Catholic Church,* Image, New York, 1995.

Cox, Harvey, *Fire from Heaven: The Rise of Pentecostal Spirituality and the Reshaping of Religion in the Twenty-First Century,* Da Cap Press, Cambridge, MA., 2001.

Crystal, David, *The Cambridge Encyclopedia of Language,* Cambridge University Press, Cambridge, 1997.

———, *Linguistics, Language, and Religion,* Hawthorn, New York, 1965.

Doniger, Wendy, ed., *Merriam-Webster's Encyclopedia of World Religions,* Merriam-Webster, Springfield, MA, 1999.

Eck, Diana L., A New Religious America: How a "Christian Country" Has Become the World's Most Religiously Diverse Nation, HarperSanFrancisco, 2002.

Eco, Umberto, *Five Moral Pieces,* trans. Alistair McEwen, Harcourt, New York, 2002.

Eidan, Klaus, *The True Life of J. S. Bach,* trans. Hoyt Rogers, Basic Books, New York, 1999.

Everitt, Anthony, *Cicero: The Life and Times of Rome's Greatest Politician,* Random House, New York, 2003.

Flannery, Austin, *Vatican Council II: The Conciliar & Post Conciliar Documents,* Costello Publishing, Northport, New York, 1987.

Frank, Philipp, *Einstein: His Life and Times, trans.* by George Rosen, Da Capo Press, Cambridge, MA., 2002.

Franklin, Benjamin, *Benjamin Franklin's The Art of Virtue: His Formula for Successful Living,* ed. George L. Rogers, Acorn, Eden Prairie, MN, 1990.

Freud, Sigmund, *The Freud Reader,* Peter Gay, ed., Norton, New York, 1995.

Geldard, Richard, *The Spiritual Teachings of Ralph Waldo Emerson,* intro, by Robert Richardson, Lindisfarne Books, Great Barrington, MA, 2001.

Glenn, John, with Nick Taylor, *John Glenn: A Memoir,* Bantam Books, New York, 2000.

Heiler, Friedrich, *Prayer: A Study in the History and Psychology of Religion,* Oneworld, Oxford, 1997.

Jones, Chesly; Wainwright, Geoffrey; Yarnold, SJ., Edward, *The Study of Spirituality,* Oxford University Press, Oxford, 1986.

Kohler, K., *Jewish Theology, Systematically and Historically Considered,* Ktav, New York, 1968.

Küng, Hans, *Judaism: Between Yesterday and Tomorrow,* Continuum, New York, 1995.

———, *On Being a Christian,* trans. Edward Quinn, Doubleday, New York, 1976.

Lachman, Gary, *A Secret History of Consciousness,* intro, by Cohn Wilson, Lindisfarne Books, Great Barrington, MA, 2003.

Leo XIII, Pope, "Divinum illud munus: Encyclical of Pope Leo XIII on The Holy Spirit," on the web at www.papalencyclicals.net/Leo13/l13divin.htm.

Lerner, Robert E., *The Heresy of the Free Spirit in the Later Middle Ages,* University of Notre Dame Press, IL, 1972.

Lesser, Elizabeth, *The New American Spirituality* (now published as *The Seeker's Guide: Making Your Life a Spiritual Adventure*), Random House, New York, 1999.

Lindbergh, David C., and Numbers, Donald L., eds. *God and Nature: Historical Essays on the Encounter between Christianity and Science,* University of California Press. Berkeley, 1986.

Lopes, Antonino, *The Popes: The Lives of the Pontiffs through 2000 Years of History,* Futura Edizioni, Rome, 1997.

Loyola, St. Ignatius, *The Spiritual Exercises,* trans. by Anthony Mottola, introduction by Rober W. Gleason, S. J., Image Editions, New York, 1989.

Marsden, George M., *Jonathan Edwards: A Life,* Yale University Press, New Haven, 2003.

Martin, Malachy, *Three Popes and the Cardinal: The Church of Pius, John and Paul in its Encounter with Human History,* Farrar, Strauss, and Giroux, New York, 1972.

Martyn, V. Carlos, *The Life and Times of Martin Luther,* Moody, 1983.

Merton, Thomas, *Witness to Freedom: The Letters of Thomas Merton in Times of Crisis,* ed. William H. Shannon, Farrar Straus & Giroux, New York, 1994.

Miles, Jack, *Christ: A Crisis in the Life of God,* Alfred A. Knopf, New York, 2001.

Octopus Books, *The Occult and the Supernatural,* in Association with Phoebus, Crescent Books, New York, 1975.

Okawa, Ryuho, *The Golden Laws,* Lantern Books, New York, 2002.

———, *The Laws of the Sun: The Spiritual Laws & History Governing Past, Present & Future,* Lantern Books, New York, 2001.

Origen, *An Exortation to Martyrdom, Prayer, and Selected Works,* Rowan A. Greer, trans., Paulist Press, New York, 1979.

Pagels, Elaine, *The Gnostic Gospels,* Vintage, New York, 1979.

Pelikan, Jaroslav, *The Christian Tradition: A History of the Development of Doctrine,* vol. 2: *The Spirit of Eastern Christendom (600–1700),* The University of Chicago Press,

Chicago, 1974.

———, *The Christian Tradition: A History of the Development of Doctrine,* vol. 3: *The Growth of Medieval Theology (600–1300),* The University of Chicago Press, Chicago, 1978.

———, *The Christian Tradition: A History of the Development of Doctrine,* vol. 4: *Reformation of Church and Dogma (1300–1700),* The University of Chicago Press, Chicago, 1983.

———, *Christianity and Classical Culture: The Metamorphosis of Natural Theology in the Christian Encounter With Hellenisms,* Yale University Press, New Haven, 1993.

Pernoud, Regine; Clin, Marie-Veronique, *Joan of Arc: Her Story,* trans. by Jeremy Duquesnay Adams, St. Martins Griffin, New York, 1998.

*Pilgrims Hymnal,* The Pilgrim Press, Boston, 1958.

Pinker, Steven, *The Blank Slate: The Modern Denial of Human Nature,* New York, 2002.

Pinn, Anthony B., *The Black Church in the Post-Civil Rights Era,* Orbis Books, Maryknoll, New York, 2002.

Pritchard, Evan T., *Native New Yorkers: The Legacy of the Algonquin People of New York,* Council Oak Books, San Francisco, 2002.

Randall, Willard Sterne, Thomas Jefferson: A Life, Harper Collins, New York, 1993.

Robinson, George, *Essential Judaism: A Complete Guide to Beliefs, Customs, and Rituals,* Pocket Books, New York, 2000.

Runes, Dagobert D., *Pictorial History of Philosophy,* Philosophical Library, New York, 1959.

Salomon, Julian Harris, *Indians of the Lower Hudson Region: The Munsee,* Historical Society of Rockland County, Suffern, NY, 1982.

Santayana George, *The Realm of Spirit: Book Fourth of Realms of Being,* Scribner's, New York, 1940.

Seneca, Seneca's Morals, ed. Sir Roger L'Estrange, Lovell, Ceryell, & Company, New York.

Shepherd, Canon A. P., "The Council of Constantinople," *Golden Blade,* 1963.

Smethurst, Arthur F., *Modern Science and Christian Beliefs,* Abingdon Press, New York, 1955.

Steiner, George, *After Babel: Aspects of Language & Translation,* Oxford University Press, Oxford, 1988.

Steiner, Rudolf, *The Festivals and Their Meaning,* Rudolf Steiner Press, London, 1981.

Susuki, Daisetz T., *Zen and Japanese Culture,* Princeton University Press, Princeton, NJ, 1970.

Tillich, Paul, *Dynamics of Faith,* Perennial, New York, 2001.

Turner, Frank M., *John Henry Newman: The Challenge to Evangelical Religion,* Yale University Press, New Haven, 2002.

Updike, John, *More Matter: Essays, and Criticism,* Knopf, New York, 1999.

Weigel, George, *Witness to Hope: The Biography of Pope John Paul II,* Cliff Street Books, New York, 2001.

Williams, Charles, *The Descent of the Dove: A Short History of the Holy Spirit in the Church,* Regent College Publishing, Vancouver, 1995.

Williams, Paul L., *Everything You Always Wanted To Know About the Catholic Church, But Were Afraid to Ask,* Doubleday, New York, 1989.

Wilken, Robert Louis, *The Spirit of Early Christian Thought: Seeking the Face of God,* Yale University Press, New Haven, 2003.

Wilson, Colin, *Access to Inner Worlds: The Story of Brad Absetz,* Celestial Arts, Berkeley, CA, 1990.

Yahlop, David, *In God's Name: An Investigation Into the Murder of Pope John Paul I,* Bantam, 1984.

Zimmerman, Fr. Benedict, *Life of St. John of the Cross,* Sheed and Ward, London, 1936.

# Index

## A



## B

D

K



L



M

## S

RUFUS GOODWIN attended Yale and Georgetown universities. He has been a United Press International correspondent to the Vatican, an author, a freelance journalist, a poet, and a novelist. He lives in Boston. He is also the author of several books, including *Dreamlife: How Dreams Happen; Give Us This Day: The Story of Prayer; Ocean Reporter,* a book of poetry; and *North Flame: A Magical Fable for All Ages.* He is also the translator of *The Illustrated Calendar of the Soul: Meditations for the Yearly Cycle* by Rudolf Steiner with illustrated by Anne Stockton.